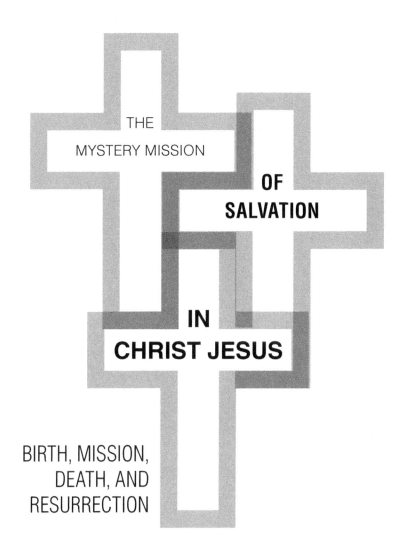

THE
MYSTERY MISSION

OF
SALVATION

IN
CHRIST JESUS

BIRTH, MISSION,
DEATH, AND
RESURRECTION

# DR IBIM ALFRED

authorHOUSE®

*AuthorHouse™ UK*
*1663 Liberty Drive*
*Bloomington, IN 47403  USA*
*www.authorhouse.co.uk*
*Phone: 0800.197.4150*

*Scripture quotations marked KJV are from the Holy Bible, King James Version (Authorized Version). First published in 1611. Quoted from the KJV Classic Reference Bible, Copyright © 1983 by The Zondervan Corporation.*

*Scripture quotations marked NIV are taken from the Holy Bible, New International Version®. NIV®. Copyright © 1973, 1978, 1984 by International Bible Society. Used by permission of Zondervan. All rights reserved. [Biblica]*

*Published by AuthorHouse  08/26/2017*

*ISBN: 978-1-5462-8117-7 (sc)*
*ISBN: 978-1-5462-8116-0 (e)*

*Print information available on the last page.*

# Contents

To Samba, my wife

# Preface

For the past twenty years, I have thought and developed an interest in what I call "the mystery mission of salvation in Christ Jesus." This curiosity has intensified over the past three years, and I am compelled by the divine spirit of Christ Jesus to put my belief and faith in ink on paper. Apostle Paul, the greatest theologian, stated: "Yet when I preach the gospel, I cannot boast, for I am compelled to preach" (1 Cor. 9:16). Like Paul, I am writing this book not of my own choice, but of necessity. I believe I have been entrusted with this assignment to unveil the mystery mission of salvation in Christ Jesus.

Paul stated: "For Christ's love compels us, because we are convinced that one died for all, and therefore all died" (2 Cor. 5:14). The love shown by Christ Jesus (Gal. 2:20, Rom. 8:35–38) is the model of authentic existence and compels believers like Paul, who taught that he had no choice but to imitate the selflessness of Christ Jesus to preach the Gospel of salvation in Christ Jesus. As a believer in the Saviour, our Lord and God Christ Jesus, I am obliged to write this book about the Son of God who wrought salvation to the universe through his birth on the first Christmas Day, his mission on earth for about three years, his cruel death on the cross on the first Good Friday, and his ultimate resurrection on the first Easter Sunday morning.

My purpose in this book is not to boast on human intelligence or ability; on the contrary, it is to show the love of Christ Jesus who condescended and descended humbly from his divine heavenly city to this sinful earthly city in order to bring eternal salvation to all those who believe in him.

I do hope and pray ardently and fervently that this book might help just one person to come to know salvation in Christ Jesus for the first time or open the spiritual eye and mind of a believer to have a deeper and more holy understanding of the amazing grace and love of Christ Jesus, who brings salvation to humanity by his wonderful and mysterious mission of salvation, which is unveiled in this book. That person in either situation could be you.

# Acknowledgements

With a very great pleasure, I record my sincere thanks to Rev Dr Martin G. Poulsom SDM – my lecturer and supervisor in my MA in Christian theology study at Heythrop College at the University of London – for his wonderful contribution, care, and love, which helped me to successfully complete my course. I wholeheartedly thank all the members of the Herne Hill Baptist Church (including Revd Andrew Miles) for the opportunity accorded me to serve as deacon, elder, service leader, and lay preacher, all of which helped me to develop some of the topics/titles in my sermons which are incorporated in this book. Many thanks to some of the members who perceived the potential in me and encouraged me to write this book. My special thanks to Peter Chodel (elder, HHBC) for the marvellous design of the cover page of this book.

Finally, special gratitude and appreciation to my wife, Samba; children Ari-ibite, Tamuno-korinama, Tamuno-dikibujiri, and Daa-ebube; and granddaughter, Ayibadiekepiriye. They perceived that God wants me to work for him. They did everything to encourage me and sponsored me to complete a certificate of higher education in religious studies at Birkbeck College and an MA in Christian theology at Heythrop College (University of London) in 2010 and 2015 respectively.

Above all, to God be the glory.

# PART 1

# SALVATION IN CHRIST JESUS

# Chapter 1

# INTRODUCTION

The birth, mission, death, and resurrection of Christ Jesus are the precious quadruplet cornerstones for the sure foundation upon which the church of Christ Jesus is built. It is divinely necessary and of paramount importance for church leaders in various denominations and congregations to impress these four holy pillars in the heart, mind, and soul of individual members of the body of Christ Jesus.

These four sanctified elements help all believers (who are "like a wise man") from the beginning of their spiritual pilgrimage on this earth to build their spiritual "house on the rock" (Matt. 7:24–27). And that rock is Christ Jesus, who wrought salvation for all people in all the nations that believe in his name. Once these four hallowed constituents are spiritually engraved and embedded in the heart of the believer from the start of his or her earthly journey as a Christian, the believer will never be shaken and will not lack divine wisdom and spiritual understanding. These four celestial elements equip, arm, and help the believer to develop faith that makes him or her to stand firm in all situations and circumstances, and avoid false teachers and prophets who teach erroneous doctrines and deceitfully misinterpret the texts in the Holy Bible for their own selfish personal aggrandizement. The hypocritical and mendacious activities of false prophets are well analysed in subsequent parts of this book.

Like the three persons (trinity) of the Godhead, Christ Jesus himself is of one nature and substance with the Father. These four sacred components – birth, mission, death, and resurrection – of salvation are consubstantial. In other words, they are of one and the same substance.

They are all together for the same purpose, the same mission, and the same saviour who is our Lord and God, Christ Jesus. Distinctively, among them, there is no change, no separation, and no confusion. Rather, they spiritually fuse and amalgamate to make a whole and integral part of eternal salvation for human beings in Christ Jesus.

It is necessary for all Christian ministers of all denominations and worship centres to put an emphasis on these mystical units in sermons in Sunday worship. It is also important to Sunday school teachers and youth workers to make sure that they teach, nurture, and help their teams to have a divine knowledge and understanding of these heavenly units. Leaders of regular Bible study groups should devote time and prayerfully search the scriptures both in the Old and New Testaments regarding the subject matter in order to make spiritual gain and understanding. Devout individual Christians who want to grow strong spiritually should spend devotional quiet time studying the Bible on this heavenly topic. Christians who work in the media should make provisions for readers and viewers to have an opportunity to gain knowledge and understand the spiritual importance of these four elements that bring salvation in Christ Jesus.

These four celestial constituents should be treated as equal in size, weight, and degree. Just as all the parts of the physical human body have to function and be active together in order to make a human being physically strong and healthy, these four transcendent spiritual features have to function and be active together in order to make the believer spiritually strong and healthy in heart, mind, and soul. This leads to salvation in Christ Jesus.

Any Christian minister of God or layperson in any Christian affiliation who does not accept and believe wholeheartedly all these heavenly four pillars of the Christian faith and doctrine, but neglects any one of these four, has gone astray and become an antichrist cut off from the way of salvation. In ages past and still today, ministers of God and Christian theologians who occupy high positions in churches and departments of theology in universities have often cast doubts on the virgin birth of Christ Jesus, his death on the cross, and especially his resurrection. These theologians muddle up their natural human experience and secular understanding with the divine plan of God for the salvation of human beings in Christ Jesus. They try to postulate, formulate, and hypothesize all sorts of negative theories (which do not hold up) to support their diabolical and delusive ideas. And of course, I suppose this trend of negative attitudes and ideas will continue till the second advent of Christ Jesus himself.

All believers in Christ Jesus should, from the beginning of their Christian earthly pilgrimage, believe and have faith in the virgin birth of Christ Jesus on the first Christmas Day. They should accept and believe all his teachings, the miracles he performed, and his proclamation of the good news of the kingdom of God or kingdom of heaven in his earthly mission. And last but not the least, all Christians should wholeheartedly believe and accept that Christ Jesus of his own volition went to the cross as a suffering God; went through the cruel and shameful death; and died for sinners. He was buried on the first Good Friday and gloriously resurrected as a sovereign God on the first Easter Sunday morning that wrought salvation for all those who believe in his name.

In summation, salvation in Christ Jesus starts from his virgin birth and includes his divine mission, his cruel and shameful death on the cross, and his final glorious resurrection as a sovereign God. This is salvation from the beginning to the end of the true plan of the triune God for all the people in the world who believe in the name of Christ Jesus. This mystical plan of salvation, with its constituent quadruplet of birth, mission, death, and resurrection, has been transferred to all Christians who go through the same process and experience.

For the spiritually unborn and carnal person to receive salvation, he or she first must be born again:

> Jesus said to Nicodemus, "I tell you the truth, no one can see the kingdom of God unless he is born again" again [Jesus] said to [Nicodemus]; "I tell you the truth, no one can enter the kingdom of God unless he is born of water and spirit. Flesh gives birth to flesh, but the spirit gives birth to spirit. You should not be surprise at my saying, you must be born again." (John 3:3–7)

Please observe the word *must*, which Jesus Christ used to express the necessity of being born again to Nicodemus and all subsequent followers of Christ Jesus. To be born again is the first fundamental condition that is required by any person who wants to be saved and follow Christ Jesus. It is an absolute prerequisite that the spiritually unborn person is obliged to go through and fulfil before coming to accept Christ Jesus. Remember that John the Baptist used the same word *must* to emphasise and reaffirm the messiahship of Christ Jesus and John's subordinate position. John said, "He must become greater; I must become less" (John 3:30).

Christ Jesus' statement, "Flesh gives birth to flesh, but the Spirit gives birth to spirit" means that the person of the flesh, which is the carnal person, must be born again spiritually by water baptism as a starting stage to receive Christ Jesus' redeeming work of salvation. In fact, Paul figuratively juxtaposed baptism, death, resurrection, and new life:

> Or don't you know that all of us who were baptised into Christ Jesus were baptised into his death? We were therefore buried with him through baptism into his death in order that, just as Christ was raised from the death through the glory of the Father, we too may live a new life. If we have been united with him like this in his death, we will certainly also be united with him in his resurrection. (Rom. 6:3–5)

All these heavenly quadruplet blessings come together to the Christian through belief and faith that unite the believer with Christ Jesus. When the believer is united with Christ Jesus, he or she becomes a disciple mandated to do missionary work in order to obey "the Great Commission" of the Lord (Matt. 28:16–20).

These celestial features of salvation become part of the Christian immediately upon conversion and conviction. The Lord proclaims to the new convert, "I am Jesus," and Jesus gives his command, "Now get up and go into the city, and you will be told what you must do." Every Christian is obliged to carry out mission work and preach Jesus as the Son of God who came to bring salvation (Acts 9:1–23).

To have a divine understanding, absolute faith, and belief in the work of salvation in Christ Jesus in his birth, mission, death, and resurrection, you must put yourself in the spiritual realm. There is a need for you to make an incorporeal journey to all the holy sites in Israel where these divine events took place, as recorded in all four gospels. The spiritual tour will divinely open your heart, mind, and soul, making it possible to have a celestial experience that will create permanent photographic images of all the scenes of events that wrought salvation in Christ Jesus.

You might have made a pilgrimage to Jerusalem, had a holy tour, and seen those places where the birth, mission, death, and resurrection of Christ Jesus took place. If that is the case, thank God for providing such an opportunity for you. However, it could just be a secular and Christian obligation that would not have given you the spiritual experience and heavenly understanding of the quadruplet that wrought salvation in Christ Jesus. It is only a spiritual or a combination of physical and sacred pilgrimages that will help you grasp the incomprehensible-to-the-human-mind salvation in Christ Jesus.

It is not compulsory to make physical pilgrimage to Jerusalem if you have not had the opportunity to do that already. If God blessed you and made the provision, thank him and take the opportunity to see all the historic holy places where the Christian faith began. However, it is paramount and necessary for you to make a spiritual journey (which does not cost you any money) to Israel and have a firm faith and belief in the work of salvation in Christ Jesus.

I bring this introductory chapter to a close and state that:

- If there was no virgin conception in the virgin womb of Mary, there would no virgin birth of Christ.
- Had there been no virgin birth of Christ, there would no divine Christ Jesus, and Christ Jesus would not have been both God and man.
- The same is true that if Christ Jesus had not been both divine and human, there would no divine gospel mission of salvation.
- It is also true that if there had been no divine gospel mission of the kingdom of God by Christ Jesus, there would have been no suffering death of God on the cross of Calvary.
- If Christ Jesus had not suffered and died on the cross and been buried, there would no resurrection.

- It is paramount to understand that if Christ Jesus did not rise as a sovereign and concurring God, there would be no work of salvation.
- Finally, if there was no work of salvation in Christ Jesus, there would be no Christianity today. Thanks be to God the Father who planned the work of salvation from the very moment Adam and Eve sinned, and executed and implemented every aspect that was fulfilled in God the Son, our Lord and God Christ Jesus, who is the saviour of the world.

This is but a précis prelude to this book. In the following chapters, an in-depth analysis and amplified version of the mystery mission of salvation in Christ Jesus (birth, mission, death, and resurrection) will be presented.

# Chapter 2

# NOMENCLATURE

In this chapter, I will classify and explain the meaning of the terms *mystery* and *mission* and the names *Christ* and *Jesus* as expressed and used in this book.

## MYSTERY

There are several similar meanings of the word *mystery*. Here, I will put forward the ones that are most relevant to how the term will be used in this book. Other words I choose that are similar to *mystery* are *enigma*, *puzzle*, *question*, and *riddle*.

Theologically, a mystery is a religious truth known only by divine revelation. It is a doctrine of faith involving puzzles that human reason is incapable of solving. It is a hidden or secret thing—something beyond human knowledge or comprehension. According to Paul, the mystery that had been hidden or kept secret from the beginning has now being revealed in Christ Jesus. Paul explained this mystery to the Ephesian Church in helpful and hopeful words: "And he made known to us the mystery of his will according to his good pleasure, which he purposed in Christ" (Eph. 1:9). In his letter to the Romans, Paul stated, "I do not want you to be ignorant of this mystery, brothers, so that you may not be conceited" (Rom. 11:25).

Paul used the word *mystery* to refer to something formerly hidden or obscure but now revealed by God for all to know and understand. The word is used in relation to the following:

1. the incarnation of Christ (1 Tim. 3:16)
2. the death of Christ on the cross (1 Cor. 2:1, 7)
3. God's purpose to sum up all things in Christ (Eph. 1:9) and especially to include both the Jews and the Gentiles in the New Testament Church (Eph. 3:3–6)
4. the change that will take place at the resurrection (1 Cor. 15:51)
5. the plan of God by which both the Jews and the Gentiles – after a period of disobedience by both – will by his mercy be included in his kingdom (Rom. 11:25). The meaning of the word *mystery* outlined in Ephesians 1:5, 9, and 10 indicates that wisdom and understanding are divine qualities underlying the revelation of God's will. This mystery of God's will has an ecclesiological focus, and it refers to the summing up of all things in Christ Jesus on behalf of the Church.[1]

## MISSION

The word *mission* is the second dominant term in this book. As it will be used in this book, *mission* means an act of sending or being sent to perform some function or service. The word has been used to denote key activities of the Church since the seventeenth century, but it is not a biblical term. It emerged in common parlance only when the Jesuits began using it in the sixteenth century to denote the assignments given to their rapidly growing fellowship. From then on, *mission* has been the shorthand term to describe Christians being sent to work among persons of other faiths as missionaries.

Ecclesiastically, *mission* means the action of sending men and women forth with authority to preach the Christian faith and administer the sacraments. This authority fundamentally and originally comes from God himself who ordains men and women to preach the good news of his kingdom. Theologically, *mission* means the sending of the second person of the Trinity (God the Son) by the first (God the Father), or of the third

---

[1] Mauvya P. Horgan, "Ephesians", in *The New Jerome Bible Commentary*, ed. Raymond E. Brown, Joseph A. Fitzmyer, Roland E. Murphy (London, 2013), 886.

(Holy Spirit) person of the Trinity by the second, for the proclamation of the kingdom of God that leads to salvation through Christ Jesus.[2]

In this book, I use the word *mission* to denote the sending of God the Son, Christ Jesus, by God the Father to the world in order to "take away the sin of the world" (John 1:29). Please note that this is just the prelude of the book; therefore, it will not be appropriate to discuss the Trinitarian dogma or the mission of Christ Jesus in detail. These will be analysed in subsequent and relevant chapters.

## CHRIST

Luke recorded the message of the angel of the Lord to the shepherds: "Today in the town of David a Saviour has been born to you; he is Christ the Lord" (Luke 2:11). At the very period of this divine annunciation, many Jews in Israel were looking forward to a political and warlord-like messiah – someone like David who would deliver them from the imperial rule of Rome. Others were looking and hoping for a saviour to deliver them from sickness and physical hardship. But this announcement concerns Christ the Lord and Saviour who delivers humankind from sin and eternal death (Matt. 1:21; John 4:42), and this is my main theme in this book. I shall examine the meaning of the title "Christ the Lord and Saviour" shortly, but I will firstly analyse the origin of Christ in the following paragraphs.

When I say "origin of Christ", am I implying that Christ had a beginning like Adam and Eve, who were the beginners of the beginning of the universe? Here I give a decisive and absolute *no* to that question. One of the most perplexing and intriguing questions by both theologians and laypeople of the Christian faith, as well as people of other faiths through the ages, is how and when Christ came to exist? It is humanly impossible and beyond the scope of this writing to provide biblically satisfactory answers to both questions, as even the Bible is inexplicit regarding this divine mystery of Christ.

Dear reader, please be encouraged and understand that it is faith and not sight that helps the Christian believe the holy scriptures from Genesis

---

[2] *Christianity: The Complete Guide*, ed. John Bowden (London, 2005), 762.

to Revelation. As it is ungodly to proof how and when God the Father came into existence, so it is infidel to attempt to ascertain the beginning of Christ the Lord and saviour.

The Bible is full of descriptions, names, and titles of Christ that can be traced from Genesis to Malachi, with several citations. It will be wearisome to cite and elaborate on all the Bible passages, and this is not my interest here. According to the Christian doctrine and faith in Christ the Lord and Saviour, it suffices to state that both God the Father the Creator of the universe and God the Son, who is Christ, have no beginning. Both of them existed before the beginning and are the beginners of the beginning both in heaven and on earth.

In this paragraph, I will analyse the citation from Luke that I have already presented: "Today in the town of David a Saviour has been born to you; he is Christ the Lord." *Lord* refers to God the Father in the original meaning. This meaning was later applied to the Messiah as well (Acts 2:36, Phil. 2:11). The full meaning of the announcement of the angel to the shepherds is that he is a Saviour, and he is Christ the Lord.

It is important to note here that it is "Christ the Lord" (not Jesus) who is the Saviour introduced to the shepherds. It is "Christ the Lord" (not Jesus) who came down from the throne of the Almighty God in heaven to be the Saviour of the world. In other words, there was no Jesus in heaven, but Christ the Lord who came to the world to be incarnated in the physical body of Jesus. I think Hendriksen is right to state that "without Christ the Lord, there is no genuine commemoration of Jesus' birth, no real Christmas and no formal Christianity as a religion."[3]

In this text, it is Christ the Saviour who has been born (not Jesus) and who will save. This Saviour was introduced to the shepherds and the cosmos as "the Christ" – that is, the Messiah or the anointed one. I join Hendriksen to state that Christ is the one anointed by the Holy Spirit to be his people's great prophet, sympathetic high priest, and eternal king of heaven and earth.

In Matthew 22:41–46; Mark 12:35–37, and Luke 20:41–44, Jesus himself raised an important theological question regarding Christ which goes to the heart of the divine Christological foundation on which the Christian faith stands. Matthew recorded that "while the Pharisees were

---

[3] William Hendriksen, *New Testament on Luke* (Edinburgh, 1978), 159.

gathered together, Jesus asked them, 'What do you think about the Christ? Whose son is he?'" (Matt. 22:41–42). Jesus' questions, unlike those of his opponents, go to the heart of things, for they concern Christology.[4]

Dear reader, please observe and understand that Jesus himself wanted to make a divine distinction between *Jesus* and *Christ*; and he wanted to bring to the fore the pre-eminence and pre-existence of Christ before the world was created (as I have stated earlier) and to reveal the truth about Christ that:

- Christ being David's son does not mean he is merely David's descendant but actually predated David and David's Lord and existed before the creation of the world.
- Christ being David's Lord, he is the Son of God the Father.
- Since Christ is the Son of God, everyone should place his or her trust in him as the Saviour who is "the Lamb of God, who takes away the sin of the world" (John 1:29).

Jesus raised a similar question to his disciples regarding "the Christ" on their way to the villages around Caesarea Philippi. Jesus asked his disciples: "Who do people say I am?" (Mark 8:27). Jesus was not satisfied with the answers his disciples gave him of what "people say" about him in 8:28. He then put the question directly to the disciples. This time, Jesus did not want the disciples to tell him what "people" (the general public of Israel) were saying about him; Jesus specifically and directly asked the disciples, "But what about you?" – my disciples who have been with me and know all I have taught and done, both in public and in private, for the whole of my ministry. "Who do you say I am?" he asks in 8:29.

Dear reader, please pause a while and meditate on the reason Jesus asks this Christological question. Jesus is Jesus, but what did Jesus want to know about Jesus (himself)? The most likely answer here is that Jesus wanted to reveal to his disciples that he is more than Jesus and that there is something – or to put it more appropriately, *someone* – inside him who is greater and more powerful than Jesus himself. It is God the Father who revealed the divine superior being who is in Jesus to Peter as Peter answered, "You are the Christ" in 8:29. Luke recorded "The Christ of

---

[4] Dale C. Allison, "Matthew", in *The Oxford Bible Commentary*, ed. John Barton and John Muddiman (Oxford, 2011), 874.

God" (Luke 9:20). Matthew gave a fuller answer to the same question: "You are the Christ, the Son of the living God" (Matt. 16:16).

In human terms, I think this single statement – or rather, the appropriate answer to Jesus' question which revealed Jesus as the Christ – is the pinnacle of Jesus' earthly ministry, because "from that time on Jesus began to explain to his disciples that he must go to Jerusalem and suffer many things at the hands of the elders, chief priests and teachers of the law, and that he must be killed and on the third day be raised to life" (Matt. 16:21). In response to Peter's answer, Christ Jesus confirmed the establishment of the Christian Church and its faith and belief.

Understand that Jesus was divinely satisfied that God, his "Father in heaven", had revealed to Peter that he (Jesus) is "the Christ, the son of the living God." With that beatitude, he blessed Peter and gave him the divine authority and right to lay the foundation of the Christian Church and to perform miracles, which the Holy Spirit enabled Peter to fulfil on the day when the Holy Spirit came to the Apostles on Pentecost and onwards (Acts 2).

Hendriksen stated that when Peter declared Jesus to be "the Christ" (Matt. 16:16), he meant the long awaited anointed one, the one who is to be the mediator between God and humanity, who was set apart or ordained by God the Father and anointed with the Holy Spirit to be his people's chief prophet (Deut. 18:15, 18; Isa. 55:3–4; Luke 24:19; Acts 3:22, 7:37); holy high priest (Ps. 110:4; Rom. 8:34; Heb. 6:20, 7:24, 9:24); and eternal king (Ps. 2:6; Zech. 9:9; Matt. 21:5, 28:18; Luke 1:33; John 10:28; Eph. 1:20–23; Rev. 11:15, 12:10, 11; 17:14, 19:6). I share the opinion of Hendriksen that Peter's declaration that Jesus is "the Son of the living God" can mean no less than that in a unique sense which is not applicable to any mortal. Jesus was, is, and always will be the son of the God who not only is himself the only living one, over and against all the so-called gods of the then-and-now pagans (Isa. 40:18–31), but also the only source of life for all humankind.[5]

Note that Matthew's addition of "the son of the living God" to Mark's "the Christ" interprets it in the direction of Jesus' unique consciousness of sonship. By invoking the father-son relationship, Matthew directs our attention away from the concept of a military or nationalistic connotation

---

[5] William Hendriksen, *New Testament Commentary on Matthew*, 643.

of the title "Messiah" and points us to "the Christ" who takes away the sin of the world.

I share the same viewpoint as Harrington who, in commenting on Mark 8:27–30, said, "Peter's confession of Jesus as the Messiah/Christ is pivotal." The passage suggests that this identification is correct when compared to what the "people say" about him being John the Baptist, Elijah, or one of the prophets. Jesus knew that the Christ in him was more and far greater than John the Baptist, Elijah, or all the other Old Testament prophets, including Moses, and even the establisher of the earthly royal throne in Israel, King David. The confession of Peter brings us to the very heart of the meaning of Messiah/Christ as applied to Jesus. That was the turning point which became a divine watershed between what he had done in his earthly mission and what was about to take place thereafter. The fact is that from this point onwards, Jesus taught the disciples to learn and understand how the passion and death of Christ fit in with his real revealed identity as the Jewish Messiah. The confession of Peter paved the way for Jesus to teach or bring to the disciples the meaning of Christology and its implication of discipleship to them and to all subsequent followers of Jesus through the ages.[6]

In comments on Matthew 16:13–20, Allison stated that the primary function of this passage is to record the establishment of a new community, one which will acknowledge Jesus' true identity and thereby become the focus of God's activity in history. Jesus is confessed as both Christ and Son of God who builds a church or temple, and he gave Peter the keys of the kingdom of heaven.[7]

I bring this evaluation of the use of the word *Christ* to an end by saying that what has been presented in the above paragraphs is just a summation, and my purpose is not to critically analyse Christological theology but to provide an introduction to the topic. As I finish this section about *Christ*, please do not think that this is the last place in this book where you will read about that majestic name; on the contrary it is just the beginning. You will see the wonderful name of Christ on almost every page of this book, if not all. There are more than 113 (depending on the version of the Bible)

---

[6] Daniel J. Harrington, "The Gospel According to Mark", in *The New Jerome Bible Commentary*, 614.

[7] Allison, 865.

citations in the New Testament which refer to Christ, and this could be more than double that if the names of Christ and Jesus are combined. I reiterate my point to state that it is ungodly to proof how and when God the Father, the Creator of the world, began to exist; it is infidel to try to probe into the beginning of the Christ, the Son of the living God who is the Saviour of the world. Here I stand on holy ground to say that both God and Christ have no beginning. They co-exist before the beginning of the universe.

Finally, before I turn to the next section, please ponder and ask yourself why this divine Christ who is God himself left his glorious and sin-free heavenly kingdom of Yahweh and came to this sinful universe. I think there is no satisfactory answer to those two and similar questions, and I will not make any attempt to do that here, but I can say in faith that the overwhelming and convincing answer is because of love. Paul put emphasis on the unconditional love in his epistle to the Romans: "'But God demonstrates his own love towards us, in that while we were still sinners, Christ died for us" (Rom. 5:8). Paul in his epistle to Timothy stated: "'Beyond all question, the mystery of godliness is great: He appeared in a body, was vindicated by the Spirit, was seen by angels, was preached among the nations, was believed on in the world, was taken up in glory" (1 Tim. 3:16).

This "mystery of godliness" is God's divine plan of salvation – from the beginning of the fall of Adam and Eve – which was keep secret for some time. The concealed secret was revealed in Christ Jesus in his birth, mission, death, and resurrection, which wrought salvation for all human beings who have faith and believe in him. God the Father did this wonderful and divine salvation through Christ Jesus because of the love he has for all humankind he created. Christ Jesus who is God the Son put emphasis on this love which compelled his Father to send him to this world (John 3:16).

This brief overview of the name *Christ* is the mystery of God which will be unveiled in the appropriate sections of this book. What prompted Christ who is God the Son and the second person of the Trinity to come to this misery-filled word, and live and die a shameful and cruel death on the cross in order to complete and fulfil his work of salvation, is the mystery of all mysteries since the creation of the universe.

In human terms, I will never have a satisfactory explanation for Christ coming to this world to die for sinners. The blissful reason came from Christ himself, who said to Nicodemus, "For God so loved the world that he gave his one and only Son, that whoever believes in him shall not perish but have eternal life" (John 3:16). Here I conclude that the great truth which motivated God to send "his one and only Son" to wrought salvation for humankind is love.

Christ came to redeem us because of the love of the father and the son. Let us sing praises to glorify his name, for:

1.  "Christ hath redeemed us"; sing the glad word!
    Mercy's sweet message be telling,
    How, through the ransom made by His blood,
    Christ now within us is dwelling.
    "Christ hath redeemed us"; Praise His name!
    Praise him, ye angels in glory!
    "Christ hath redeemed us", bearing our shames;
    Tell out the wonderful story!

2.  "Christ hath redeemed us", marking us free,
    Free from the sins that enslaved us;
    Never in bondage more can we be,
    Trusting in Him who hath saved us.

3.  "Christ hath redeemed us", we are His own,
    Purchased by blood – He will hold us;
    Nor will he ever leave us alone,
    Safely His arms shall enfold us.

4.  "Christ hath redeemed us", soon with the throng
    Gathered in glory we'll meet Him;
    Oh, with what rapture join in the song,
    When face to face we shall greet Him![8]

## JESUS

Jesus is the most appropriate name that our Lord and saviour could receive. The name *Jesus* is divinely given and expounded by the angel in holiness

---

[8] Ira D. Sankey, *Sacred Songs and Solos* (London, 1987), no. 118.

and reverence to Joseph. The name portrays and tells every aspect of his earthly missionary work as a saviour of the world.[9] The name of Jesus is above all other names on earth because at his name "every knee should bow and every tongue confess that Jesus Christ is the Lord" (Phil. 2:10–11). The name *Jesus* is Jesus, and there is no other name which is holier; and there is no better mediator both in heaven and earth between God and humanity, and no name more worthy to do the work of salvation than the saviour's name of Jesus.

Dear brother or sister, please understand that in this passage you can find the truth of divine God's purposeful bestowing of the wonderful name Jesus. Dear believer, please allow the Holy Spirit right now to help you to understand the deeper spiritual meaning of the sweetest name both in heaven and on earth, which is Jesus.

It is marvellous to observe that the angel of God gave the holy name *Jesus* (meaning "Saviour") to Joseph. The angel of God the Father also made a holy proclamation and said "[Jesus] will save his people from their sins" – not from the hardship and the brutal imperial rule of Rome. This was contrary to the expectation of the vast majority of the populace in Israel. There is a pun here to say that saviour saves (Jesus saves) his people from their sins. Theologically, I state that the evangelist exploited the popular etymology of Jesus' name. Jesus is the Greek form of *Joshua*, and in popular etymology it means "Saviour" or "God saves." The original and more correct meaning is "Yahweh help."

It is of paramount importance to state here that the name *Jesus* explicitly means that he is the saviour of the world, for "Salvation is found in no one else, for there is no other name under heaven given to mankind by which we must be saved" (Acts 4:12).

I will bring this brief prelude of the meaning of the name Jesus to a close by joining Spurgeon to say that the name *Jesus* is given to our Lord because he saves. His saving power and grace is not according to any temporary and common salvation from enemies and troubles (although these are all included in his grand and total package of salvation); he saves primarily and ultimately from spiritual enemies and specifically from the most dreadful and violent enemy, which is sin. The Old Testament records

---

[9] Charles Haddon Spurgeon, *Spurgeon's Commentary on the Bible,* ed. Robert Backhouse (London, 1997), 160.

many famous but temporary saviours God used occasionally in their own generation – such as Noah, Joseph, Moses, Joshua, Gideon, Samson, Deborah, David, and Esther – but, it is noticeable that their acts of saving were limited and confined to the people of Israel. Here, the title of saviour is given to our Lord above all the known and unknown saviours because Jesus is the grand and ultimate saviour, in a sense, who wrought universal and eternal salvation to his people. His saving grace is unique because it has elements of the past, present, and future.[10]

Dear sister or brother, join me to adore and worship and bow down to this awesome and miracle-performing name of Jesus. Feel the presence of the marvellous name of Jesus and breathe in his pervading holy aroma where you are right now. This aroma of Jesus is incomparable to the fragrant anointing oil that was poured over Aaron's head (Ps. 133:2).

I encourage you to:

1. Take the name of Jesus with you,
   Child of sorrow and of woe;
   It will joy and comfort give you—
   Take it then where're you go.
   Precious name … oh, how sweet!
   Hope of earth and joy of heaven!
   Precious name … oh, how sweet!
   Hope of earth and joy of heaven.

2. Take the name of Jesus ever,
   As a shield from every snare;
   If temptations round you gather,
   Breathe that holy name in prayer.

3. Oh, the precious name of Jesus!
   How it thrills our souls with joy,
   When His loving arms receive us,
   And His songs our tongues employ.

4. At the name of Jesus bowing,
   Falling prostrate at His feet,
   King of kings in heaven we'll crown Him,
   When our journey is complete.[11]

---

[10] Spurgeon, 161.
[11] Sankey, no. 91.

## CHRIST JESUS

In the preceding paragraphs, I have examined the glorious and divine meanings of the names of both *Christ* and *Jesus* separately, as if they were two different entities without connection or relationship. Before I bring this chapter to an end, it is necessary to state in absolute terms that *Christ* and *Jesus* are in perfect and holy union with one another. The two names combined as the compound name Christ Jesus or Jesus Christ make a beatific whole both on earth and in heaven.

It was Christ's mystery of incarnation in Jesus in this transcendent, pure, and without blemish complete union that makes Jesus uniquely fully God and fully human. It is this nature of being fully divine (God) and fully human (man) that makes it possible for Christ Jesus to be the grand and ultimate mediator between God the Father and human beings. The writer of the fourth Gospel did not spend time giving an account of the birth of Jesus as recorded in Matthew and Luke; but John forcefully and unequivocally stated, "The Word became flesh and made his dwelling among us. We have seen his glory, the glory of the one and only, who came from the Father, full of grace and truth" (John 1:14). I think this is the summation account by John regarding the virgin and divine birth of Jesus, with Christ (the Word) incarnated and become flesh in the human body of Jesus.

The analogical conclusion here is that "The Word becomes flesh but remained the Word, even God."[12] In a nutshell, the second person (Christ) of the Trinity assumed human form, yet he did not lay aside his divinity, which is why Christ Jesus was fully divine and fully human in union without been fused. This divine and enigmatic relation of the two natures to one another has been, is now, and will forever remain a mystery far above the comprehension of humankind. It is this mystery which Paul enthusiastically proclaimed to the Colossians (4:3), to the Ephesians (3:4), and to the entire Gentile world.

---

[12] .William Hendriksen, *New Testament Ccommentary on John*, 84.

# FAITH

It may be appropriate and useful to cite the definition of faith that was stated in the Council of Chalcedon, convened by the emperor Marcian (450–57) in 451, which affirmed the divinity and humanity of Christ Jesus on parity. The definition states:

> So following the saintly fathers, we all with one voice teach the confession of one and the same Son, our Lord Jesus Christ: the same perfect in divinity and perfect in humanity, the same truly God and truly man, of a rational soul and a body; consubstantial with the Father as regards his divinity, and the same consubstantial with us as regards his humanity; like us in all respect except for sin; begotten before the ages from the Father as regards his divinity, and in the last days the same for us and for our salvation from Mary, the virgin God-bearer, as regards his humanity; one and the same Christ, Son, Lord, only-begotten, acknowledged in two natures which undergo no confusion, no change, no division, no separation, at no point was the difference between the natures taken away through the union, but rather the property of both natures is preserved and comes together into a single person and a single subsistent being; he is not parted or divided into two persons, but is one and the same only—begotten Son, God, word, Lord Jesus Christ, just as the prophets taught from the beginning about him, and as the Lord Jesus Christ himself instructed us, and as the creed of the fathers handed it down to us.[13]

Please observe that the above definition of faith is the summation of my analysis of Christ Jesus regarding his divine and human natures, and upon this faith I shall base my hope and belief to proceed and develop this mystery mission of salvation in Christ Jesus.

---

[13] *The Christianity Reader,* ed. Mary Gerhart and Fabian E. Udoh (London, 2007), 341.

As you read this book, please put your present and eschatological hope of salvation in Christ Jesus, the "Wonderful Counsellor, Mighty God, Everlasting Father, Prince of Peace" (Isa. 9:6). It is only in Christ Jesus that you shall obtain salvation with eternal glory in all fullness of joy and serenity which come to you through his mystery mission of salvation. Christ Jesus is the one and only divine mediator between God and human beings because of the two natures in him (being God as well as being human). As both God and human, he is the one and only divine and legitimate advocate between God and human beings.

Christ Jesus is uniquely placed to understand both the holy mind of God the Father who is "The Lord, the Lord, the compassionate and gracious God, slow to anger, abounding in love and faithfulness, maintaining love to thousands, and forgiving wickedness, rebellion and sin" (Exod. 34:6–7) and the sinful nature of humans. It is only Christ Jesus who mediates and reconciles both the holy God and sinful human beings by his atonement for sin which wrought salvation for all who believe in him.

The mystery mission of salvation in Christ Jesus is finally and ultimately accomplished in his resurrection. Therefore, let us join Lyra Davidica and proclaim the finished work of salvation of Jesus Christ as we sing:

Jesus Christ is risen today, Hallelujah!
Our triumphant holy day; Hallelujah!
Who did once upon the cross; Hallelujah!
Suffered to redeem our loss; Hallelujah!

Hymns of praise then let us sing; Hallelujah!
Unto Christ our heavenly King; Hallelujah!
Who endured the cross and grave; Hallelujah!
Sinners to redeem and save: Hallelujah!

But the pains, which He endured; Hallelujah!
Our salvation have procured; Hallelujah!
Now above the sky He's King; Hallelujah!
Where the angels ever sing: Hallelujah![14]

---

[14] Lyra Davidica *Mission Praise* (London, 1990) 357.

# Chapter 3

# THE VIRGIN BIRTH OF JESUS

In the previous two chapters, I presented an overview of the theme of this book and clarified some of the theological terms I will apply for the rest of my analysis. My main aim in this chapter is to analyse the virgin birth of Jesus as recorded in all the gospels generally, but the majority of text and analysis will focus on the record of Luke.

The writer of the Gospel of Matthew gave the following account of the virgin birth:

> But after [Joseph] had considered this, an angel of the Lord appeared to him in a dream and said, "Joseph son of David, do not be afraid to take Mary home as your wife, because what is conceived in her is from the Holy Spirit. She will give birth to a son, and you are to give him the name Jesus, because he will save his people from their sins." (Matt. 1:20–21)

In contrast, the writer of the fourth Gospel did not spend time giving a detailed account of the virgin birth of Jesus but forcefully and unequivocally stated: "The Word became flesh and made his dwelling among us, we have seen his glory, the glory of the one and only, who came from the Father, full of grace and truth" (John 1:14). I think this is the summation account by John regarding Jesus' virgin birth when Christ (the Word) was incarnated and became flesh in the human body and personality of Jesus.

Hendriksen gave an inspirational explanation of "The word became flesh",[1] stating that "the verb *became* has a very special meaning in this context". He gave an illustration to explain that when "The Word" (Christ) "became flesh", Christ did not cease to be what he was before in his heavenly kingdom; Christ remained Christ when even he became flesh in the human body of Jesus in incarnation. Hendriksen made reference to Lot's wife and Lot, stating, "When the wife of Lot became a pillar of salt, she ceased to be the wife of Lot. But when Lot became the father of Moab and Ammon, he remained Lot" (Gen. 19).

## THE BIRTH OF JESUS FORETOLD

For the rest of this chapter, I will depend on the record of Luke, who gave the following detailed account of the birth of Jesus:

> In the sixth month, God sent the angel Gabriel to Nazareth, a town in Galilee, to a virgin pledged to be married to a man named Joseph, a descendant of David. The virgin's name was Mary. The angel went to her and said, "Greetings, you who are highly favoured! The Lord is with you." Mary was greatly troubled at his words and wondered what kind of greeting this might be. But the angel said to her, "Do not be afraid, Mary, you have found favour with God. You will be with child and give birth to a son, and you are to give him the name Jesus. He will be great and will be called the Son of the Most High. The Lord God will give him the throne of his father David, and he will reign over the house of Jacob for ever; his Kingdom will never end." "How will this be," Mary asked the angel, "since I am a virgin?" The angel answered, "The Holy Spirit will come upon you, and the power of the Most High will overshadow you. So the holy one to be born will be called the Son of God. Even Elizabeth your relative is going to have a child in her old age, and she who

---

[1] John 1:14; Rom. 1:3, 8:3; 2 Cor. 8:9; Gal. 4:4; Phil. 2:5–11; 1 Tim. 3:16; Heb. 2:14.

was said to be barren is in her sixth month. For nothing is impossible with God." "I am the Lord's servant," Mary answered. "May it be to me as you have said." Then the angel left her. (Luke 1: 26–38)

The text cited above clearly shows the divine and virginal conception of Jesus in the virgin womb of Mary (see Matt. 1:18–25). It is indisputably recorded by both Matthew and Luke, as well as John and Paul, that Mary's conception was the work of the Holy Spirit who made it possible for Christ the Messiah-God to incarnate in the holy womb of Mary and be born as Jesus. According to John, "The Word was with God, and the Word was God" and "The Word became flesh and made his dwelling among us" (John 1:1, 14).

## THE BIRTH OF JESUS

I implore you to religiously read Luke 2:1–20 on the birth of Jesus for deeper spiritual understanding and spiritual gain which will feed your soul for holy development and growth in Christ Jesus who alone wrought salvation because of his holy birth. Luke was the only gospel writer who linked the birth of Jesus to the world history of the Roman Empire during the reign of the emperor Caesar Augustus (31 BC–14 AD). Both Joseph and Mary were of the household of David, and Mary was also probably required to enrol for the census. In the lifetime of Joseph and Mary, in Syria – the Roman province in which Palestine was located – women of 12 years old and older were required to pay a poll tax and therefore to register. Since both Joseph and Mary were required to register, and since both of them were of the household of David, they both went to the town of Bethlehem, the town where David himself was born (1 Sam. 17:12, 20:6).

Luke 1:5 mentions Herod the King, and 2:1 refers to Caesar Augustus the emperor as stated above. To a certain extent, there was a difference between malevolent Herod and benevolent Augustus. However, there were two similarities between them: both were heathens and both were men of superior ability.

Caesar Augustus was a heathen emperor of Rome, but his definitive decretal order "that a census should be taken of the entire [Roman] world" unwittingly triggered and contributed to the fulfilment of the prophecy of Micah, who prophesied in about 750 BC about the birth of Jesus in Bethlehem. Micah prophesied a promised ruler from Bethlehem and stated: "But you Bethlehem Ephrathah, though you are small among the clans of Judah, out of you will come for me one who will be ruler over Israel, whose origins are from of old, from ancient times" (Mic. 5:2).

In contrast to the prediction of doom in 5:1, Micah shifted his prophecy to a positive future, not only for Israel, the people of God, but also for the Gentile nations. The "ruler" is Christ, who condescended and descended to earth and entered into Mary's virgin womb and was born as Jesus more than two millennia ago, and now rules and will rule forever. The beginning of Christ has no beginning in heaven, but his beginning began on earth when he was born as Jesus on the very first Christmas Day in Bethlehem (John 8:58).

The prophecy of Micah was fulfilled through Joseph as the impeccable historian Luke recorded: "So Joseph also went up from the town of Nazareth in Galilee to Judah, to Bethlehem the town of David, because he belonged to the house and line of David. He went there to register with Mary, who was pledged to be married to him and was expecting a child" (Luke 2:4–5). In the Jewish tradition, it was very important that they should know their line of descent, their family tree. Both Matthew and Luke realised how the Jews valued their family tree, and it was because of this that Matthew and Luke recorded the genealogy of Jesus to start the mystery mission of salvation in Christ Jesus.

It is necessary to note that there are textual difference between Matthew 1:2–16 and Luke 3:23–38 recording the genealogy of Jesus. Matthew begins the genealogy with Abraham, who is the father of the Jewish people and the founder of the nation of Israel. Luke, on the other hand, traced the lineage of Jesus in reverse order and went back to Adam, the first man on earth. Matthew was a Jew, and I think that he tried to emphasize that the salvation of the world came from Christ Jesus who was a descendent of Abraham, who was a Jew. Meanwhile, Luke was a Gentile, and he put in effort to point out that salvation of the world did not originate from Abraham; salvation came from Christ Jesus who is God himself, who created Adam the son of God. It is worth noting that the very moment Adam and Eve sinned against God, the Lord God in his mercy planned and set in motion the programme of salvation immediately.

The work of salvation in Christ Jesus had been a work in progress before the call of Abraham. In fact, forgiveness of sin which leads to salvation is initiated by God and started with Adam and Eve. After Adam and Eve committed the sin of disobedience, God's anger was poured upon them, and he pronounced punishment on them which affected all human beings throughout the ages and in all the world. But take note, dear child of the merciful and the tender-hearted God. Immediately after the condemnation and pronouncement of punishment upon Adam and Eve, "The Lord God made garments of skin for Adam and his wife and clothed them" (Gen. 3:21). God graciously provided for Adam and Eve with more effective clothing to cover their shame (Gen. 3:10). This is the beginning of the process of the work of salvation which continued through all ages and ultimately and divinely culminated in Christ Jesus. I believe, I am on holy ground to state that Luke was right to trace the genealogy of Jesus to the first created human being: "Adam, the son of God."

However, it is important to note that both Matthew and Luke traced the lineage of Jesus to the same ancestor, David. It had been divinely planned that both Joseph and Mary "belonged to the house and line of David." In 1 Samuel 20:6, the author stated that Bethlehem was David's home town and "annual sacrifice had been made for his clan." The text implied that for a long time, David and his relatives held a yearly sacrificial fest—a kind of sacred family reunion in Bethlehem. In fact, David was "tending the sheep" in the field around Bethlehem when Samuel asked Jesse (the father of David) to send someone to the field in order to bring David home. "So he sent and had him brought in" and "Samuel took the horn of oil and anointed [David] in the presence of his brothers, and from that day on the Spirit of the Lord came upon David in power" (1 Sam. 16:1–13).

David was in the same vicinity of Bethlehem tending the same sheep of his father when Jesse instructed David to take provisions to his three elderly brothers in the camp of Israel who were fighting against the Philistines. It is necessary to religiously read 1 Samuel 17 for your spiritual growth and development, and to have a firm faith in Yahweh Lord of Israel, because

"The Lord saves, for the battle is the Lord's," and the Lord God Almighty helped David to triumph over the Philistine.

Finally, I conclude here that Bethlehem is the "city of David." David himself said to Saul, "I am the son of your servant Jesse of Bethlehem" (1 Sam. 17:58). Joseph and Mary were from the line and household of David, and there was no better town in Israel which had been divinely planned and prepared to receive the Messiah-King (Christ Jesus) who is the saviour of the world than the "city of David" of Bethlehem.

Luke recorded the story of the birth of Jesus and brought it to its finest climax and most intended purpose when he stated: "While [Joseph and Mary] were [in Bethlehem], the time came for the baby to be born, and she gave birth to her first born, a son. She wrapped him in cloths and placed him in a manger, because there was no room for them in the inn." (2:6–7).

According to Hendriksen,[2] the words "while they were there the time came for the baby to be born" may have the following meanings:

1. "While they were there" – This may mean that Joseph and Mary spent a few days in Bethlehem before Jesus was born. On the other hand, it may simply place special stress on the fact that Jesus was indeed born in Bethlehem, and that the greatest event the world had ever seen took place while they were there.

2. "The time came" – The birth occurred "in the fullness of time" (Gal. 4:4). The meaning may simply be that the birth took place when the normal period between conception and delivery had expired. Although the conception itself was a miracle, the process of development within the womb was allowed to run its usual course.

3. "Her first born, a son" – Note it is not "her only son", but "her first born." The natural explanation is certainly that after Mary gave birth to Jesus, she continued to bear other children. The very names of Jesus' brothers are mentioned in the New Testament (Matt. 13:55). The fact that Jesus had brothers is also clear from Matthew 12:46–47: Mark 3:31–32; Luke 8:19–20; John 2:12, 7:3, 5, 10; and Acts 1:14.

---

[2] William Hendriksen, *New Testament Commentary on Luke*, 143–146.

4. "She wrapped him in cloths" – Note that this does not mean that Mary, having just given birth to her first born, immediately had the strength to wrap her baby with her own hands. It is likely that Mary gave instructions to Joseph, who carried it out, or to one of the women who would have been around during the delivery process.

5. "And placed him in a manger, because there was no room for them in the inn". Hendriksen makes a critical and comprehensive analysis about "the inn" where Jesus was born. He postulates five theories about "the inn", and finally asks two self-imposed questions: "Why was there no room in the inn?" and "Was it because Bethlehem was overcrowded with people that wanted to be registered for the census?" According to Hendriksen, the second question refers to the reason often given, which may be right but is probably wrong or at least incomplete.

Hendriksen's own opinion is that at the birth of Jesus, Bethlehem was filled with men (officials and soldiers of the Roman government) charged with the responsibility of taking the census. Augustus, who enacted the imperial decretal order of the census, and the soldiers who carried it out were well aware that the Jews, because of religious scruples, were terribly afraid of coming into contact with non-Jews. Predominantly because of this, non-Jewish census officials were to be quartered not in Jewish private homes but in public places such as inns. It is not surprising, therefore, that it was exactly in the inn that there was no room for Joseph and Mary.

It cannot be emphasised too strongly that our Lord God Jesus was born in a stable and was laid down in a manger – that is, a feeding trough for animals, possibly a niche carved out in the cave wall. There was no room for Joseph and Mary in the inn. This was not because the innkeeper was cruel or inhospitable, but because the inn was already overcrowded.

Dear beloved child of God, please empathise with Mary. Think for a moment and ponder her feelings about the situation and circumstance in which she found herself. As an expecting mother for the first time, she would have liked and wanted to be in the best possible place to deliver her baby, especially her firstborn child. Or she might have contemplated having her first child in a house where human beings normally lived; but definitely, she would not have imagined having her first son in a place where animals were kept.

Did she see the animals around her and baby Jesus? Yes. Did she hear the blare of the animals that disturbed the sleep of the tender and weak baby Jesus and herself, and was she concerned and worried? Yes. But what could she do? Nothing. It was very likely that Mary had a restless and sleepless night and went back to memory lane. Perhaps she recalled the voice of the angel Gabriel telling her about the greatness and the divine nature of the child she carried in the very first month of her conception. Did Gabriel tell her that "the son of the Most High" who was in her virgin womb would be born in an ignominious, dehumanised place full of animals? No.

All the negative, depressing thoughts that have been raised are for you to think and speculate about the likely mindset of Mary in the situation and circumstance in which she found herself. Whatever thoughts she might have had, I believe Mary had confidence and trusted the words of the angel who said to her: "Greetings, you who are highly favoured! The Lord is with you. … Do not be afraid, Mary, you have found favour with God." As you read this passage, confidently and sincerely claim the words of the angel which were pronounced upon Mary. Whatever situation and circumstance (whether adverse or favourable) you find yourself currently in, be sure and certain that "you are highly favoured and have found favour with God."

Please note that when Jesus was born, practically and physically "there was no room" for Joseph and Mary; and therefore, there was no room in the inn for Christ (God), maker of heaven and earth and all the good things (including the best palaces) in them. Spiritually, there were hearts and minds in Israel (the teachers of the law, religious leaders, high priests including the Sanhedrin) that did not make room for Christ Jesus in Israel. Of course, there are those who do not make room for Christ Jesus not only in his lifetime in Israel but in all ages all over the world. As I write, there are billions of people in the universe who have not and will not make room for Christ Jesus in their hearts and minds; and of course, this trend will continue until the second advent of Christ Jesus himself.

It does not really mean that all those who do not make room in their hearts actually definitely hate Christ Jesus—although some absolutely do have hatred for Jesus for whatever reasons. Those who do not have room for Christ Jesus in their hearts and minds are not too busy, but they have already overcrowded their hearts, like the inn, with thoughts of riches, honour, prestige, fame, pleasure, business, political affairs, and so on. They have no room for Christ Jesus, no time to reflect on his will, and no desire to go out of their way to do his pleasure. They do not have room in their hearts to embrace the work of salvation for which he was born in Bethlehem, when "a great company of the heavenly host appeared with the angel, praising God" and singing the first Christmas carol.

I do hope and believe that you have made room for Christ Jesus in your heart. I presume that this is true of you, as you have being reading this book, and especially about the birth of Jesus who came to save you and wrought eternal salvation. If what I said about you is the truth, praise God and continue in your daily life in Christ Jesus, and tell others about this wonderful saviour. If you have not made provision in your heart and mind, however, I ardently pray that the Holy Spirit of the living God will open your spiritual eyes to see him and embrace him. May he open your spiritual ears to hear his tender voice, receive his call, and take his instruction to live and walk with him on a daily basis all through your life. Above all, may you open your heart and ask Christ Jesus to come and take control of all aspects of your life. He is right at the door of your heart waiting and saying to you now, "Here I am! I stand at the door and knock. If anyone hears my voice and opens the door, I will come in and eat with him and he with me" (Rev. 3:20).

## THE SHEPHERDS AND THE ANGEL

In the preceding paragraphs, I have stated that Jesus was born and placed "in a manger because there was no room for them in the inn." Now I continue with the story of the birth of Jesus as recorded by Luke and discuss the first group of people who made room for Jesus in their hearts and celebrated the first Christmas. They were the originators of the divine epoch-making nativity play shared by all Christian denominations in all ages.

These shepherds saw the celestial being and heard the songs of the angels who sang the original and first carol while watching their flocks at night around the blessed fields of the town of Bethlehem. Luke states: "And there were shepherds living out in the fields nearby, keeping watch over their flocks at night" (2:8). Luke also recorded the scene when Jesus went to the synagogue in Nazareth on a Sabbath day:

> The scroll of the prophet Isaiah was handed to him. Unrolling it, he found the place where it is written: "The Spirit of the Lord is on me, because he has anointed me to preach good news to the poor. He has sent me to proclaim freedom for the prisoners and recovery of sight for the blind, to release the oppressed, to proclaim the year of the Lord's favour." (Luke 4:16–19; Isa. 61:1–2).

Luke's account of the birth of Jesus is impeccably recorded, and it is certainly in divine harmony with God, who is the master planner. Take note that it is not a coincidence that the announcement of the birth of a messiah-saviour who has "the spirit of the Lord" and was sent and "anointed to preach good news to the poor" by the Lord God Almighty was first and foremost made known to poor shepherds. In the lifetime of Jesus (and probably now), shepherds were at the very bottom of the social, religious, and economic strata and despised. Because of the very nature of their occupation and profession, they were not able to participate in all the Jewish religious festivals and observe all the regulations of the Mosaic Law, especially the man-made rules superimposed upon the law. However, on a positive note, Hendriksen[3] suggested that the particular shepherds to whom the first proclamation of the saviour's birth was made were different. These shepherds were devout men, probably acquainted with the messianic prophecy, and like Simeon were "waiting for the consolation of Israel" (2:25). This statement is supported by the positive godly exemplary reaction of the shepherds (2:15–20).

Luke recorded the awe-inspiring event, described and presented it as though heaven and earth came together in the vicinity of the little town of Bethlehem, and stated: "a great company of the heavenly host appeared

---

[3] Hendriksen, 149.

with the angel" on earth (2:13–14). The birth of Jesus was one of the greatest events in the history of the universe, and something God the Creator had promised man the creature at the very moment Adam and Eve committed the sin of disobedience. It was an extraordinary heavenly event that resulted in a supernatural reaction both in heaven and on earth. I am standing on holy ground and state that Christ-Messiah (God the Son), who is a heavenly being, condescended and descended to the earth and was born as Jesus. Therefore, the only befitting, appropriate beings both in heaven and on earth to proclaim this long-awaited and glorious news would have been the "great company of the heavenly host" of angelic beings. It would not have been proper for an ordinary human being in Israel—even the high priests, teachers of the law, Pharisees, or Sadducees—to proclaim the birth of Jesus to the shepherds.

At the time when Jesus was born, many religious leaders and even ordinary frustrated, oppressed people were seriously expecting a secular political leader and warlord like King David who would deliver them from the iron rule of Rome and give them back their religious freedom, while others were hoping for the arrival of a saviour who would save them from sickness and economic hardship. But this proclamation of the birth of Jesus by the angel concerns a Messiah-saviour who delivers Israel and the Gentile nations from sin and eternal death (Matt. 1:21).

Luke stated that "an angel of the Lord appeared to them, and the glory of the Lord shone around them, and they were terrified" (2:9). "An angel of the Lord" is a designation used throughout the birth of Jesus narratives (Luke 1:11; Matt. 1:20, 24, 2:13, 19). The angel in Luke 1:11 is identified as Gabriel (1:19, 26). This divine phenomenon happened with a dramatic swiftness. These shepherds had never seen anything like it. I go back through memory and think of Moses, who was a shepherd and saw and experienced an awesome burning bush where "the angel of the Lord appeared to him in flames of fire from within a bush" (Exod. 3:2). In that scene, "I Am Who I Am" made his name and himself known to Moses and assured him that he would rescue the Israelites "from the hand of the Egyptians and to bring them up out of that land into a good and spacious land, a land flowing with milk and honey" (3:8). I am uncertain of whether the shepherds in Luke's narrative knew or had heard about the experience of Moses. As unschooled men ostracized by the elite of Israel's religious, political, and social groups, it was very unlikely that they had any knowledge of the experience of Moses and the burning bush.

The angel of the Lord in all his holiness, brilliance, and heavenly power appeared to them as close as divinely possible. "And the glory of the Lord shone around them, and they were terrified. But the angel said to them, 'Do not be afraid. I bring you good news of great joy that will be for all people. Today in the town of David a saviour has been born to you, he is Christ the Lord. This will be a sign to you: You will find a baby wrapped in cloths and lying a manger" (Luke 2: 9b–12). The angel came to the shepherds with the glory of the Lord, which brought heavenly brightness that was rightly regarded as the manifestation of God's presence and power. The glory of the Lord flashed all around the shepherds and illuminated the dark night in the fields in the vicinity of the town of Bethlehem.

Prior to the appearance of the angel and proclamation of the birth of Christ the Lord, the shepherds had no knowledge that Christ the saviour of the world had been born. Christ brings light and life to the world, and the shepherds were the first to see that light and life. John stated: "In him was life, and that life was the light of all men. The light shines in the darkness, but the darkness had not understood it" (John 1:4–5). Christ came to give light and life to both the God people of Israel and the whole Gentile world. From his birth, he gave light to the shepherds and continues to give light which illuminates spiritually the hearts and minds of all those who accept him as their personal Lord and saviour.

Christ Jesus himself in his earthly ministry said to his audience, "I am the light of the world. Whoever follows me will never walk in darkness, but will have the light of life" (John 8:12). Christ Jesus proclaimed himself to his audience as "I Am Who I Am", the name Yahweh used to introduce himself to Moses. Christ Jesus referred to himself as "I am" seven times (all in the gospel of John) as self-description. Both physical and spiritual light are indispensable to human beings, and for that reason, the omniscient God on the first day of creation said: "Let there be light … and there was light" (Gen 1:3). Because of the primacy of the light, God's first creative word called forth the light in the midst of primeval darkness. Light is necessary for making God's creative works visible and makes life possible and pleasant.

It is imperative to note that from the beginning of creation, the first universal element God gave to the world was light. Therefore, it is proper that during the birth of Christ Jesus, God gave light to the shepherds. The record of Luke on the birth of Jesus states that "an angel of the Lord appeared to the [shepherds] and the glory of the Lord shone around them" (2:9). This is in perfect harmony with the account of Matthew on the resurrection: "There was a violent earth quake, for an angel of the Lord came down from heaven and going to the tomb, rolled back the stone and sat on it. His appearance was like lightning, and his clothes were white as snow" (Matt. 28:2–3).

I rejoin the nativity story of Luke, who stated, "But the angel said to them, 'Do not be afraid, I bring you good news of great joy that will be for all people. Today in the town of David a saviour has been born to you, he is Christ the Lord. This is will be a sign to you: you will find a baby wrapped in cloths and lying in a manger" (2:10–12). The statement "Do not be afraid" is given many times in both the Old Testament and the New Testament.[4] Fear was (and is) the common human reaction to angelic appearance, and encouragement and assurance from the same celestial being was (and is) needed.

Observe that the main purpose or mission of the appearance of the angel to the shepherds was to bring "good news of great joy that will be for all people." Were the shepherds expecting to hear the good news the angel brought to them? Probably yes, as had been explained before. Did the "good news" make any material difference in the situation and circumstance they found themselves in as shepherds? What was the meaning of this "good news"? The "good news" the angel proclaimed to the shepherds did not instantaneously change their material well-being, or their social or religious stance in Israel. Nevertheless, the angel brought the "good news" of salvation through Christ Jesus and declared it as "of great joy." There is no greater joy for both the shepherds and you than the realisation that "a Saviour has been born to you; he is Christ the Lord."

As the shepherds did, you have wholeheartedly accepted him as your saviour. This "Christ the Lord" is Godself who came down from heaven to earth to give the greatest joy to the shepherds, you, and "all people", regardless of nationality, sex, age, or social or economic status.

---

[4] Gen. 15:1, 21:17, 26:24; Deut. 1:21; Josh. 8:1; Matt. 28:5; Luke 1:30, 2:10, 5:10, 8:50, 12:7, 32.

Note the following:

- The good news proclaimed by God to Moses – "So now go. I am sending you to Pharaoh to bring my people the Israelites out of Egypt" (Exod. 3:10) – was meant for only for the descendants of Abraham, Isaac, and Jacob.

- Not all the Hebrews who left Egypt reached the promised land: "All those who came out of Egypt – all the men of military age – died in the desert on the way after leaving Egypt" (Josh. 5:4), except Joshua and Caleb.

- Even for Joshua and Caleb, the promised land was not immediately realised and fulfilled in their lifetime. Rather, it took a long period of forty-odd years of wilderness wandering.

- The "good news" that was proclaimed by the angel to the shepherds is for "all people", which includes God's people of Israel as well the sinful nations of the Gentiles.

- This "good news of great joy" does not take forty years or even forty seconds to be realised or fulfilled in the person who believes in the saving grace of "Christ the Lord." The fulfilment of the "good news" of "Christ the Lord" is without any procrastination; it is an instantaneous fulfilment. It is today and now as Christ Jesus said to Zacchaeus the tax collector: "Today salvation has come to this house" (Luke 19:9); and to the criminal who was crucified with [Jesus]: "I tell you the truth, today you will be with me in paradise" (Luke 23:43).

- The promise of the "great joy" must be accepted through personal belief and faith in Christ Jesus, who is the saviour of your soul.

- The "good news of great joy" of salvation should be proclaimed by every believer in Christ Jesus to all unbelievers in all nations.

- Those who do not believe and reject the salvation message cannot be saved, and the "great joy" will not bubble in their hearts.

- The wonderful and marvellous heavenly blessing of salvation that gives "great joy" is only and solely for those who believe in the one and only Son of God: Christ Jesus (John 3:16).

- The saviour who was introduced by the angel to the shepherds is "Christ the Lord" who is the Messiah or the anointed one. He is the one anointed by the Holy Spirit to be his people's great prophet, great sympathetic high priest, and eternal king.

- "Christ the Lord" is the "Wonderful Counsellor, Mighty God, Everlasting Father, and Prince of Peace" (Isa 9:6b).
- "Christ the Lord" is the "son of Man" Daniel saw in his dream (Dan. 7:13). That was the first time a reference was made to the Messiah as the Son of Man, a title which Christ Jesus applied to himself eighty-one times in the Gospels. It is never used by anyone but Christ Jesus.

## Pax

At the end of the angel's proclamation of the birth of Jesus, Luke continued: "Suddenly a great company of the heavenly host appeared with the angel, praising God and saying, 'Glory to God in the highest, and on earth peace to men on whom his favour rests'" (2:13–14).This brief hymn is called the "Gloria in Excelsis Deo", from the first words of the Latin Vulgate translation (meaning "Glory to God in the Highest")[5]. Christ condescended and descended from God's highest heaven and came down to earth below. So it was divinely appropriate that "a great company of the heavenly host" should also come down from heaven to earth and give "Glory to God in the Highest" who sent his son Christ to bring salvation to all people on earth. The heavenly angelic host knew and recognised the glory and majesty of both God the Father who sent his one and only son Christ to the world and God the Son who willingly and voluntarily came down and wrought salvation to all the people on the earth. And for that holy reason, the heavenly host praised and honoured both God the Father and God the Son.

The proclamation of the heavenly host "and on earth peace (*pax*) to men on whom his favour rests" mean exactly and precisely that, without any ambiguity. It does not require interpretation. As has been explained and emphasised in other sections in this book, peace and salvation in Christ Jesus is free for all, but not assured for all. Peace from or of God is given to only those "on whom his favour rests", and it is only those who wholeheartedly accept Christ Jesus as their saviour who receive his favour

---

[5] The NIV Study Bible (London, Sydney, Auckland, Toronto, 1985) 1,508.

and peace. Christ was born to bring peace from his Father in heaven to all people on earth.

Christ was born into the Roman world, and Israel was part of the Roman Empire. The Roman world experienced the "Roman Peace" (*Pax Romana*), an external tranquillity probably obtained by suppression that forced all subject states into false obedience. The *Pax Romana* was not permanent, and it was not present in all the subdued states at the same time in the Roman Empire. In the lifetime of Christ Jesus, there was no *Pax Romana* in Israel in the Roman Empire. Several freedom fighters and agitators for independence who opposed imperial Roman rule were executed by crucifixion. During the trial of Jesus before Pilate, "A man called Barabbas was in prison with the insurrectionist who had committed murder in the uprising" (Mark 15:7). In fact, Jesus was accused (in this case by his own people of Israel) of insurrection and being a ring leader against Pilate and Caesar, which Luke recorded in the following terms:

> Then the whole assembly (the Council of the elders of the people, both the Chief priests and teachers of the law-the Sanhedrin) rose and led him off to Pilate. And they began to accuse him, saying, "We have found this man subverting our nation. He opposed payment of taxes to Caesar and claims to be Christ, a King" (Luke 23:1–2).

All the accusations brought against Jesus were purely political attempts to portray Jesus as a violent man and rebel gang leader in opposition against Caesar and the Roman authority.

Contrary to all the false allegations, Christ came down from heaven to earth with a divine peace right from his birth. He talked about peace, and he lived an exemplary life as a peacemaker throughout his earthly mission. At his birth, the angels proclaimed a holy, deeper, more lasting peace which was in him during his earthly mission. The secular *Pax Romana*, which was not really peace, ended with the collapse of the Roman Empire, but divine and celestial peace from the Prince of Peace endures forever. He is the peace of life, and he is the Davidic Messiah, the "Prince of Peace" (Isa. 9:6).

Dear child of the Prince of Peace, please devote some quiet time to read the Sermon on the Mount, the first of the five great discourses in Matthew chapters 5–7. This sermon was from the holy lips of Christ Jesus and expressed the inner and deeper feeling of peace in the Prince of Peace. It is the grand bulwark upon which all the peace movement of all sorts and in the entire world, both ancient and modern, stand. Christ Jesus preached peace and practiced peace all the time in his earthly ministry. Even in his agonising final hours on earth, he prayed for peace for his disciples and you, and said, "Peace I leave with you, my peace I give you. I do not give to you as the world gives" (John 14:27).

The "peace" Christ Jesus spoke of here is the heavenly peace between God and human beings and the salvation that his redemptive work on the cross and his ultimate resurrection will achieve for his first disciples and for you. This peace is the total well-being and inner rest of the spirit in a holy fellowship and daily relationship with God. Christ Jesus himself is your peace, because he is the fountain and source of your inner peace and being.

After his resurrection, he appeared to his disciples, and the first greeting from him to them was, "Peace be with you" (John 20:19). Dear child of the God of peace, be assured that right now at this moment in time, the Prince of Peace stands by you and is saying to you, "Peace be with you." His peace is with you in whatever circumstance and situation you find yourself.

After the brief but glorious and inspirational Christmas hymn "Gloria in Excelsis Deo", which was first sang by the "great company of the heavenly host", Luke stated:

> When the angels had left them and gone into heaven, the shepherds said to one another, "Let's go to Bethlehem and see this thing that has happened, which the Lord has told us about." So they hurried off and found Mary and Joseph, and the baby, who was lying in the manger. When they had seen him, they spread the word concerning what had been told them about this child, and all who heard it were amazed at what the shepherds said to them. But Mary treasured up all these thing and pondered them in her heart. The shepherds returned, glorifying and praising God for all the things they had heard and seen, which were just as they had been told. (2:15–20).

Please observe that the shepherds heard the good news of the birth of Jesus as well as the angelic praise; and without hesitation they encouraged one another to see for themselves the thing that had been said to them about Jesus. Actually, the angel did not tell them to go to Bethlehem to see Jesus; but the angel was sure that the shepherds would go. So he gave them the road map and signpost to follow to see the saviour of all the people of the world. It is the Holy Spirit who prompted the shepherds to go to Bethlehem to seek and find the saviour, and they did find him just as had been said by the angel.

As you read this nativity story at this moment in time, my ardent prayer is that the same Holy Spirit who prompted the shepherds and galvanised them to action will help you to take a positive step for Christ Jesus. I fervently pray that the Spirit of the living God will help you either make it possible for Jesus to be born or reborn in your heart right now, or assist you to proclaim the birth of Jesus to others who do not realise that he came to save them. I also sincerely pray that the saviour, Christ Jesus, will help you to have a deeper and inner personal relationship with him and give you that peace which he gives to all who believe in him.

The shepherds gladly told Mary and Joseph of the wonderful celestial figure who appeared to them and what he said to them about Jesus and the rest of the holy phenomenon, all of which pointed to the divinity of Jesus. Of course, Mary and Joseph were not surprised by the testimony of the shepherds, because both of them had separately received similar messages from angels regarding Jesus. However, the shepherds did not confine their story and experience to Mary and Joseph but enthusiastically and sincerely shared the good news of the birth of Jesus the saviour with all those they met on their trip back from the town of Bethlehem to the fields where they came from.

Unlike Mary and Joseph, who had prior revelation about Jesus, "All who heard it were amazed at what the shepherds said to them" (2:18). The good news of the angel to the shepherds is compared to the parable of the sower who scattered his seed that "fell on good soil, where it produced a crop – a hundred, sixty or thirty times what was sown" (Matt. 13:8). The shepherds honestly shared their story with many people they met in Bethlehem and as stated before, Bethlehem had its highest population at the time when Christ was born because of the decretal census order in Israel.

Note the positive entry of how the testimony of the shepherds was received: "all who heard it were amazed." Not some, but all. This "all" could be hundreds or possibly thousands of people who heard the testimony of the shepherds. In other words, all received their testimony with amazement and wanted to see Jesus.

It is imperative to note that "all who heard" were not ambivalent about the good news of the birth of Jesus; they were all amazed and certain, convinced without doubt that what had been prophesied about their town of Bethlehem seven centuries earlier by the prophet Micah had come to fulfilment in their lifetime. Micah prophesied regarding a promised ruler from Bethlehem and stated: "But you Bethlehem Ephrathah, though you are small among the clans of Judah, out of you will come for me one who will be ruler over Israel, whose origin are from of old, from ancient times" (Mic. 5:2).

The magnanimous characters of the shepherds takes me back to memory lane and reminds me of the four lepers of Samaria. They too made a wonderful and marvellous discovery, though theirs was material – unlike the shepherds, who received spiritual eternal blessings. The lepers did not want to keep the good news of the abandoned booty they found but went and shared it with the people who were besieged in the city and facing great famine. Like the shepherds, the four lepers said to each other, "We're not doing right. This is a day of good news and we are keeping it to ourselves. If we wait until daylight, punishment will overtake us. Let's go at once and report this to the royal palace" (2 Kgs 7:9).

Dear child of the prince of peace, I have more to write about the good example of the missionary character that was displayed by both the shepherds and the lepers. However, I will end my discussion here. But on a serious note, it suffices to state here that it is necessary and obligatory for all believers in Christ Jesus to spread the good news of salvation which he brings with him to the world right from his birth.

# Chapter 4

# THE MISSION OF CHRIST JESUS

The virgin birth of Jesus, which was the focus of Chapter 3, is linked to his earthly mission which he came to fulfil. Therefore, in this chapter, I will evaluate and analyse the mission of Christ Jesus in the land of Palestine and its divine role in the work of salvation. The mission of Christ Jesus is the single most important ministry in the history of the universe, since the Creator God the Father and God the Son (Christ) created the world, and it will remain so until the second advent of Christ Jesus himself.

It is vital to state from the beginning here that the sole and overarching divine purpose of Christ Jesus' mission to Israel and the world is to bring salvation to the Jewish people of Yahweh as well as the Gentile nations of the pagans. All the Christians from the Apostolic age to the current era believe that Christ Jesus transformed and renewed their lives and gave to them salvation through his birth, mission, death on the cross, and ultimate resurrection on the third day. Christ Jesus is presented as the Son of God (the Messiah, Christ, Saviour) even before his virgin birth. The Gospel writer of Matthew recorded the purpose of the mission of Christ Jesus which was revealed to Joseph by an angel of the Lord before his birth. Joseph was in a dilemma of what to do with Mary because of her uncomfortable condition of been pregnant but not by him when the angel of the Lord appeared to him in his dream:

But after he had considered this, an angel of the Lord appeared to him in a dream and said, "Joseph son of David, do not be afraid to take Mary home as your wife, because what is conceived in her is from the Holy Spirit. She will give birth to a son, and you are to give him the name Jesus because he will save his people from their sins." (Matt. 1:20–21).

This message of the angel is marvellous and wonderful in the sight of God the Father, who sent the divine figure to speak to Joseph. These assuring statements from the angel allayed Joseph's fear, concern, and worry, and helped him make decisions in obedience to God's will to fulfil the grand plan for salvation wrought by the birth, mission, death, and resurrection of Christ Jesus.

As you read this fascinating cited scripture, think about the circumstances in which you find yourself. Perhaps you are trapped in a situation and cannot make any decision or take action, and it seems that there is no way forward at the moment. If that is your position, please do not make a hasty decision, but rather wait patiently on the Lord, and he will direct and guide you just as the angel did to Joseph.

Joseph was a righteous man of God, and I do believe that you are also a believer and a saved soul in Christ Jesus. I strongly believe that Joseph was a righteous man; he sought the face of God, and it was because of this that the angel appeared to him in his dream in order to communicate God's purpose and plan for him regarding the unborn Jesus and virgin Mary. As the angel of the Lord appeared to Joseph and spoke to him, so the Holy Spirit of God will communicate to you in order to settle all your fears, uncertainties, and worries if you continue to seek his face and wait without murmuring.

Christ Jesus said to his audience in the great Sermon on the Mount: "Ask and it will be given to you; seek and you will find; knock and the door will be opened to you. For everyone who asks receives; he who seeks finds; and to him who knocks, the door will be opened" (Matt. 7:7–8). Read the living testimony of King David who had absolute faith and confidence in God: "I waited patiently for the Lord; he turned to me and heard my cry" (Ps. 40:1). Read again and take note of the instruction and conclusion of David: "Wait for the Lord; be strong and take heart and wait for the Lord" (Ps. 27:14).

It is imperative to note in the message of the angel that he gave the name "Jesus", meaning saviour, to Joseph. The angel also made a holy annunciation and said to Joseph: "[Jesus] will save his people from their sins." Here I stand on a solid and holy ground to state that the words of the angel are also the main focal point of this book, which is salvation. It will also be part of my conclusion that Christ came humbly in the human bodily form of Jesus to save as many as would believe in him.

In relating the statement of the angel, Matthew exploited the popular etymology of Jesus' name. Note that the word "save" from sins is applied because oppression, exile, and foreign domination were often regarded as punishment for sins in the Old Testament viewpoint. Oppression also involved separation from God. The essence of sin was that it hindered obedience to the commandments of Yahweh.

Please observe that at the time of this holy annunciation of the angel, Israel had been forcefully occupied by imperial Rome and oppressed and ruled with an iron fist. Christ Jesus came to this world in order to obtain salvation for humankind through his proclamation of the kingdom of God; and above all by his death on the cross and resurrection. I am safe to state here that there are heavenly connections between the birth of Jesus; the proclamation of the kingdom of God; the death and resurrection; and the work of salvation.[1]

Luke recorded the beginning of the ministry of Christ Jesus and stated:

> He went to Nazareth, where he had been brought up, and on the Sabbath day he went into the synagogue, as was his custom. And he stood up to read. The scroll of the prophet Isaiah was handed to him. Unrolling it, he found the place where it is written: "The Spirit of the Lord is on me, because he has anointed me to preach good news to the poor. He has sent me to proclaim freedom for the prisoners and recovery of sight for the blind, to release the oppressed, to proclaim the year of the Lord's favour." (Luke 4:14–19)

---

[1] Benedict T. Viviano, "The Gospel According to Matthew", in *The New Jerome Bible Commentary*, ed. Raymond E. Brown, Joseph A. Fitzmyer, and Roland E. Murphy (London, 2013), 635.

This text is the executive summary of the mission statement of Christ Jesus. Did Christ Jesus successfully complete his mission on earth? Of course, the answer is yes, and you will agree with me as you read in subsequent chapters in this book how he fulfilled the purpose of his mission and ultimately brings salvation to all those who accept the good news he proclaimed.

The writer of the fourth Gospel recorded what came from the lips of Christ Jesus himself when he said to Nicodemus: "For God so loved the world that he gave his one and only Son, that whoever believes in him shall not perish but have eternal life. For God did not send his Son into the world to condemn the world, but to save the world through him" (John 3:16–17). The greatest truth that motivated God's plan of salvation even to the extent of sending his only and one son Christ Jesus is love. The verses shed light on the following aspects of this holy love:

- its character ("so loved")
- its author (God the Father himself)
- its object (the whole world, not just the Jewish nation of the only people of God)
- its gift (God the Son, the only and one begotten Son of God the Father, Christ Jesus)
- its purpose (that whoever believes in his name, whether Jews or Gentiles, shall not perish but have eternal life)

The last part of the statement (its purpose, which is eternal life) is the main interest of this book (salvation), and it is necessary to expand on this here. First, I will summarise the background of events which made Christ Jesus embark upon his mission in the land of Palestine.

After the fall of man as recorded in the third chapter of Genesis, God did not abandon humankind forever. God had a grand plan to save humankind from the moment Adam and Eve lost Paradise because of disobedience, which led to their sin and spread to all their descendants. In passing judgement on the serpent who deceived Eve to disobey God's order, God said to him "and I will put enmity between you and the woman, and between your offspring and hers; he will crush your head, and you will strike his heel" (Gen. 3:15). This passage seems to explain the antagonism between people and snakes which symbolises the outcome of the titanic struggle between God and the evil one, a struggle played out in the hearts and history of humankind.

God's promise is divinely clear that the offspring of the woman would eventually crush the serpent's head, a promise that has been faithfully and truly fulfilled in Christ Jesus' victory over the power of Satan through his death on the cross and resurrection. This is a victory in which all believers in the Lord and saviour Christ Jesus now share (Rom. 16:20).[2] It came to humankind when God – who did not lie but made his promise good – sent Christ Jesus, his one and only son, at the appropriate and appointed time to save the seed of Adam and Eve from the original sin. No matter the longevity, God brought his promise to be fulfilled in Christ Jesus.

Paul, writing to the Galatians in his epistle, stated: "But when the time had fully come God sent his Son, born of a woman, under the law, to redeem those under the law, that we might receive the full rights of Sons" (Gal. 4:4). Christ Jesus is the offspring of the fallen woman Eve who God promised would crush the head of the offspring of the serpent. This was materialised in the birth, mission, death, and resurrection of our Lord and saviour Christ Jesus on the first Christmas Day; the first Good Friday; and the first Easter Sunday Morning. The offspring who is Christ Jesus brings eternal life (salvation) to all those (both Jews and Gentiles) who believe in him.

John 3:16 is the interface between the Old and the New Testaments, and it is the key passage which explicitly explains the divine reason for God the Father to send God the Son to the world. John the evangelist analysed the narrative with a discourse on the sending of Christ Jesus mainly and only to bring salvation to the whole world. What prompted God the Father to do this is his own Fatherly love for the world he created. The three key terms from the lips of the one who was sent (Christ Jesus) are *love*, *believe*, and *eternal life*. This small trinity intermingles and is interwoven inseparably. The sinner must know that God loves him or her so much that he sent his one and only beloved son. The sinner must believe in the name of Christ Jesus who alone gives eternal life (salvation). And the sinner must constantly, on a daily basis, love the giver of eternal life and praise him here on earth as well as in the kingdom of God forevermore.

---

[2] NIV Study Bible, 12.

Spurgeon commented on John 3:16 under different subheadings. Here I will concentrate on just one – the divine plan of salvation and the divine choice of the people to whom salvation comes – which is most relevant to my motif in this chapter.

## THE DIVINE PLAN OF GOD'S SALVATION

In commenting on John 3:16, Spurgeon regarded it as the divine plan of salvation and said, "Note the love of God in the plan of salvation. He has put it thus: 'that whosoever believeth on him should not perish, but have everlasting life.'" Spurgeon stated that the way of salvation is extremely simple to understand and exceedingly easy to practise, when once the heart is made willing and obedient.

Spurgeon generated a question on belief, asking, "So what is it to believe in Jesus?" Spurgeon himself provided the answer, stating that, "What is to believe in Jesus is to give your firm and cordial assent to the truth by accepting that God did send his Son, born of a woman and bear the punishment of our transgressions." According to Spurgeon, you must accept for yourself that Jesus offered an atonement, and that atonement becomes yours when you accept it by putting your trust in him as well as your personal truest. First comes assent to the truth, then acceptance of that truth for yourself, and then a simple trusting of yourself wholly to Christ, as a substitute. The essence of faith is trust, reliance, and dependence, Spurgeon emphasised.

The divine choice of the people to whom salvation comes is described in these words: "whosoever believeth in him." There is in the text a word which has no limit – "God so loved the world" – but then comes in the descriptive limit, which Spurgeon begs you to notice with care: "He gave his only begotten Son that whosoever believeth in him should not perish."

It is my opinion that God loving the world does not mean that every person and all people – including those who do not believe in Christ Jesus – shall be saved; neither did God send his only son to the world so that even those who do not acknowledge and refuse to accept him as their personal Lord and saviour should be saved. Read how John put it: "For God so loved the world that he gave his one and only Son, that whosoever believes in him shall not perish but have eternal life." Note the compass of the love: while every unbeliever is excluded, every believer is included in this grand plan of God's salvation.[3]

The writer of the fourth Gospel recorded the first public appearance of Christ Jesus to Israel and stated: "The next day [John the Baptist] saw Jesus coming towards him and (after Christ Jesus returned from the desert where he had been tempted). As John saw him approaching, he exclaimed to his audience, while he looked or pointed towards Jesus) "Look the Lamb of God; who takes away the sin of the world" (John 1:29). Please observe that here John the Baptist formally and publicly introduced Christ Jesus to the Jews who were with him and listening to his answer for his mission of baptism.

It is true that by his voluntary submission to the rite of baptism and by his victory over Satan in the desert of temptation (in Matthew's account), Christ Jesus had indeed vicariously taken upon himself the curse of the law and of rendering perfect obedience. And by these very acts and by those that were to follow, he was divinely prepared to take away the sin of the world. Please note that according to John the Baptist, it is the sin of the *world* – men and women from every tribe and people, by nature lost in sin (John 11:51, 52), which the Lamb of God is taking away, and not only the sin of a particular nation, such as God's people of Israel.

It is of paramount importance to emphasize here that John 3:16 does not teach or even insinuate a free-for-all universal atonement for salvation. John the Baptist did not teach such unscriptural doctrine, nor does John the evangelist or Christ Jesus himself.[4] Read the first citation: "Yet to all who received him, to those who believed in his name, he gave the right to become children of God" (John 1:12). The imparting of the gift (salvation) is dependent on humankind's reception of it, as the words "received" and "believed" make absolutely clear.[5]

Salvation in the fullest sense of the term is what God has in mind for the whole world into which he sent his one and only son. This universal but individually obtained salvation must only be received by those who believe

[3] Charles Haddon Spurgeon, *Spurgeon's Commentary on the Bible*, ed. Robert Backhouse (London, 1997), 189 –190.

[4] John 1:12, 13; 3:16; 10:11, 27, 28; 17:9;

[5] William Hendriksen, *New Testament on John*, 98–99.

in Christ Jesus. Once again, I cite John the evangelist, who recorded the words from the holy lips of Christ Jesus. According to John, Christ Jesus said: "The thief comes only to steal and kill and destroy; I have come that they may have life, and have it to the full" (John 10:10). Here, John insisted that Christ Jesus is the only source of salvation. "Those who came before" is probably a reference to the false prophets and Jewish teachers of the law and tradition to which they appealed, who did not bring eternal salvation. They are rejected and regarded as thieves. Take note of the contrast between the thieves who "steal" and "kill" and "destroy" for their own personal gain and Christ Jesus' self-denial and sacrifice solely for the interest of his followers. Christ Jesus has come that his followers might "have life and have it to the full." The life which Christ Jesus offers is salvation for the present age as well as the age to come; and this salvation is free and complete only in Christ Jesus.

Finally, I make reference to Luke's account in this all-important subject of the word *salvation*. According to the recording of Luke, when the teachers of the law and those who strictly adhered to Mosaic Law objected to Christ Jesus' conduct of association with a section of the population that had been ostracized (case in reference: Zacchaeus the tax collector), Christ Jesus seized the opportunity and made his divine mission statement: "Today salvation has come to this house, because this man, too, is a son of Abraham. For the Son of Man came to seek and to save what was lost" (Luke 19:9–10).

Observe another important "mission statement" in Luke 19:10 which summarises Christ Jesus' purpose of coming to the world: that is, to bring salvation ("eternal life", John 18:18) and the kingdom of God (John 18:25). Dear loved child of God, observe that firstly Christ Jesus offered himself to stay with Zacchaeus; and Zacchaeus's unconditional willingness to accept Christ Jesus as his humble host changed the life of Zacchaeus for good and brought salvation to his entire household. Note that Zacchaeus wholeheartedly and without any hesitation and reservation confessed his sin and promised to pay four times, which was extreme repayment, to all those he had disproportionately collected tax from by deception.

It is wonderful and marvellous to notice that the presence of Christ Jesus makes possible what is humanly impossible. A wealthy and rich man such as Zacchaeus went through the "needle's eye", but not without some radical change wrought by the work of the Holy Spirit. Like God the Father portrayed as a shepherd in Ezekiel 36:14, Christ Jesus (God the Son) who is the "good shepherd" (John 10:14) also seeks out the lost sheep to save them.[6]

This salvation which Christ Jesus brought to Zacchaeus meant emancipation from the greatest evil and being in possession of the greatest good. This salvation can only be construed as nothing less than "eternal everlasting life" in Christ Jesus in his glory in his kingdom. Today, Jesus called the chief publican out in that tree and with blessing entered his home. Today, therefore, the great spiritual miracle had taken place. The greatest physical and spiritual shepherd had found his lost sheep.

Note that Zacchaeus did not seek out Christ Jesus; it was Christ Jesus who lifted up his divine eyes and found him, and asked him to come down, and offered to be his guest in order to bring salvation to him and his family. After a few days of the jubilation of salvation, the good shepherd was going to lay down his life on his own accord for his sheep, including Zacchaeus, to complete the way to salvation.

My ardent prayer is that as you read this book of salvation, whatever happened to Zacchaeus for his salvation and his entire family will also be fulfilled in your life and in your household in the name of Christ Jesus, the bringer of salvation to all those who put their faith and focus on him through the ages.

---

[6] Robert J. Karris, "The Gospel According to Luke," in *The New Jerome Bible Commentary*, 711.

# Chapter 5

# SALVATION

In the preceding four chapters, I have given an overview of the theme of this book and explained some of the theological terms which I will apply to the rest of my writing. I have also presented both the birth and mission of salvation in Christ Jesus.

That settled, in this fifth chapter, I will without much ado and procrastination dive straight into the main theme of this book in order to explain the mystery mission of Christ Jesus in the land of Palestine. In order to put this chapter on its divine and appropriate track from the beginning, it is necessary to state that the one and only transcendental tenacity of Christ Jesus' unfathomable mission to the people of God of Israel is to bring salvation to the Jews as well as to the ungodly Gentile nations. The perplexing and puzzling question is, how does Christ Jesus bring this redemptive work of God the Father?

It is likely that I will spend some time and energy giving a satisfactory answer to the above question later in the appropriate sections in this book; but in a nutshell, the reverberating answer is that Christ Jesus brings salvation "to all the nations of the earth" by the grand and ultimate atonement on the cross at Calvary on the first Good Friday (Gen. 22:18; Isa. 53:7; John 19:30). All Christians from the apostolic age to the current era believe that Christ Jesus has transformed their lives and has given to them salvation through his death and resurrection on the first Good Friday and on the first Easter Sunday respectively. The question of how this amazing grace of salvation has been possible in particular and how it relates to the history and story of Christ Jesus has been the subject of intense and immense discussion throughout Christian history from the time of the patristic era (and even in the apostolic era). It is very likely that this trend of debate will continue in the near and far distant future as new generations of theologians develop new hermeneutical presuppositions regarding certain texts in the Bible.

I state from the very beginning of this chapter that without the resurrection phenomenon on the first Easter Sunday morning, there would be no work of salvation, and it is Christ Jesus who wrought both of them through his birth, mission, and death on the Calvary cross on the first God Friday. It is necessary to confine the word *salvation* to its divine meaning in this book, which is to "save from sin and lead to eternal life in Christ Jesus." This is my understanding and meaning of salvation in this book.

That is to say, salvation in this book will not be concerned with a worldwide range of view that includes liberation and black theology, and involves secularised and comprehensive materialistic topics like prosperity gospel, politics, economics, sociology, human rights, injustice, and all other related intractable and complicated issues. All these are very good and worthy of discussion. However, it is necessary to state that they are beyond the scope and dimension of this book, as I only and mainly focus on the spiritual aspect of salvation. This eternal message of salvation of sin in Christ Jesus is the greatest liberation of all liberation movements that lead to freedom from every bondage in the whole wide world.

Christians hold that the birth, mission, death, and resurrection of Christ Jesus has changed things in their lives for good forever. Humanity has fallen into disorder since the fall of Adam and Eve. Things were not what they were meant to be at the beginning and origin of creation. Something had to be done to restore the divine order as it was from the beginning under the control of the Creator God before the fall of Adam and Eve. The same God who made the good and perfect world from the beginning therefore acted to renew and reorder the disordered world.

The Christian doctrine of sin tries to give an account of what went wrong after Adam and Eve disobeyed God, fell into sin, and lost Paradise. On the positive side, the doctrine of salvation deals with the restoration of the original created order – and above all, returning humanity to its proper relationship to God through the birth, mission, death on the cross, and resurrection of Christ Jesus, who brings salvation to all those who believe in him. The Christian doctrine of salvation focuses on Christ Jesus as the redeemer and saviour of the world.

The Christian belief and faith in salvation is understood to be grounded in the life and death of Christ Jesus on the cross and his resurrection. This salvation which was for the first Jewish Christians and Gentiles of the early church is the same salvation that is for all the believers now and the same salvation that will be for all the future believers in Christ Jesus. Salvation is salvation for all believers in all generations in all nations, as there is no adjective that is good or adequate enough for it. It is good to praise and worship Christ Jesus who does what he is (Saviour) and has done the greatest thing in the history of human beings by freely giving present and eschatological eternal salvation to all who have faith and belief in him.

In the following sections, I will analyse the term *salvation* from the perspective of both the Old and the New Testaments.

## SALVATION: OLD TESTAMENT PERSPECTIVE

In a nutshell, the Old Testament denotation of salvation is to "bring into a spacious environment" (Ps. 18:36; 66:12). It is the viewpoint of this book that the term *salvation* carries from the start a metaphorical sense of "freedom from limitation" (in Egypt) and "deliverance from factors which constrain and confine." Salvation is also a notion of deliverance from diseases (Isa. 38:9, 20); from trouble (Jer. 30:7) or from enemies (2 Sam. 3:18; Ps. 44:7). God is the author of salvation who saved the fathers from Egypt (Ps. 106:7–10) and their sons from Babylon (Jer. 30:10).

Generally, the Old Testament denotation of salvation is deliverance from danger, from fatal illness (healing), and from captivity. One of the most noticeable citations in the Old Testament relevant to the word *salvation* is the statement of Moses to the Israelites who were fleeing from their Egyptian slave masters and pursued by the almighty army of Pharaoh. The Israelites who had camped by the sea near Pi Hahiroth opposite Baal Zephon were trapped in between the Red Sea and the Egyptian army, which was marching after them and about to overtake them. The Israelites in their panic and confusion blamed and rebuked Moses for bringing them out of Egypt: "Didn't we say to you in Egypt, leave us alone; let us serve the Egyptians? It would have been better for us to serve the Egyptians than to die in the desert." But Moses had confidence and trust in the omnipotent Yahweh and made a positive response with all certainty to his faint-of-heart fellow Hebrews: "Do not be afraid. Stand firm and you will see the deliverance the Lord will bring you today. The Egyptians you see today you will never see again. The Lord will fight for you; you need only to be still" (Exod. 14:8–14).

Note that Moses exhorted the fleeing Israelites to stand firm and prepare for a holy war. The understanding of the people in the ancient world was that in war, the gods fought in heaven in support of their armies on earth (Exod.17:8–16). Since Yahweh was Israel's only true deity even in Egypt, Israel's victory was assured. The people had only to avoid panic and be confident in the coming victory.[1] The fleeing Israelites were in a panic because of the seemingly superior enemy (the Egyptians) who was pursuing and closing in on them; but Moses told them to trust in Yahweh's deliverance for their safety.[2]

It is necessary to note that although Israel was "armed for battle" (Exod. 13:18) and "marching out boldly" (Exod. 13:18), Moses instructed them to put their faith in God who gave them the victory alone. In this instance, Moses gave the only and best divine instruction to the Israelites to stand firm and wait for the salvation of the Lord because it was the only option for them. As stated earlier, although Israel was "armed for battle and marching out boldly", their army and arms were physically infinitesimal compared to the Egyptian army, which had all the advanced sophisticated arms and technology of the era and was of course a regional military power. It was good for the Israelites not to trust in chariots and horses (which in fact they did not have). The only available way forward for them was to trust God Almighty (El Shaddai) who had appeared to father Abraham and promised to "greatly increase [Abram's] number (Gen. 17:1–2). The Almighty God of Abraham truly and trustily brought the Egyptians to their knees (they perished in the Red Sea) but raised up the Israelites and helped them to cross the Red Sea on dry land (Ps. 20:7–8). It is good to

---

[1] Richard Clifford, "Exodus", in *The New Jerome Bible Commentary,* ed. Raymond E. Brown, Joseph A. Fitzmyer, and Roland E. Murphy (London, 2013), 49.

[2] Walter Houston, "Exodus", in *The Oxford Bible Commentary,* ed. John Barton and John Muddiman (Oxford, 2011), 76.

trust the invisible chariots of God which are available to the children of God in tens of thousands and thousands (Ps. 68:17).

This is the essence of the OT idea of salvation. It is important to stress that the idea of salvation emerged from the exodus indelibly stamped with the dimension of God's mighty and powerful acts of deliverance in the life and fabric of the history of the Jews. "God" and "salvation" are virtually identical terms in the Old Testament, which is expanded and deepened in terms of a particular instrument of this salvation. The Old Testament perspective of salvation finally leads to the understanding in the New Testament that God delivers his people (Israel) through the Messiah, God and saviour, who is Christ Jesus.

From the above citation, it is very well established and factual that the Hebrews were in utter pandemonium and confusion. Moses told them to trust in Yahweh's absolute deliverance. And of course, God did deliver the Jews, and they did not see the Egyptians again as Moses had precisely predicted. God reminded the Israelites in subsequent events of the extraordinary and super-heavenly deliverance he brought to them and said, "You yourself have seen what I did to Egypt and how I carried you on eagles' wing and brought you to myself (Exod. 19:4; Deut. 1:30–31; Isa. 63:9). God and deliverance (salvation) are inseparable; and this is the understanding of the Old Testament idea of salvation which comes from Yahweh, the Creator God of the universe and the God of Abraham, Isaac, and Jacob. The terms *God* and *saviour* are virtually identical and synonymous in the Old Testament.

It is vital to stress that the idea of deliverance (salvation) emerged from the exodus phenomenon indelibly engraved with a dimension of God's mighty and powerful acts of deliverance in the life and fabric of the history of the people of God, and established the nation of Israel. *Yahweh* and *saviour* were identical in the Old Testament, which expanded and deepened them in terms of a particular instrument of this salvation. As stated above, *salvation* means "bring into spacious geographical location", which could imply both physical and spiritual freedom by bringing the Israelites from their prison-like confinement in limited and restricted location in Egypt and settling them in the vast land in Canaan, which flowed with "milk and honey." God had given the Israelites several successes against their enemies, who attempted to dislodge and annihilate them in the fertile and good land he placed them in. God fought for Israel and put their enemies to shame. In the same way, many a time the persecutors of the Christian Church and those who hate it have been put to shame by the power of the truth of the gospel of Christ Jesus.[3]

This is what "I Am Who I Am" said to Moses about the Promised Land: "I have indeed seen the misery of my people in Egypt. I have heard them crying out because of their slave drivers, and I am concerned about their suffering. So I have come down to rescue them from the hand of the Egyptians and to bring them up out of that land into a good and spacious land, a land flowing with milk and honey" (Exod. 3:7–8).

Dear beloved and precious child of God, pause for one moment and examine "the Egyptians" that are pursuing you and closing in on you. "Egyptians" here represents all sorts of trials, temptations, and physical and spiritual problems in your Christian life. It is likely that right now you may be facing matrimonial problems (such as singleness, infidelity, divorce, childlessness), family-related issues, financial difficulty, unemployment, work-related issues in the office, ill health, bereavement, academic-related matters, and innumerable other intractable problems. Your only solution is to stand firm and fix your eyes upon Christ Jesus. Be immoveable and gaze on the divine and holy grace of the bringer of both physical and spiritual deliverance who is your Lord Christ Jesus.

"Focus" here means to totally fix all your heart, soul, and spirit and remain in Christ Jesus, because he alone is able to stop the Egyptians or any act or plan of the devil which tends to prevent you from gaining your freedom and liberty in the Lord Christ Jesus, and any device of Satan through agencies of human beings and environment, which may include even your place of worship and leaders in your local church who stop you from realising your potential in the Lord.

Please be encouraged to know and understand that I am not for a moment blaming Satan whenever something goes wrong in your life and environment. If I do that, I am actually giving Satan credit that he does not deserve, and I am attributing to him the power to determine and control every aspect of your life all the time, which he does not have and will never get. However, I also know that he is the father of lies and the prince of this

---

[3] Matthew Henry, *Matthew Henry's Commentary on the Whole Bible* (Peabody, Massachusetts, 2008), 640.

world, and can of course occasionally cause confusion and distress in order to discourage you to focus on Christ Jesus (John 8:44, 16:11). But Christ Jesus gave you absolute assurance and said "the prince of this world [Satan] now stands condemned" (John 16:11). Christ Jesus also said, "I have told you these things, so that in me you may have peace. In the world you will have trouble. But take heart! I have overcome the world" (John 16:33).

Note here that even before his arrest, death on the cross, and final and ultimate victory in resurrection, Christ Jesus declared that "I have overcome the world." Does this statement stand to the test, and does Jesus make good his assurance to the disciples? Without much ado, the answer is definitely yes. Problems, trials, and temptations which are but temporal will certainly come our way and cause temporal disruption in some or possibly all aspects of our lives, but they cannot and will not be able to defeat us. Christ Jesus stands before you now and whatever situation or circumstance you find yourself in. He is saying to you, "Take courage; I have conquered the world." Since Christ Jesus has gained victory over the world (Satan and his devilish earthly activity), you are also a victor over all your problems.

Be assured that your negative fear and worries will not materialise. Christ Jesus is saying to you right now, "Come to me, all you who are weary and burdened, and I will give you rest" (Matt. 11:28). He is talking to you and saying again, "Take my yoke upon you and learn from me, for I am gentle and humble in heart, and you will find rest for your souls. For my yoke is easy and my burden is light" (Matt. 11:29). Christ Jesus who makes these holy promises is faithful to you and capable of fulfilling them because all power and authority, both in heaven and on earth, has been given to him (Matt. 28:18). The "rest" Christ Jesus promises you today is an eternal heavenly one, which is for now as well as eschatological (Rev.14:13).

## FALSE PROPHETS

Dear believer, watch out for the spiritual Egyptians in your environment (nowadays they are very common in Christian fellowship centres). Our Lord and saviour Christ Jesus has already given warning to his disciples regarding false prophets and said to them, "Watch out for false prophets.

They come to you in sheep's clothing, but inwardly they are ferocious wolves" (Matt. 7:15). There are similar warnings regarding false prophets in the New Testament.[4] The Egyptians (the enemies of the children of God) are many and shrewd.

True prophets are God's mouthpiece. They are commissioned by God and convey God's message to all human beings. False prophets are self-appointed persons who, though pretending to proclaim God's truth, actually proclaim their own lie for their personal aggrandizement.

Jesus warned his hearers regarding false prophets more than two millennia ago, and his message is even more relevant and of primary importance to us today. The number of false prophets has multiplied by several millions since then. One of the main reasons for Jesus' warning about these false prophets is that although they "come in sheep's clothing", on the inside they are actual and real wolves who are very dangerous and destructive. In order words, they are evidently pretenders and hypocrites.

That the scribes and the Pharisees were included among those whom Christ Jesus was thinking is well obvious (Matt. 6:2, 5, 16; 15:7; 23). However, in view of Matthew 7:21 and John 10:8 and 12, it is clear and obvious that the description fits many others besides. It applies, in fact, to all those whose influence tends to lead God's children astray, especially to those who selfishly and maliciously lead people astray for personal financial aggrandizement.

As indicated earlier, the Gospels, the book of Acts, the Epistles, and the book of Revelation are all full of numerous warnings of false prophets. In fact, one of the dragon's (Satan's) allies is "the beast out of the earth" (Rev. 13:11), who is called "the false prophet" (Rev. 16:13, 19:20, 20: 10). Dear reader, please note that Christ Jesus' description of false prophets who come in sheep's clothing but inwardly are ferocious wolves, and the picture presented in Rev. 13:11 of "the beast with two horns like a lamb but spoke like a dragon", closely resemble each other. In both cases, the inner essence is in conflict with the outward manifestation. Dear beloved child of God, please note that false prophets are representative of the power of darkness (Col. 1:13, Luke 22:53, Acts 26:18, Eph. 6:12) masquerading as angels of light (2 Cor. 11:14).

---

[4] Matt. 24:11, 24; Mark, 13:22; Luke 6:26; Acts 13:6; 2 Pet. 2:1; 1 John 4:1; Rev. 16:13, 19:20, 20:10; 2 Cor. 11:26; Gal. 2:4; 2 Cor. 11:13; 1 Cor. 15:15; 1 Tim. 4:2.

The characterisation of false prophets as people who lack divine authorisation, bring their own message, and tell people what they want to hear is well rooted in the Old Testament (Isa. 30:10; Jer. 6:13, 8:10, 23:21). These are the kind of prophets who will shout "Peace, peace!" when there is no peace" (Jer. 6:14, 8:11; Ezek. 13:10). Their words are "softer than oil" (Ps. 55: 21; John 10:1, 8).[5]

Concerning these false prophets, John wrote to the believers of his time: "Dear friends do not believe every spirit, but test the sprits to see whether they are from God, because many false prophets have gone out into the world" (1 John 4:1). As stated above, true prophets hear and speak from God, being "carried along" by the Holy Spirit (2 Pet. 1:21). False prophets such as the Gnostics of John's day speak under the influence of spirits alienated from God (1 Tim. 4:1; 2 Pet. 2:1). John gave a divine blueprint of how to identity false prophets (1 John 4:3).

In adding to John's blueprint, I will present other characteristics of false prophets which are very prevalent in this era. It is likely that all of these or some of these may be applicable to a Christian fellowship centre (church) where false prophets who are deceitful workmen and workwomen masquerade themselves as angels of light (2 Cor. 11:14).

## *Ecclesiastical Authority*

False prophets are self-imposed individuals who are not under a recognised divine ecclesiastical authority and are not practically responsible or accountable to any authentic Christian body or organisation, not even to their own members. They do not belong to any of the mainstream of Christian churches and denominations. They have the absolute and ultimate right to appoint or promote any member to an office. They have the power to demote or even remove any member of their congregation who disagrees with their teaching to protect their own personal selfish interest. Some of them have not attended any recognised and reputable Christian theological institution and do not have a basic and formal qualification in Christian theology.

In fact, quite a few of them set up their own mushroom Bible colleges and issue their own certificates in theology to their candidates after few months of a crash programme. They arrogantly grant to themselves and

---

[5] William Hendriksen, *New Testament Commentary on Matthew*, 371–373.

also to their members all sorts of ecclesiastical titles, such as evangelist, apostle, prophet, bishop, and any other title that portrays them as super and superior clergy. It is interesting to note that these false teachers claim to have more divine authority than the rest of the mainstream Christian denominations, such as Baptists, Roman Catholics, Church of England, or Methodist. They do this by claiming to be the Pentecostal Church and/ or born-again Christians. They tend to show manifestations of the Holy Spirit by speaking in tongues in their preaching and prayers without the divine inspiration and interpretation. (Please note that I am not against speaking in tongue as stipulated and authorised in the New Testament).

## Biblical Hermeneutics

In most cases, the messages of false prophets are not contextual and are in contradiction with the full and divine purpose and meaning of the scriptures. A majority of the time, false prophets cite and misinterpret the scripture in their false message to their congregation for their own evil personal reasons. Like Satan who misused Ps. 91:11–12 while tempting Christ Jesus, these false prophets misuse Holy Scripture either because of lack of divine understanding or a deliberate act instrumented by Satan himself (or both together).

These false prophets definitely belong to their father the devil. Concerning the devil and his followers, Christ Jesus said, "You belong to your father, the devil and you want to carry out your father's desire. He was a murderer from the beginning, not holding to the truth, for there is no truth in him. When he lies, he speaks his native language, for he is a liar and the father of lies" (John 8:44). I can say here that the problem of the false prophet is not a lack of divine understanding of the wisdom of God in the scriptures; James's advice for his fellow believers of "the twelve tribes (of Israel) scattered among the nation" is still very relevant to us today. This divinely inspired instruction is that "If any of you lacks wisdom, he should ask God, who gives generously to all without finding fault, and it will be given to him" (Jas. 1:5). The wisdom of God is not just acquired information, but practical insight with spiritual implications which can be given by God to all those who sincerely and diligently seek him in order to serve and worship him in spirit and in truth.

Going back to John 8:44, Christ Jesus said "you want", which points to a show of determination of will. The problem of the false prophets is basically spiritual and not intellectual. They are being orientated towards Satan, "the father of lies", and are determined to carry out the work of the evil one to murder. By telling lies in citing and misinterpretation of Holy Scripture from both testaments in order to deceive and mislead members of their congregation and ultimate audience, the false prophets are deliberately spiritually (even at times practically) killing some believers in the Lord.

The false prophets preach what they think their vulnerable audience wants to hear and not what they receive from God. Their main themes are prosperity, good health, becoming a millionaire without much labour, having a problem-free and easy life, family or generation curse, first son curse, witchcraft, evil spirits and related themes which can attract people to their church. They magnify the power and the name of Satan and see the devil even in the four corners of every room in houses and in a dinner plate on a dining table. They see the devil even in the life of a few-months-old baby and claim that the baby is possessed by demonic forces. They claim that the baby is responsible for any family misfortune, and they believe that they have the spiritual power to cast out the evil spirit in the child. By trying to force out the so-called devil from the child, they subject the child to very cruel and physical punishment and maltreatment, which in most cases leads to death of the innocent child.

They tell their audience that they have unlimited power for both spiritual and physical healing. Single women and married women who seek the blessing of the womb are their common target. These women become prey because the false prophets tell and promise to give them husbands and children through their so-called divine power.

Some of these false prophets are very influential and powerful among their members, who reverence and elevate them even to the level of gods. Some false prophets encourage their branch churches to put a chair at the front stage or altar which none of the officers is allowed to sit at any time, especially during worship. Members believe that the spirit of the false prophet (founder/owner) of a particular Christian church sits on that empty chair and spiritually controls the service while the false prophet is physically at the headquarters or in another branch hundreds of miles away.

False prophets trap their members by telling them of the misfortunes and dangers which await them if they leave; and at the same time promise them prosperity and everything that will give them comfort if they continue to be part of the congregation.

## Membership

A majority of the members of fellowship centres or churches which are established by false prophets can be traced to the ethnic background or local area of the prophet. Appointment of any office or position is also mainly influenced by ethnicity, tribalism, and nepotism. Any member who is in a better financial position and always puts a big envelope in the offertory bag in the congregation can be appointed as an officer and given an ecclesiastical title.

## Love of Mammon

One of the common and prevailing characteristics of false prophets is the love of mammon. They tend to satisfy their inordinate yearning for earthly treasure and at the same time pretend to serve God. The impossibility of combining these two opposite and contrary goals (promoting and glorifying God and satisfying the yearnings of the flesh) is stated very tersely and unambiguously in the teaching of Christ Jesus in the Sermon on the Mount: "No one can serve two masters: for either he will hate the one, and love the other; or else he will hold to the one, and despise the other. Ye cannot serve God and mammon" (Matt.6:24, Luke 16:13). Here, *mammon* represents all earthly material things, including money, real estate, victuals, clothes, and other luxurious goods which bring temporal earthly pleasures to an unspiritual person.

In my opinion, there is nothing wrong for a Christian to be rich or wealthy. A rich Christian who loves God will show this by being devoted to him – placing everything including money, time, and talents at his disposal to serve God. Loving God is not merely a matter of the emotions but of heart, soul, mind, and strength (Matt. 22:37; Mark 12:30). To love God requires service and even sacrifice (Matt. 10:37–39). So described, it becomes all the more evident that this supreme, self-sacrificing, enthusiastic allegiance to the Supreme God cannot be rendered to two unequal parties

(God and mammon). Whoever renders it is no longer a worshiper of God Almighty but a worshiper of Satan. The one to whom it is rendered becomes god. Moreover, since there is only one true and supreme Almighty God the Creator, it follows that mammon-worship is idolatry.[6]

It is not an exaggeration to state that many false prophets (especially those who have branches in Europe and the United States) are millionaires. Quite a few either have their own private jets or hire one to operate their domestic and international ministries. The main theme of their message is tithing, offering, and giving. They are well-equipped with scriptures, especially Malachi 3:8–12 and Luke 6:38, to support their message and convince their vulnerable audience. They tell their members that the more they give, the more they will receive from God. The false prophets pray their so-called "special prayer" for their members and tell them that their prayer is panacea and omnipotent and able to solve all physical and spiritual problems.

These false prophets deceive their members to amass wealth for their personal aggrandizement instead of using it to help poor members of their congregation and serve God. They plan their management structure to make sure that they are in firm control of the money in their ministry. The main and only aim of their daily, weekly, monthly, and annual programmes is to generate funds for their personal interest.

## Mission

From what has already been stated above, it is not surprising that false prophets do not engage in any form of missionary (both home and foreign) activity for the propagation of the Gospel. Some of them make an effort at church planting within their catchment areas in the main cities and urban places in order to make financial gain. They are not interested in going to the local and rural areas where they will not make any financial benefit.

Those false prophets who are based in the developed countries of Europe and the United States have no interest in the mission field in Africa and other developing countries in rural areas because such mission fields will be a financial burden rather than a benefit. On the other hand, those false preachers who are based in Africa and other developing countries are

---

[6] Hendriksen, 347–348.

very enthusiastic to get an opportunity to open a foreign mission in the developed countries of Europe and North America, mainly because of the financial benefit. Such missionary activities do not even spread among the citizens of the host country but are confined to the people (immigrants) from the country the false prophet came from. Just as in the home country, mission activity in the host country is based on ethnicity which can be traced to the ethnic background of the leader.

## SALVATION

What has been presented above about false prophets is just the tip of the iceberg of the activities of Satan and his fallen angels of evil spirits that are roaming around deciding who to devour. The purpose of the summation of the false teachers of the scripture is to help you understand who they are and pray for the Holy Spirit to make you spiritually vigilant in your environment so that you do not become their prey. If you are already familiar with these things as a mature child of Christ Jesus, thank God, and in his holy name continue in your faith as you journey through this earthly city to the celestial city of God.

If you are a young and growing believer in the Lord, I implore you in the name of Christ Jesus to watch out for false preachers wherever you are, as they are in every nook and corner of the world. Be careful and do not allow them with their words (which are "softer than oil") to prevent you from receiving all the wonderful blessings which the Lord Almighty has promised you before the foundation of the world. These false teachers are trying to be stumbling blocks to God's original and divine plain of universal salvation through Abraham in Christ Jesus. Please spend time in your devotion or Bible-reading period learning more about the false prophets, the shepherds, and the sheep in Ezekiel 13 and 34 respectively, as compared with Christ Jesus saying "I am the good shepherd" in John 10:14.

When God called Abraham to leave Ur of the Chaldeans; he made a grand and everlasting promise to him, saying, "I will make you into a great nation and I will bless you, I will make your name great, and you will be a blessing. I will bless those who bless you, and whoever curses you I will Curse; and all the peoples on earth will be blessed through you" (Gen.

12:2–3). The New International Study Bible explains this passage and states explicitly that God's promise to Abraham has a sevenfold structure:

1. "I will make you into a great nation"
2. "I will bless you"
3. "I will make your name great"
4. "You will be a blessing"
5. "I will bless those who bless you"
6. "Whoever curses you I will curse"
7. "All peoples on earth will be blessed through you"

In Genesis 1:27–28, Moses stated, "So God created man in his own image, in the image of God he created him; male and female he created them. God blessed them and said to them, 'Be fruitful and increase in number." This divine original blessing which was pronounced by God the Creator upon Adam and Eve was partially and temporarily suspended when they lost Paradise because of disobedience as recorded in the third chapter of Genesis. God promised Abraham that his original blessing pronounced on Adam and Eve would be restored and fulfilled through Abraham and his offspring. Peter cited the seventh promise to his fellow Jewish listeners and said, "And you are heirs of the prophets and covenant God made with your fathers. He said to Abraham, 'through your offspring all peoples on earth will be blessed" (Acts 3:25).

Please note that Peter was making a direct reference to Christ Jesus as the promised offspring of Abraham. In his passage about the genealogy of Christ Jesus, Matthew started with an executive summary: "A record of the genealogy of Jesus Christ the Son of David, the Son of Abraham" (Matt. 1:1). It is the same Son of Abraham who is Christ Jesus that John the Baptist introduced to his disciples and listeners and said, "Look the Lamb of God, who takes away the sin of the world" (John 1:29). Abraham himself saw Christ Jesus as "the Lamb of God" in spirit and assured his son Isaac, saying, "God himself will provide the lamb for the burnt offering" (Gen. 22:8). The immediate fulfilment of Abraham's trust in Yahweh was God's response in the provision of the ram in Genesis 22: 13, but its ultimate fulfilment is the Lamb of God who is Christ Jesus who John the Baptist proclaimed (John 1:29, 36).

As stated earlier, the Egyptians tried to stop the Israelites from going to the land which God had promised to Abraham and his descendants. The purpose of the Egyptians pursuing the Israelites after they had left Egypt was not to destroy the entire fleeing group of Israelites and throw their bodies into the Red Sea, but to stop them from leaving the Egyptian land of slavery and force them back into perpetual bondage and impose heavier burdens on them. Had the Egyptians been successful in their diabolical desire, that would have abrogated all the holy promises and blessings (including the seventh) which God promised to Abraham and his offspring. But holy people of Yahweh, let us give all the glory, honour, and praise to the Almighty God, because he is the Ebenezer of Israel and the ultimate saviour of the Israelites as well as the Gentiles. The El Shaddai (God Almighty) nullified the hellacious plan of the Egyptians, and they failed abysmally because the El Shaddai is the God Almighty, the King of Glory, the Lord strong and mighty, the Lord mighty in battle (Ps. 24:7–10).

My earnest and fervent prayer is that the Holy Spirit of God will open your spiritual eyes to see the Egyptians (the false prophets) in your environment. May he give to you the power and courage to stand firm in the name of Christ Jesus who has given you the victory over Satan and his fallen angels.

It is necessary to assert that God and salvation are inseparable. This is the essence of both the Old and New Testaments' dogma of salvation which comes from the Creator God, who is the God of Abraham, Isaac, and Jacob – the same trio-God of the Father, Son, and Holy Spirit. The term *God* and *saviour* are virtually identical and synonymous in the Old Testament.

*Salvation* also means to bring into a spacious place or environment. The Psalmist said: ("You (God) brought us into prison and laid burdens on our backs. You (God) let men ride over our heads, we went through fire and water, but you (God) brought us to a place of abundance") (Ps. 66:11–12). The Psalmist claimed that the Israelites went through several types of suffering: captives thrown into prison; prisoners of war turned into slaves; and going through fire and water, both of which are metaphors for severe suffering and trials. Despite all these, the Lord brought them to a place of abundance and a spacious environment. The psalmist concluded that God brought them out of a situation of distress into a situation of overflowing well-being.

Isaiah made a similar statement and encouraged the Israelites to have faith in their Creator, the God of Jacob, who made the nation of Israel. Isaiah said to his fellow Jews: "When you pass through the waters, I will be with you; and when you pass through the rivers, they will not sweep over you. When you walk through the fire, you will not be burned; the flames will not set you ablaze" (Isa. 43:2). This passage is likely to be an allusion to the Israelites when they crossed the Red Sea, thanks to the awesome power of El Elyon, the God Most High (Exod.14:21–22) and the Jordan River (Josh. 3:14–17). Isaiah's prophecy to "walk through fire" was literally fulfilled in the dreadful situation experienced by Shadrach, Meshach, and Abednego (Dan. 3:25–27). Salvation, which also means to bring into a spacious place or environment, could also imply both physical and spiritual freedom by bringing the Israelites from their prison of confinement in a small parcel of land in Egypt to a vast and spacious land. This is what "I Am Who I Am" unequivocally said to Moses: "So I have come down to rescue [the Israelites] from the hand of the Egyptians and to bring them up out of that land into a good and spacious land, a land flowing with milk and honey" (Exod. 3:8).

Salvation also indicates spiritual freedom from the rigid and perpetual offerings, sacrifices, and all other burdens of Mosaic Law in favour of salvation in Christ Jesus that comes by the grace, love, and mercy of God. This is the salvation gospel that Paul enthusiastically wrote in his epistle to the Galatians, saying: "It is freedom that Christ has set us free. Stand firm, then, and do not let yourselves be burdened again by a yoke of slavery" (Gal. 5:1). Paul spoke of the unconditional and divine freedom in Christ Jesus and encouraged Gentile Christians in Galatia to stand firm in the freedom of Christ and that they should not allow themselves to be deceived by listening to messages from others who preached about Mosaic Law, which was the yoke of the law that led to a yoke of slavery.

It is imperative to state here that Paul was the most qualified person in all aspects of life among the Apostles in his day and had the appropriate vantage point to talk on these subjects of the "yoke of slavery" in Mosaic Law and "freedom in Christ Jesus." He had practical experience of what he was talking about as a former defender of Mosaic Law and a violent persecutor of the followers of Christ Jesus – one who was later dramatically and mysteriously called by Christ Jesus himself to become an Apostle specifically for the Gentiles. As prescribed in the Old Testament (mainly in Leviticus and Deuteronomy), the Mosaic Law of salvation – which is humanly impossible to fully adhere to, fulfil, and implement – imposes merciless and rigorous demands, while Christ's message of salvation in the New Testament, as Paul sums up "freedom in Christ Jesus", does not involve any kind of "work by man or woman" but simply by faith in the Spirit of the believer in Christ Jesus.

Paul sent the same good news of salvation to the Christians in Rome and stated in his letter that Mosaic Law had come to an end because "Christ is the end of the law so that there may be righteousness for everyone who believes" (Rom. 10:4). Christ Jesus himself said in his great Sermon on the Mount to his listeners,[7] "Do not think that I have come to abolish the Law or the Prophets; I have not come to abolish them but to fulfil them" (Matt. 5:17). Jesus fulfilled the Law in the sense that he gave it its full meaning. He emphasised its deep, understanding principles and need for total commitment rather than mere external acknowledgement and obedience. In a more spiritual and divine meaning, Christ Jesus is the fulfilment of the law in the sense that he brought it to completion by obeying perfectly its demands and by fulfilling its types and all the prophecies.

The climax of Christ Jesus' fulfilment of the law came when he voluntarily and willingly went to the Calvary cross; suffered and died; made the grand and ultimate sacrifice for all humanity; and above all, rose from the dead and made the final triumph that brings salvation to both the Jews and the Gentiles who have faith in him. Dear believer, it is vital for you to know that since Christ Jesus is the fulfilment of the law, you are no longer "under the Law" (Rom. 6:15) because Christ Jesus has set you free and you are free indeed. Here I am not confining the phrase "under the law" just to the Mosaic Law of the Old Testament but to all other laws, rules, and regulations which are imposed by false prophets in their local churches in order to prevent their members from leaving and receiving freedom in Christ Jesus and his saving grace.

Salvation in the Old Testament is also a notion of deliverance from disease (Isa. 38:9, 20), from trouble (Jer. 30:7), and from enemies (2 Sam. 3:18, Ps. 44:7). God does physically deliver his people from troubles,

---

[7] NIV Study Bible, 1419.

diseases, and enemies; but the worst and most deadly of all troubles, diseases, and enemies is sin. The greatest and best thing the good and gracious Creator God has done for his people is deliverance from all their sins through the death and resurrection which wrought salvation in Christ Jesus. It is possible for a believer in Christ Jesus to die in times of trouble, die as a result of illness or sudden death, or die in the hands of enemies; but the dead in Christ Jesus still have eternal salvation. On the other hand, if an unbeliever die in sin, this leads to both physical and spiritual death. The ultimate result is the destruction of both soul and body (Matt. 5:22).

Finally, I bring this section of the Old Testament perspective on salvation to a close by citing yet one more text from the prophet Isaiah which captured the mind and soul of Charles Haddon Spurgeon and brought him to meet his God. Spurgeon stated:

> I was in the gall of bitterness and in the bonds of iniquity, but had yet, by divine grace, been led to feel the bitterness of that bondage, and to cry out by reason of soreness of its slavery, seeking rest and finding none, I stepped within the house of God, and sat there, afraid to look upward, lest I should be utterly cut off, and lest his fierce wrath should consume me. The minister rose in his pulpit, and as I have done this morning, read this text, "Turn to me and be saved, all you ends of the earth; for I am God and there is no other" (Isa. 45: 22). I looked that moment; the grace of faith was vouchsafed to me in the self-same instant. I shall never forget that day, while memory holds its place; nor can I help repeating this text, whenever I remember that hour when first I knew the Lord.

Spurgeon felt that God has a special way of teaching salvation. I join Spurgeon to say that salvation is God's greatest divine work and is completed in Christ Jesus. God calls his people to focus and depend on him for their salvation. Christ Jesus is the only and one source of salvation for all the nations of the earth.[8]

---

[8] Charles Haddon Spurgeon, *Spurgeon's Commentary on the Bible,* ed. Robert Backhouse (London, 1997) 123–124.

In conclusion, I consider two final texts from the Old Testament. First, again from Isaiah: "It is too small a thing for you to be my servant to restore the tribes of Jacob and bring back those of Israel I have kept. I will also make you a light for the Gentiles, that you may bring my salvation to the ends of the earth" (Isa. 49:6). This together with Genesis 12:1–3, Exodus 19:5–6, and Isaiah 49: 6 is sometimes called the "great commission of the Old Testament", and it is quoted in part by Paul and Barnabas in Acts 13:47. The Jews were the bearers of God's light to the Gentiles, but that light was not bright enough to give divine light to all the Gentile nations. God's light was waiting for the ultimate and true bearer who would illuminate for all peoples of the earth. I am on holy ground to state that Christ Jesus is that heavenly and holy bearer of the true light of the triune God which shines now in every nook and corner of the world (Luke 2:30–32; John 8:12 and 9:5). With this "light to the Gentiles", I will turn to the New Testament in order to meticulously examine its panorama of salvation.

My final citation from the Old Testament regarding salvation is Isaiah 12, a short chapter that puts an emphasis on giving thanks and praising God mainly because of his mighty power and grace of salvation and deliverance. Observe the second half of 12:2: "The Lord, the Lord, is my strength and my song; he has become my salvation".This is quoted almost verbatim from Exodus 15:2, the song of the man of God Moses and his sister Miriam. It is a hymn which celebrates God's spectacular victory over Pharaoh's army when the Israelites miraculously crossed the Red Sea on dry land, while the Egyptian army perished in the same Red Sea as explained earlier (see also Ps. 118:14). Just as the "Song of the Sea" rounded off the account of God's salvation of his people at the Exodus, so here the second part of Isaiah 12:2 is rounded off with the all-embracing and surpassing word *salvation*. Also observe that the word *salvation* is striking because of its close similarity with the name "Isaiah." Please note that generally, the words of the prophet Isaiah are potentially words of salvation.[9]

---

[9] R. Coggins, "Isaiah", in *The Oxford Bible Commentary,* 449.

## SALVATION: NEW TESTAMENT PERSPECTIVE

Having made a summation of the Old Testament perspective on salvation, it is necessary to state from the beginning of this section that the Old and New Testaments are intertwined and woven together. This does not suggest structuralism, but a synchronism, harmonization, and understanding of textual fact and hermeneutics throughout the whole Bible. My focal point in this section is to meticulously examine the New Testament perspective on salvation.

In the New Testament, I begin with a general observation that the "religious" usage of a moral/spiritual deliverance becomes almost wholly dominant as far as the idea of salvation is concerned. The word *salvation* is mentioned by Christ Jesus the saviour and the bringer of salvation only once, when he said to the tax collector, "Today salvation has come to this house, because this man, too, is a son of Abraham" (Luke 19:9). It is imperative to note that although Zacchaeus the tax collector was of the lineage of Abraham, he did not walk in the footsteps of Abraham, and of course he did not have the faith of the Father of faith Abraham (Rom. 4:12). Hence, Zacchaeus had no salvation till that moment when the saviour Christ Jesus, who is salvation himself, pronounced salvation to Zacchaeus and his household.

Christ Jesus gave salvation to Zacchaeus (who was excluded from Jewish society and regarded as a sinner) because of the instantaneous and spontaneous spiritual transformation which took place in his life. This contrite heart of repentance is recorded in Luke 19:8: "But Zacchaeus stood up and said to the Lord, 'Look Lord! Here and now I give half of my possessions to the poor, and if I have cheated anybody out of anything, I will pay back four times the amount.'" Zacchaeus promised the extreme repayment required under the law in case of theft (Exod. 22:1, 2 Sam. 12:6, Prov. 6:31), but it was Christ Jesus' pardon of sin to Zacchaeus which brought salvation to the publican and his household.

Isaiah also stated: "With joy you will draw water from the wells of salvation" (12:3). It is likely that this is an allusion to God's abundant provision of water for Israel during the desert wanderings (Exod. 15:25, 27). Note that here, God's future saving act is itself the "well" from which Israel would draw "life-giving water."

God provided this life-giving water through his son, Christ Jesus, who talked to the Samaritan woman at "Jacob's well." In the dialogue between Christ Jesus and the woman, Jesus answered her, "If you knew the gift of God and who it is that asks you for a drink, you would have asked him and he would have given you a living water" (John 4:10). Christ Jesus came to give eternal life (salvation), which is free for all who believe in him. The water Christ Jesus who is God the Son offers is the divine free gift of God the Father. Those who put their trust in him and drink this divine water will spiritually never thirst. Christ Jesus wanted the woman to realise that he is the everlasting life or salvation as well as the author of salvation.

In response to the woman's question in John 4:13, Christ Jesus said, "Everyone who drinks this water will be thirsty again, but whoever drinks the water I give him will never thirst. Indeed, the water I give him will become in him a spring of water welling up to eternal life" (4:13–14). Note the contrast Jesus draws here between physical water from Jacob's well and the living water Jesus provides. Consider the following facts about the physical water from the well:

- It cannot prevent one from becoming thirsty, but rather makes the person thirsty again and again because it helps and satisfies just on temporarily hourly bases.
- The physical water is only for the physical body, which is outside the soul and is not concerned with the spiritual aspects of the person, of which the soul is most valuable and important. This physical water is useless, incapable, and powerless when it comes to filling the needs of the soul.
- To some extent, this physical water is limited in quantity, and in fact it may not be available when needed. In Africa and other developing countries, human beings as well as animals die because of lack of water or contaminated and poisoned water. In such places, people drill holes deep into the earth to get drinkable water or walk miles to reach pure and clean water to drink.
- It is laborious and costly to obtain good, clean water that is always available for both human beings and animals.

Meanwhile, the following is true about the living water which Jesus bestows:

- It makes one lose physical thirst and gain spiritual water for all time; that is, it gives lasting satisfaction. Once a believer, always a believer. Once reborn, always reborn (John 6:35; Isa. 49:10; Rev. 7:16, 17; 21:6; 22:1, 17).
- The living water enters into the soul and remains within as a source of spiritual refreshment and satisfaction.
- This living water from Christ Jesus is a self-perpetuating spring (John 1:12). Here on earth, it sustains a person spiritually with a view to the everlasting life in the realm above ("welling up to eternal life").[10]

Christ Jesus offered this free water of salvation to his fellow thirsty Jews and said in a loud voice, "If anyone is thirsty, let him come to me and drink. Whoever believes in me, as the scripture has said, streams of living water will flow from within him." (John 7:37–38).

Salvation also suggests turning from the rigid and impracticable Mosaic Law to spiritual freedom in Christ Jesus that comes through the love, grace, kindness, and mercy of God. This is also the viewpoint of Paul, which he expressed in his corpus to the Romans: "Therefore, there is now no condemnation for those who are in Christ Jesus, because through Christ Jesus the law of the spirit of life set me free from the law of sin and death" (Rom. 8:1–2). Paul used the word *law* in several different ways in Romans to mean, for example, a controlling power which is its meaning, as is applicable here; God's law (2:17–20; 9:31; 10: 3–5); the Pentateuch (3:21b); the Old Testament as a whole (3:19); and a principle (3:27).[11] Paul asserted in Romans 8:1–2 that there is no condemnation for those united with Christ Jesus, and it is no longer levelled by the law against those not observing it, nor is there any condemnation resulting from sin.

"Condemnation" means the same as the "curse" in Gal. 3:10 (Deut. 27:26). A curse or condemnation clung to the spiritually unborn human beings and tore them in two, because they were "flesh" and were dominated by sin (Rom. 5:16–18) but still had a "mind" that recognised God's law. But this condition does not affect the Christian, who no longer lives under that dispensation of condemnation (2 Cor. 3:9) or of death (2 Cor. 3:7).

---

[10] William Hendriksen, *New Testament Commentary in John*, 163.
[11] NIV Study Bible, 1681.

According to Paul, it is the law of the spirit of Christ Jesus which sets him and all subsequent believers in Christ Jesus free as a result. The Mosaic Law which leads to sin and death has been made redundant and irrelevant. The law of the spirit of Christ Jesus supplies the spiritual vitality that Mosaic Law could not give. The law of the spirit through Christ Jesus is the life-giving power of God himself. The freedom of the Christian is achieved either through Christ (instrumental) or in Christ (unitive). Either way, Christ Jesus is the only and ultimate source of the freedom of humanity.[12]

One of the most perplexing question on the subject of salvation in the New Testament is, "What must I do to be saved?" (Acts 16:30b). This divine heart-searching question was uttered by a jailer in Philippi when Paul and Silas, who were prisoners of the jailer, were dramatically and miraculously released by the divine act of the omnipotent God who triggered an earthquake in the middle of the night. Note that the jailer had heard that Paul and Silas were preachers of "the way to be saved" (Acts 16:17).With the earthquake and his own near death, he wanted to know about "the way to be saved."

Stop for a moment and observe the sincerity of this man of authority. The jailer was desperate and was really willing to do anything and everything within his capacity to be saved. The question from the jailer is the grand question and the starting point which leads to the heart and fabric of the Christian community. Paul and Silas were very sincere in their response to the question of the jailer and said to him, "Believe in the Lord Jesus, and you will be saved – you and your household" (Acts 16:30–31). This answer from Paul and Silas is one of the simplest and most rudimentary, but it is also one of the most theologically sophisticated. What they share is the heart and soul of salvation and the way to salvation in Christ Jesus. It is wonderful and marvellous to observe the work of God the Holy Spirit which prompted the mind of the jailer to ask for the way to be saved on one hand, and Paul and Silas to give a divine and appropriate answer that points the way to salvation.

The question about salvation came from the heart and soul of the jailer, and the rejoinder came from the pure and sincere hearts and souls of Paul and Silas. But once again, observe the single most important question

---

[12] Joseph A. Fitzmyer, "The Letter to the Romans," in *The New Jerome Bible Commentary*, 852.

regarding salvation from the heart of the jailer: "What must I do to be saved?" The jailer totally surrendered and submitted his life to Paul and Silas and was prepared to take instructions from them and do anything in order to be saved. What was the spiritual impact of the answer of Paul and Silas on the jailer? The spiritual effect sets a good moral example to all humankind on the subject matter of salvation: "At that hour of the night the jailer took them and washed their wounds; then immediately he and his family were baptised. The jailer brought them into his house and set a meal before them; he was filled with joy because he had come to believe in God – he and his whole family" (Acts 16:33–34).

It is necessary to highlight the astonishing and outstanding purity of the hearts and souls of Paul and Silas in the situation and circumstance in which they found themselves. Luke earlier stated, "A mob was quickly formed against Paul and Silas, and judges ordered them stripped and beaten with wooden whips. Again and again the rods slashed down across their backs; and afterwards they were thrown into prison. The jailer was threatened with death if they escaped, so he took no chances, but put them into the inner dungeon and clamped their feet into the stocks" (Acts 16:22–24).

The jailer made sure that Paul and Silas were not just in the inner cell of the prison, but for maximum security, he used the stocks. More sinisterly, he made them face hideous torture and maximum suffering. They were in serious pain and agony as a result of the wounds they sustained because of the beating and flogging. Observe the Christlike spirit of the two evangelists. Despite their personal physical pain and suffering, Paul and Silas focused on the salvation of the jailer (their tormentor and enemy), and instructed and directed him to the divine way of salvation, which is, "Believe in the Lord Jesus, and you will be saved – you and your household." Their physical pain and suffering did not pollute the purity of their hearts because they had focused their hearts and minds on God, as Christ Jesus said that those who are pure in heart are blessed and shall see their God.

In the beginning and formal occasion of the laying of the foundation of the Christian faith on the day of Pentecost, Peter had already made a similar plea to the crowd. Luke recorded: "When the people heard this, they were cut to the heart and said to Peter and the other Apostles,

'Brothers, what shall we do?' Peter replied, 'Repent and be baptised, every one of you, in the name of Jesus Christ for the forgiveness of your sins. And you will receive the gift of the Holy Spirit'" (Acts 2:37–38).

Salvation calls for a contrite heart, a childlike attitude, a receptive spirit, helplessness, and total and unreserved renunciation of all and every sundry of sin in order to follow Christ Jesus who brings eternal salvation to all those who believe in him. Salvation comes upon a person with a divine, spiritual, and eternal power. It melts down all physical and worldly power in that person. The departure of the carnal body and the arrival of spiritual power must take place at a point in time for every child of God who has received or will receive salvation of the Lord Christ Jesus. That moment is a period of titanic struggle and spiritual battle between Christ Jesus and Satan in the life of the spiritually degenerated person.

This spiritual warfare between good and evil may last just for few minutes or sometimes much longer, depending on the situation, circumstance, and disposition of individuals. However, whatever may be the background of a person, it is imperative to say, "But thanks be to God! He gives us the victory through our Lord Jesus Christ" (1 Cor. 15:57). Immediately, the victory has been won, all the materialistic elements of the person disappear, and the person becomes a newborn baby (born again), helpless and weak. Like a newborn baby who must rely and depend upon the mother or nurse, so also a born-again person must totally and wholeheartedly depend upon Christ Jesus through the Holy Spirit in all aspects of daily life.

The power of the resurrected Christ Jesus comes with a divine mighty force of salvation and first of all disarms the most powerful and violent evil spirit in a person and brings that person to his or her knees in prayer like Paul, asking, "Who are you Lord?" (Acts 9:15), or the jailer "Sirs, what must I do to be saved?" (Acts 16:30), or the story in Mark in the lifetime of Christ Jesus: "When [the demon-possessed man] saw Jesus from a distance, he ran and fell on his knees in front of him" (Mark 5:1–20).

Salvation comes instantaneously and unconditionally. It brings transformation of character in the heart of those who acknowledge and confess Christ Jesus as their personal Lord and saviour. Saul, who "was still breathing out murderous threats against the Lord's disciples" a few moments earlier, at once began to preach in the synagogues that Jesus is the

Son of God and "the Jews conspired to kill him." Notice here the effectual positive impact of the power of salvation on Paul in Damascus, who was transformed from a persecutor of the Lord's disciples to one persecuted as the Lord's disciple, and even on the demon-possessed man in Decapolis, who "no-one could bind any more, not even with a chain. For he had often been chained hand and foot, but he tore the chains apart and broke the irons on his feet. No-one was strong enough to subdue him." This violent "man who had been possessed by the legion of demons" sat at the feet of his saviour Christ Jesus "dressed and in his right mind [and] went away and began to tell in the Decapolis how much Jesus had done for him. And all the people were amazed."

One of the significant physical transformations that takes place in the life of the transformed person is baptism in Christ Jesus. Saul "got up and was baptised." Like Paul, there must be spiritual changes in the inner being of the transformed person who has received salvation from the Lord and saviour Christ Jesus. In fact, Christ Jesus must take control of all and every aspect of the new believer. Saul, who had obtained a letter of authority from the high priest (authority from humans) and who was in command and in control of his followers, suddenly came under the authority and control of Christ Jesus and took instruction from his Lord. Instead of being a commander, he was commanded; instead of giving instruction, he was instructed by the most powerful instructor who is: Christ Jesus.

In the case of the jailer, I notice a similar trend of saving grace and power which came upon him. Paul and Silas "spoke the word of the Lord to him and to all the others in his house" regarding the salvation of the Lord Jesus. "At that hour of the night the jailer took them and washed their wounds, then immediately he and all his family were baptised" (Acts 16:32–33). Please note the divine spontaneous positive impact of the power of salvation which turns the jailer, who was the master of the prison and the controller of his guards, into a slave of Paul and Silas, addressing them as "sirs" and even doing the service of a base servant by washing their wounds (including washing their feet). This change of character and position from a master to a servant was followed by another physical symbol of the sacred sacrament of baptism.

The subject of baptism will be discussed later in this book; here, it suffices to state that salvation of a person is immediately followed by a symbol of the sacred sacrament of public baptism in the name of Christ Jesus. Salvation is also accompanied by both a spiritual and a physical feast. In the case of the jailer, he brought Paul and Silas into his home and set a meal before them because "he was filled with joy because he had come to believe in God – he and his whole family." Salvation is a priceless precious free gift from Christ Jesus, and its value immeasurably outnumbers all the wealth and affluence of the world. I think that this jailer was a rich and influential man in his society, but notice that his wealth and power did not give him joy in his inner being. What ultimately made him and his household jubilant was the salvation that came to them in their new faith in God in Christ Jesus.

This mini trinity – salvation, baptism, and joy – are interwoven and inseparable. They work together in synchronization, indirectly or directly, in the life of every Christian when that person finds new faith in God through the saving grace of Christ Jesus. A similar trio event was recorded earlier in Acts 8:26–40 with regards to the mysterious meeting that took place between Philip and the Ethiopian eunuch. Luke recorded: "Then Philip began with that very passage of scripture and told him the good news about Jesus" (8:35). This good news of Jesus is fundamentally based on the salvation which Christ Jesus freely gives to all people in every nation and tribe who proclaim him as their Lord and saviour. As recorded, the salvation of the Ethiopian eunuch was immediately followed by water baptism, at his request. Please note the extraordinary event that took place in 8:39: "When they came up out of the water, the spirit of the Lord suddenly took Philip away, and the eunuch did not see him again, but went on his way rejoicing." Observe the small trinity – salvation, baptism, and joy – in the life of the Ethiopian, which later manifested in the same way to Saul and the jailer.

It is intriguing to observe the strange behaviour of the Ethiopian eunuch here. Luke recorded that "the spirit of the Lord suddenly took Philip away, and the eunuch did not see him again but he went on his way rejoicing" (Acts 8:39). By the conventional character of human beings, I expect the eunuch to be filled with poignancy and sorrow, missing his hero (in spiritual terms) who was his spiritual guide or pastor and unveiled the text he was reading in Isaiah 53:35, which he did not understand. Philip as a pastor to the Ethiopian eunuch even performed the symbolic salvation of the sacrament of water baptism for him. Contrary to my expectation of the eunuch to be heavy-hearted, doleful, and low-spirited, he was in an inspirational and jubilant mood of rejoicing all the way to Ethiopia.

What was the reason for his unique display of illumination and exaltation of character? The simple and true answer is that the Ethiopian eunuch found and received his eternal salvation in Christ Jesus. This "Ethiopian eunuch, an important official in charge of all the treasury of Candance, queen of the Ethiopian" had found the most important and priceless treasure – salvation – which is more valuable than all the treasury of Candance he had ever seen or had. It was likely that he dearly missed his spiritual hero and pastor and might have been very sorrowful; however, all that was immediately overtaken and overwhelmed by the everlasting joy that was in him because of the eternal salvation which he had received.

Recently, my wife and I met a friend in the gym who asked me to show him how to use the rowing machine, which I gladly and sincerely did. After that day, we did not go to the gym for about a week. When the friend saw us again, the first statement he made was, "It was good that you showed me how to use the rowing machine before you were off for a few days." He added, "I missed you, but I am happy you helped me and showed me how to use the rowing machine. Since then, I spend more time on it than any of the other machines because of the benefit of it and changes that I can feel in my body in the past few days." In other words, the help he received from me and the benefits he gained from using the machine were more valuable and important to him than missing me.

But note, the benefits my friend received from the rowing machine are physical, temporal, and infinitesimal compared to the spiritual gain of salvation which the Ethiopian Eunuch received from Phillip. Joy is always associated with the divine free gift of salvation which Christ Jesus brings to all those who believe in him. When salvation enters into the heart of a person, it occupies the most honourable, highest, most valuable place, which is the very centre of the heart, soul, and mind. Salvation takes pre-eminent place and displaces all worldly things which are not in agreement with the heavenly things the person has been called to focus on. It is possible to lose all your valuable earthly treasures and those that are closest to you, but your gracious and good God will not allow you to lose your salvation, except if you decide to walk away from it of your own volition.

This supremacy of salvation in the life of the child of God makes it possible for the saved soul to rejoice in the Lord irrespective of the situation and circumstance of the person in Christ Jesus. It is that internal and eternal joy that made the Ethiopian eunuch walk away rejoicing despite suddenly missing his pastor, Philip. He believed that the salvation he had received through hearing the good news of Christ Jesus was far better than the company of the evangelist. This Ethiopian Gentile God-fearing pilgrim went home and unwrapped his new and most important and valuable treasure of salvation in his own Gentile country. Later tradition identified the eunuch as the first Gentile convert in Africa and the founder of the Ethiopian Church.[13]

Salvation calls for a contrite heart; childlike, receptive helplessness; and the renunciation of all and every sin for the sake of Christ Jesus. Salvation turns or transforms the stony heart of the spiritually degenerated, ungodly, ungovernable, and uncontrollable person to become the fleshy heart of a new creature in Christ Jesus by keeping behind all former ways of life (2 Cor. 5:17). This is only possible because the new believer is united with Christ Jesus through faith in him and now is totally, absolutely, and unequivocally committed to him. Salvation is the restoration and fulfilment of God's purpose in creation (2 Cor. 4:6), and this takes place only and solely in a person by Christ Jesus through whom all things were made (John 1:3; Col. 1:16; Heb. 1:2) and in whom all things were restored (Rom. 8:18–23; Eph. 2:10).

Ezekiel prophesied about these contrasting hearts of stone and flesh which are belligerent to each other. When God promised the return of the Israelites from far away among the nations back to their promised land, God declared, "I [God] will give them an undivided heart and put a new spirit in them; I will remove from them their heart of stone and give them a heart of flesh" (Ezek. 11:19; 36:26). Here the Almighty God of Israel promised to deliver his people (bring salvation) from their enemies and set them free from captivity in all foreign lands. In both citations, God promised an inner spiritual and moral transformation that would result in a single-minded commitment to him and his will. Flesh in the Old Testament is often a symbol for wickedness, weakness, and frailty (Isa. 31:3), and in the New Testament it often stands for the sinful nature as a

---

[13] Loveday Alexander, "Acts", in *The Oxford Bible Commentary*, 1030.

God-opposing force (Rom. 8:5–8). However, in the context of salvation, flesh stands in opposition to stone for a pliable, teachable heart which is willing to be submissive to the good news of Christ Jesus and his saving grace and power.

All the four Gospel writers stated that salvation is present in the person and ministry of Christ Jesus and especially after his death on the cross and resurrection. All the corpora of the four evangelists, Paul's corpora, and other apostolic writers in the New Testament emphatically state that salvation calls for a contrite heart; childlike, receptive helplessness; and renunciation of every kind of sin. Observe that the jailer really portrayed the characteristics of a person who is determined to cast away every evil activity and readily embrace Christ Jesus for salvation.

Note that the Holy Spirit prompted the heart and mind of the jailer to submit himself helplessly and unconditionally to Paul and Silas in order to be saved. His life was "positively turned upside-up" for good for his salvation. His position as the jailer who was a master to Paul and Silas in his own right was changed to servant as "[the jailer] called for lights, rushed in and fell trembling before Paul and Silas" (Acts 16:29). At that hour of the night, the jailer took them and washed their wounds. He brought them to his house and set a meal before them; he was filled with joy because he had come to believe in God – he and his family (Acts 16:33–34). The meal was shared in jubilant gladness, which is a divine sign of salvation received and recreated in the jailer's home. Like the jailer, Christians are saved from sin for holiness, from death for life, from the power of evil for the power for good, and from the devil for God.

It is paramount to state that Paul saw salvation as something in the past (Rom. 8: 24), but also in the present (1 Cor. 1:18), and finally for the future (Rom. 13:11). This dimension of salvation has important implications for eschatological understanding. Christians receive the forgiveness of sins, life, and salvation, which is obtained by Christ Jesus through his incarnation, ministry, innocent suffering, hideous death, glorious resurrection, and holy ascension. The only and one solution for sin of every kind and for every human being in all the earth from every tribe and tongue is, "Believe in the Lord Jesus, and you will be saved – you and your household."

Finally, I state that the central mainstream of Christian teaching is that salvation in the Christian sense of the term is manifested in, and constituted on the basis of, the birth, mission, death, and resurrection of Christ Jesus. This is to emphasise that within the Christian tradition, the distinctive understanding of what salvation is can only be realised on the basis of who Christ is and what Christ does or has done for all humanity in all the whole wide world. Christ Jesus is the only source and basis of salvation, and the saving grace of humanity is embedded, cemented, steadfast, and grounded on the solid rock in Christ Jesus. In other words, Christ Jesus and the work of Christ Jesus – which is salvation – is woven together like the seamless dress of Christ Jesus himself. From the apostolic, patristic, or classical period to the present day, questions or rather discussion about who Christ Jesus is (saviour) has always been closely related to questions about or examination of what Christ Jesus does (brings salvation to those who believe in him).

I have presented the importance of salvation in the Christian doctrine, and it cannot be over-emphasised. I have analysed the relationship between the human and divine natures of Christ Jesus and asserted that Christ Jesus was fully God and fully man. My discussion has shown that in order to bring salvation to humans, Christ had to assume the balanced nature of God and man. I unequivocally assert that Christ Jesus is synonymous with salvation. Anyone who purports to be Christ Jesus must do the same and exact salvation he does.

Christ Jesus is the Christ, and the Christ is the salvation. As an algebraic expression, I formulate that *Christ 'C'* = *salvation 'S' (C=S)*. Salvation outside this parameter is anathema. Since the foundation of this universe, no human being has ever or will ever do the work of salvation like our saviour, Christ Jesus, who is our Lord and God.

# Chapter 6

# SOURCE OF SALVATION

I stated previously that the solution for sin is to believe in the Lord Christ Jesus as the saviour and Lord who freely gives salvation to as many as those who believe in him. John stated: "Yet to all who received him, to those who believed in his name, he gave the right to become children of God – children born not of natural descent, nor of human decision or a husband's will, but born of God" (John 1:12–13). Membership in God's family is by grace alone, which is the gift of God (Eph. 2:8–9). It has never been and will never be a human achievement, yet the imparting of the gift is dependent on individual recipients, as the words *received* and *believed* make clear.[1]

My focal point here is to trace the source of this free gift of salvation. Christ Jesus gives eternal life, which is salvation, but from where does he bring it? Does he bring it from the other persons of the trinity (i.e. God the Father and God the Holy Spirit), from heaven, or even from within the secular world? Could it even be possible that Christ Jesus brings salvation from Beelzebub – the prince of the demons – as purported by Jesus' opponents (the teachers of the law) "who came down from Jerusalem and said, 'He is possessed by Beelzebub! By the prince of demons he is driving out demons'" (Mark 3:22). Here I propose that it is necessary for Christians to know the source of this wonderful gift of eternal salvation. For instance, Christians believe "every good and perfect gift is from above, coming down from the Father of heavenly lights who does not change like shifting shadows" (Jas. 1:17).

---

[1] NIV Study Bible, 1561.

From the Christian perspective, Christ Jesus himself is the one and only source of salvation. I believe that the only divine source and shape of Christian salvation within the Christian tradition is grounded and firmly based and secured on the love and grace of Christ Jesus. The person of Christ Jesus is the historical point of departure and arrival of Christians – that is to say, departure from the Adamic original natural sin and all the negative worldly avaricious things of this earthly city which lead to eternal damnation and condemnation. Turning to Christ Jesus cleanses us from the original sin of Adam and leads us to the City of God in the eternal kingdom, where we have all the heavenly treasures of salvation and are in the presence of our God and saviour Christ Jesus forever (Rom. 5:12–21).

It is a sacred historical fact, recorded in all four Gospels that the incarnation of Christ to the world as Jesus brought the Christian community into spiritual being. The Christian community believes that their lives have been changed from spiritual death (eternal and hellish death) to eternal life (both present and eschatological salvation); from the darkness of this world and all its demonic and devilish forces to the glorious and marvellous light of heaven; and from condemnation and damnation to the divine grace and justification and eternal salvation wrought through Christ Jesus.[2]

I earnestly and tenderly state here according to my faith and belief that the faith and belief of the Christian community and the dogma of salvation is mystically and divinely linked with the birth, mission, death, and resurrection of Christ Jesus. These quadruplet elements – the manger, earthly journey, cross, and empty tomb – are inseparably interwoven and mysteriously work together for the salvation of all believers through the ages. This is the good news of the biblical gospel which has been recorded in the Pentateuch, the historical books, the poetic and wisdom literature, the prophets in the Old Testament, and in the four Gospels, the Acts of the Apostles, the letters of Paul, the Epistles of the Apostles, and the book of Revelation in the New Testament. In a nutshell, the birth, mission, death, and resurrection of Christ Jesus are the summation of the Holy Scripture in the Holy Bible.

All four Gospel writers unanimously stated that salvation was present in the person and ministry of Christ Jesus, especially in his death on the cross and his eventually resurrection power which wrought salvation. In the

---

[2]  1 Pet. 2:9; Eph. 5:8; Rom. 4:25, 13:12; Gal. 2:16, 3:24.

fourth Gospel, Jesus declared, "I am the bread of life" (John 6:35). Christ Jesus confirmed in this passage that he and only he impacts and sustains life. Christ Jesus is the consecrated real original bread who came down from heaven, which refers to spiritual eternal life and eternal salvation. It is through faith – through intimate union with Christ Jesus and assimilating him spiritually as physical bread is assimilated physically – that human beings attain everlasting life. The "I am" in John is the first of seven self-descriptions of Christ Jesus in John 6:35.

Incidentally, all seven "I ams" are from the fourth Gospel of John.[3] I call to mind that "I Am Who I Am" is the name God used to reveal himself to Moses in Exodus 3:14 and wished to be known by and worshipped as in Israel. "I Am" is the shortened form of "I Am Who I Am." Christ Jesus applied the phrase to himself in John 8:58–59 and, in so doing, he claimed to be God and risked being stoned for blasphemy.[4] It is of beatific importance to note that Christ Jesus did not in any form or kind commit blasphemy, as the Jews of his time and even some current theologians think. I stress that Christ Jesus was fully God and fully man when he was doing his missionary work of salvation on earth. Christ Jesus is the source of the Christian faith of salvation. The expression and claim of Christ Jesus of "I Am" is to indicate his eternity of transcendental being; his oneness with God the Father; and the intra-Trinitarian relationship as has been formulated by Augustine of Hippo of Africa.

Salvation can be a purely secular notion, concerned with political emancipation or the general human quest for liberation, as explained in the Old Testament perspective of salvation. On religious grounds, salvation is not specifically a Christian credo, as all the world's major religions have the concept of salvation. However, they differ enormously in relation to both their understanding of where salvation comes from, how it is achieved, and the shape and form which it is understood to take.

Of all the world's religions, it is only Christians who believe that the source of and shape of their salvation is grounded and based only on Christ Jesus, as expressed and explained in both the Old and New Testament text citations. In addition to Holy Scripture, which has been cited, I state that the classic or patristic early Christian theologians and authors confirmed

---

[3] John 6:35; 8:12; 9:5; 10:7, 9, 11, 14; 11:25; 14:6, 15:1, 5.
[4] The NIV Study Bible, 1581–1582.

that Christ Jesus is the main and only source of Christian salvation. For instance, Irenaeus Bishop of Lyon in AD 178 developed the idea of "recapitulation" or "going over again" (which is to say, starting from the beginning) of all the events in history in which humanity lost its way. According to Irenaeus, Christ Jesus recapitulates the history of Adam and succeeds where Adam failed, thereby undoing the fall of humanity.[5]

When Christ incarnated and became fully human in Jesus, he recapitulated in himself the long history of the human race and obtained salvation for us, so that we might regain in Christ Jesus what we had lost in Adam, who was "in the image and likeness of God." In the theology of the patristic or classic writers, the incarnation (birth of Jesus) is the beginning and the foundation of Christian salvation that comes to believers in Christ Jesus. However, it is paramount to stress in the same degree the importance of the resurrection with regards to salvation that Christ Jesus is the first born of the death (Col. 1:8). As a matter of angelic truth, without the resurrection phenomenon, there would not have been Christian salvation. I will explain this statement in the appropriate section in this book.

Recapitulation has its foundation in salvation as the perfection of the creation that comes from the Creator God the Son (Christ Jesus). Christ Jesus is the origin and the head of the new creation who summarises or recapitulates in himself the whole of creation. His coming is the fullness of time (Gal. 4:4) and the climax of human history. The central text for the concept of recapitulation is in Ephesians 1:10, which states "to put into effect when the times will have reached their fulfilment – to bring all things in heaven and on earth together under one head, even Christ." This states the plan of God the Father to sum up all things in Christ Jesus. The expression "under one head" is very significant; it gives the idea of a divine leadership under the headship of Christ Jesus. A contemporary way of putting it might be to say that in a world of confusion where things do not add up or make sense, we look forward to the time when everything will be brought into meaningful relationship under the headship of Christ Jesus.[6]

It is important to stress that there is an eschatological dimension of salvation which is available only from Christ Jesus. It is also necessary to

---

[5] Alister E. McGrath, *Christian Theology: An Introduction* (4th edn, Oxford, 2007), 328.
[6] The NIV Study Bible, 1757.

make a final note that salvation is a dynamic process which includes the past, present, and future. Paul saw salvation as a past (Rom. 8:24), present (1 Cor. 1:18), and future event (Rom. 13:11). I will analyse this in the appropriate part in this book.

## SOURCE OF SALVATION: THE CROSS OF CHRIST JESUS

Originally, the cross was viewed in a derogatory way as "a stake used as an instrument for punishment and execution." This is the primary usage and purpose of the cross in the New Testament. Crucifixion of live criminals did not occur in the Old Testament, where execution was by stoning.[7] However, dead bodies were occasionally hung on a tree as a warning (Deut. 21:22–23; Josh. 10:26). Such bodies were regarded as accursed (Gal. 3:13). It is also necessary to know that bodies hung on a tree had to be removed and buried before nightfall (John 19:31). This explanation accounts for the New Testament reference to Christ Jesus' cross as a "tree."[8] All in all, the cross was a symbol of an abysmal humiliation by imperial Rome, but it now stands as an emblem of victory and a sacred icon for Christians.

The New Testament writers' interest in the cross of Christ Jesus therefore is neither an archaeological nor historical one, but more Christological. They are divinely concerned with the eternal, cosmic, soteriological significance of what happened once for all in the death of Christ Jesus, the Son of God on the cross. This soteriological significance is the grace of the salvation in Christ Jesus. Theologically, the word *cross* was used as a summary description of the gospel of salvation that Christ Jesus died for the sins of the world. So the "preaching of the gospel" is "the word of the cross, the preaching of Christ crucified" (1 Cor. 1:17). It has already been explained in earlier parts in this book (Chapter 2) that the only and main mystery mission of Christ Jesus is to bring salvation to all people in all nations. That is to say that the word *cross* in this book stands for the whole glad announcement of the redemptive grace to all people of the atoning death of Christ Jesus.

---

[7] J. D. Douglas, *New Bible Dictionary: Second Edition* (Leicester, 1994), 253–254
[8] Acts 5:30; 10:39;1 Peter 2:24.

I share with you the enormous interest of Jurgen Moltmann with regards to his theological understanding and ardent faith in the cross of Christ Jesus. Moltmann stated, "The centre of my hope and resistance once again became that which, after all, is the driving force of all attempts to open up new horizons in society and the Church: the cross of Christ."[9] The theology of the cross is that "Christian faith stands and falls with the knowledge of the crucified Christ; that is with the knowledge of God in the crucified Christ, or to use Luther's seven bolder phrase, with the knowledge of the 'Crucified God.'"[10]

Moltmann points out the abandonment of Christ on the cross – at the ninth hour, Jesus cried out in a loud voice, "Eloi; Eloi lama *sabachthan*!?" which means "My God, my God why have you forsaken me?" (Mark 15:34). According to Moltmann, "By this cry, the crucified Christ brings God to those who are abandoned."

By the suffering of Christ Jesus on the cross, Christ brings salvation to those who suffer; and through Christ's death on the cross, he brings eternal life (salvation, which had been underlined earlier) to those who are suffering and dying. I share Moltmann's opinion that "the tempted, rejected, suffering and dying Christ Jesus on the cross came to be the centre of the religious of the oppressed and the piety of the lost." The main reason Christ Jesus suffered on the cross is because of God's infinite and glorious love and to bring salvation to God's creation. This is what was on the celestial lips of Christ Jesus who declared, "For God so loved the world that he gave his one and only Son, that whoever believes in him shall not perish but have eternal life. For God did not send his Son into the world to condemn the world, but to save the world through him" (John 3:16–17).

It is God's love for the world that motivated God for the plan of salvation. It is the love of God which made Christ incarnate to this world, and it is the same passionate love which made Christ Jesus went to the Calvary cross willingly to suffer and die for the sin of the world. The cross of Christ Jesus is the test of everything in Christianity. The cross alone and nothing else is the test, because the cross of Christ Jesus refutes everything and has its syncretistic divine power in Christianity. The death of Christ Jesus on the cross is the centre of all Christian theology (Christology and

---

[9] Jurgen Moltmann, *The Crucified God* (London, 2001), page xviii.
[10] Moltmann, 62.

soteriology). All Christian theology about God, creation, sin, forgiveness of sin, and salvation from death have their focal point in the crucified Christ.

The cross of Christ Jesus is a gargantuan subject; it is not possible to discuss and cover the nitty-gritty here. However, because of the splendid and unique place it occupies in the doctrine of Christianity, I set forth further statements below which may help to develop your faith in Christ Jesus and his mystery mission of death on the cross and ultimate resurrection.

- Many Christians (especially in the Roman Catholic Church) make the "sign of the cross" on varied occasions and situations. Even in the religion of Islam and other major and minor religions of the world, the cross is recognised as the main symbol of Christianity. In the Moslem and other non-Christian world, the Red Cross, which is an international charity organisation, is regarded as a Christian missionary organisation because of the symbol of the cross.

- The understanding of the cross in Israel is that it is a curse for blasphemers and breakers of God's law in general (Deut. 21:23; Gal. 3:13). In the New Testament, the Jews said that Jesus made himself "Son of God" (John 19:7). During the lifetime of Christ Jesus, Israel was occupied by imperial Rome. There were many freedom fighters and leaders of revolt, and most of them were executed by the Romans by crucifixion on the cross. The Jews regarded and recognised them as martyrs for the righteous cause of the God of Israel, and they were not rejected as blasphemers. In the case of Christ Jesus'crucifixion, he was accused of blasphemy and was labelled in a derogatory way as "The King of the Jews" who stirred up insurrection and rebellion against the temple high priest and imperial Roman authority in Israel. In other words, the cross of Christ Jesus is a curse among the Jews and in Judaism.

- The cross is not just anathema to the Jews; it was also foolishness to the Gentiles. Paul was in spiritual agony as he realised that the "religion of the cross" was not respectable and perverse to both Jews and Gentiles. In his first epistle to the Corinthians, he said "Jews demand miraculous signs and Greeks look for wisdom, but we preach Christ crucified: a stumbling block to Jews and foolishness to Gentiles" (1 Cor. 1:22–23). Christ crucified is a stumbling block to the Jews because they expected a triumphant, political leader (the Messiah) who would fight as a military leader against imperial Rome, drive away the Roman soldiers from the land of Israel, and liberate and set them free to regain independence in their economies, politics, and to some extent and more important religious affairs (Acts 1:6). The crucified Christ is also foolishness to the Greeks (especially the Greek philosophers) and the Romans because they were certain that no reputable and honourable person would voluntarily and willingly carry his own cross and allow himself to be crucified. Moreover, it was meaningless and unthinkable that a man condemned by Jewish religious leaders and crucified as a criminal because of blasphemy and ungodliness could be the saviour through whom the sins of the whole world are washed away. To the Romans, the cross was so sacrilegious that Cicero declared, "Let even the name of the cross be kept away not only from the bodies of the citizens of Rome, but also from their thought, lip, sight and hearing."[11]

- At the time of Cicero's writing, it was regarded as an offence against manners to speak of this hideous death for slaves in the presence of respectable and noble people in Rome. It was not the sign of conquest; it was not a sign of triumph that occupied the most sacred and high place in a church or an adornment on the imperial throne, nor was it the sign of order and honour as it is now used and presented in major monarchical ceremonies in England. The cross was rather a sign of contradiction and scandal, bringing expulsion, exclusion, excommunication, and ultimately death.
- Faith in the cross distinguishes the Christian faith from the rest of the world's religions and from secular ideologies and utopias.
- The crucified Christ Jesus (Messiah) on the cross now represents God's church of liberation for all people, whether Jews or Gentiles, Greeks or Barbarians, masters or servants, male or female.
- To die on the cross meant to suffer and die as one who was an outcast and rejected (Mark 8:35, 15:34).
- In Church history, the closest and most dignifying form of following the crucified Christ Jesus was to be a martyr. Those who were put to death were considered to have undergone the

[11] Moltmann, 28.

"baptism of blood" and had fellowship with Christ Jesus in his death. The cross of Christ Jesus was the basis on which the Apostles, the martyrs, and all those who show selfless love were crucified with him.

- The cross is not just an event of the past which can be contemplated in detachment. It is also an eschatological (future) event in and beyond time, for as far as its spiritual meaning is concerned, it is an ever-present reality in every aspect of the life of the believer in Christ Jesus.

- Christ Jesus was not powerless, yet he was crucified on the cross. He went voluntarily to be crucified according to the scriptures in the New Testament. He said this to his disciples on many occasions before he willingly went to the cross for the ultimate and grand sacrifice: "The reason my Father loves me is that I lay down my life only to take it up again. No-one takes it from me, but I lay it down of my own accord. I have authority to lay it down and authority to take it up again. This command I received from my Father" (John 10:17–18).

- The knowledge of the cross brings a conflict of interest between God who has become man and man who wishes to become God. The cross of Christ Jesus destroys the destruction of the human being and alienates the alienated human being, and in this way restores the humanity of the dehumanised human.

- The death of Christ Jesus on the cross is a mystery beyond natural human knowledge and understanding.

- Consider the cry of agony on the cross: "And about the ninth hour Jesus cried out with a loud voice, saying, 'Eli, Eli, lema sabachthan!?' That is, 'My God, my God why have you forsaken me?'" (Matt. 27:46). This is the fourth word from the cross, the very first one reported by Matthew and Mark. It is issued from the dying but divine mouth of Christ Jesus shortly before his last breath that makes him the saviour of the world. Just to remind us, Christ Jesus issued seven words (known as the Seven Words of the Cross) from his holy lips, which are as follows:
    1. "Father, forgive them: for they do not know what they are doing" (Luke 23:34).

2. "I tell you the truth, Today you will be with me in Paradise" (Luke 23:43).

3. "Dear woman, here is your son, Here is your mother" (John 19:26–27).

4. "My God, my God, why have you forsaken me?" (Mark 15:34).

5. "I am thirsty" (John 19:28).

6. "It is finished" (John 19:30).

7. "Father, into your hands I commit my spirit" (Luke 23:46).

Going back to the fourth item above, I notice that Christ Jesus suffered indescribably and was in intense agony because he had been "made sin" for us (2 Cor. 5:21) and "a curse" (Gal. 3:13). Isaiah said, "But he was pierced for our transgressions, he was crushed for our iniquities; the punishment that brought us peace was upon him, and by his wounds we are healed. We all, like sheep have gone astray, each of us has turned to his own way; and the Lord has laid on him the iniquity of us all" (Isa. 53:5– These words of agony on the cross initially seem to be a negative cry, but a careful spiritual understanding reveals that the outcome is definitely positive. It confirms that Christ Jesus carried all our sins on the cross and God abandoned him because of our sins. It should not be interpreted as a negative of negativity – that is to say, God was not with Christ Jesus on the cross and God actually and practically abandoned his son (God the Son) Christ Jesus and left him alone on his own on the cross to suffer and die a hopeless death. On the contrary, the positive opposite is the truth of God's original plan of salvation in Christ Jesus.

• God himself died the death of the godless on the cross of Christ Jesus, yet he did not die. God is dead, and yet he is not dead but alive. The history of Israel and God's salvation plan for the Jews and the Gentiles that was dormant for about four hundred years after the prophet Malachi in the Old Testament was opened up and activated once again in Christ Jesus through his birth, mission, death on the cross, and ultimate resurrection as recorded in the four gospels and the epistles in the New Testament.

Chapter 7

# THEMES OF THE CROSS OF CHRIST JESUS

In chapter 6, I examined the source of salvation for the Christian Religion and explained that the Christians dogma, teaching, faith and belief is that their source of salvation is from only one and main source which is Christ Jesus who is Godself and who is salvation himself. I also concluded that the cross of Christ Jesus is very significant as source of salvation and has become a holy and sacred icon and symbol which represents the Christian faith in the whole wide world.

My main aim in this chapter is to escalate the points raised in chapter 6 and analyse the themes of the cross of Christ Jesus. In this chapter, I will evaluate the following aspects of the cross: symbol of shame, place of final sacrifice for sins, demonstration of God's love, forgiveness of sin, reconciliation, victory of the cross and source of Christianity.

## THE CROSS: SYMBOL OF SHAME

In the four gospels, the cross is presented as symbol of public shame and humiliation as well as debasement. As stated earlier, imperial Rome used it not only as an instrument of torture and execution but also as an ignominious pillory reserved for the worst criminals and the lowest of the low. To the Jews, the cross was a sign of been accursed by God from the Old Testament perspective. Although the word *cross* is not directly found in the Old Testament, it bears a resemblance to the tree referred to in Mosaic Law: "If a man guilty of a capital offense is put to death and his body is hung on a tree, you must not leave his body on the tree overnight. Be sure to bury him that same day, because anyone who is hung on a tree is under God's curse. You must not desecrate the land the Lord your God is giving you as an inheritance" (Deut. 21:22–23).

Please note that those who were hung on trees had committed capital offences. The murderer was first executed (perhaps by stoning; see Deuteronomy21:21) and then his body was hung on a tree; but the body must not be left hanging on the tree overnight. Also note that the law prohibited a prolonged and procrastinated exposure of the deceased body on the tree, which gave undue attention to the crime and the criminal. Please also note that this imposed a death penalty and stressed its function as a deterrent. By association, it is followed by a regulation which limited public exhibition of an executed offender.[1] Mosaic Law casts off a person who has been hung on a tree because he is cursed by God. Hanging on a tree symbolised divine judgement and rejection.

There are unfathomable differences between a person hung on a tree who is under God's curse and Christ Jesus, who was crucified on the cross as the saviour of the world. Firstly, Christ Jesus was not guilty of a capital offence or any other similar offence that would have instigated the death penalty. In fact, Pilate proclaimed Jesus' innocence in Luke 23:4, 14, 22, and in John 18:38 and 19:4. Luke recorded: "For the third time [Pilate] spoke to them [the whole assembly of the council of the elders of the people, both the chief priests and teachers of the law] and asked "Why? What crime has this man committed? I have found in him no grounds for the death penalty" (Luke 23:22).

Secondly, the execution of the murderer was by stoning, which I think was less dehumanising, with a minimum period of pain and suffering. I also think that the person who committed murder was treated with humanity and dignity, with his clothes on him. In the case of Christ Jesus, he was stripped of his garment, given thirty-three lashes (this was worse than stoning), forced to carry his heavy cross (which weighed between thirty and forty pounds), and finally put through all the indescribable

---

[1] Christoph Bultmann, "Deuteronomy", in *The Oxford Bible Commentary*, ed. John Barton and John Muddiman (Oxford, 2011), 149.

cruelty of crucifixion. His ordeal of cruel hash treatment from the time he was arrested in the Garden of Gethsemane to his final death on the cross lasted more than twelve hours.

Thirdly, in the case of a murderer, it was just the dead body that was hung on the tree. It was not a good thing to see a dead body on a tree, but it is proper to say that the dead body on the tree did not feel any pain and was indifferent to any type of humiliation and insults (which might be genuine, especially from the relatives or next of kin of the deceased). But in the case of Christ Jesus, he was hung on the cross alive and even refused to accept the wine mixed with gall – a type of painkiller intended to alleviate his suffering – which was offered to him because he wanted to be fully conscious and fully in control of his own death. Moreover, Christ Jesus received all the mockery from the Roman soldiers, absorbed all the insults hurled at him by those who passed by, and endured the provoking words of the chief priest, the teachers of the law, and the elders of Israel.

Fourthly, one of the most important contrasts between person guilty of a capital offence and the Lord Christ Jesus, who was declared innocent and of whom was found "no ground for the death penalty", was that the guilty murderer was not willing to die even for his sin in order to "purge the evil from among" the Israelites. On the contrary, Christ Jesus, who was sinless (fully divine and fully man), voluntarily and willingly surrendered himself and accepted the full punishment of the sins of the human race. This was the universal vicarious humiliation and curse which Christ Jesus took upon himself willingly.

Paul stated in his epistle to the Galatians that "Christ redeemed us from the curses of the law by becoming a curse for us, for it is written: "Cursed is everyone who is hung on a tree" (Gal. 3:13). I join Stanton to say that the thought in this passage is Jesus acted in a representative capacity and the Mosaic law printed its curse on Christ Jesus[2]. In the death of Christ Jesus, the force of the curse was finished, completed, and totally exhausted, and those held under its power were liberated. Paul made a similar assertive statement in his second epistle to the Corinthians: "God made him who had no sin to be sin for us, so that in him we might become the righteousness of God" (2 Cor. 5:21). This is the summary of the Gospel and its logical conclusion. Christ Jesus, the entirely righteous one,

---

[2] G.N.stanton, "Galatians", in The *Oxford Bible Commentray,* 1159.

on the Calvary cross took the sins of the world upon himself and endured the punishment of the whole world on the first Good Friday. Through this divine and marvellous exchange, he made it possible for all people to receive his righteousness, which has made it possible for all who believe in him to be reconciled to God.

Christ Jesus endured the cross and despised the shame. For this holy reason, "let us fix our eyes on Jesus, the author and perfecter of our faith, who for joy set before him endured the cross, and scorning its shame, and sat down at the right hand of the throne of God" (Heb. 12:2). There are three main phrases in this citation to ponder upon as follows:

1. "fix our eyes on Jesus"
2. "perfecter of our faith"
3. "joy set before him"

What do you think of these phrases? What do they mean to you? How do you understand them, and how can you explain them to others?

The shameful spectacle of a victim carrying the cross was very familiar in the lifetime of Christ Jesus and his twelve disciples, his wider followers, and his general audience. Carrying of the cross by the victim to the place of his crucifixion was a daily common event in Israel, which reminded them that they were under the imperial rule of Rome and been treated as slaves in their own country. It is against this backdrop of melancholy and downheartedness that Christ Jesus spoke to his disciples three times and explained to them the spiritual road of discipleship, which must be cross-bearing.[3]

## THE CROSS: PLACE OF FINAL SACRIFICE FOR SINS

One of the most important sacrifices in the Old Testament which has been made and observed in the history of the Israelites is the commemorative Passover sacrifice which Moses instructed the Jews to pass from posterity to the next generation. Moses said to the Israelites: "Then tell them, it is the Passover Sacrifice to the Lord, who passed over the houses of the Israelites

---

[3] Matt. 10:38; Mark 8:34; Luke 14:27.

in Egypt and spared our homes when he struck down the Egyptians. Then the people bowed down and worshipped" (Exod. 12:27).

Moses devoted the whole of Exodus 12 to the Passover. In that event, the blood of the lamb that was slain was put on the door frame of all the houses of the Israelites in Egypt. The good news here is that Yahweh "passed over" and did not destroy the occupants (the Israelites) of the houses that were under the sign of the blood of lamb. The Passover sacrifice saved the Israelites (brought deliverance and protection) from the destruction of the firstborn of human and animal in all the land of Egypt, because all the houses of the Jews in Egypt bore the mark of the sign of the blood of the sacrificial lamb.

This extraordinary, wonderful working power of the blood of the Passover lamb which the Israelites observed and experienced is transposed to the New Testament, which is centred upon Christ Jesus as the sacrificial lamb of Yahweh (Rom. 8:3). The traditional lamb, if not provable in all instances, has a widespread precedent. It is laid down in Exodus 12:46, Numbers. 9:12, and Psalm. 34:20 that no bone of the Passover victim is to be broken. This small but significant detail is typologically fulfilled when it is reverently and appropriately applied to the crucified Christ Jesus.[4] In Psalm 43:19–20, David affirmed that, "A righteous man may have many troubles, but the Lord delivers him from them all; he protects all his bones, not one of them will be broken." It is likely that John the Divine applied these words of the ancestor David to his descendent Christ Jesus. Regarding the righteous one, John stated, "My dear children, I write this to you so that you will not sin. But if anybody does sin, we have one who speaks to the Father in our defence – Jesus Christ, the righteous one" (1 John 2:1). With regards to the bones of the righteous man (Christ Jesus), John also stated: "these things happened so that the scripture would be fulfilled: 'Not one of his bones will be broken" (John 19:36). It is marvellous, but not just a coincidence that Christ Jesus was the only one of the three people who were crucified whose legs were not broken, and although he suffered an unusual spear thrust, even that did not break any of his bones.

At the beginning of his gospel, John recorded that Christ Jesus is "the Lamb of God." John stated: "The next day John saw Jesus coming

---

[4] J. D. Douglas, *New Bible Dictionary: Second Edition* (Leicester, 1994), 881–883.

towards him and said, "Look the Lamb of God who takes away the sin of the world!" (John 1:29, 36). Here, John the Baptist did not refer to Christ Jesus as the Passover lamb which had been slaughtered in the first Passover night and saved the firstborn of human beings and animals only and mainly in the households of Israel in Egypt. The Passover lambs from the first Passover night up to the destruction of the second temple by imperial Rome in 70 AD were all chosen by the men of individual households in Israel. These lambs were "lambs of men", chosen by men, and these lambs were specifically meant to take away the sins of individuals Jews only. This did not include any of the Gentile world. These lambs could not and did not take away the sins of the Hebrews either temporarily or permanently, which is why every day the Jews had to slaughter bulls, sheep, goats, doves, or pigeons endlessly and in vain for their sins.

Please note here that the Lamb who John the Baptist introduced to his audience is "the Lamb of God" (Christ Jesus who is God the Son), chosen by God himself (not by men), who "takes away the sins of the world" (not just Israelites' sins but the sins of the whole of the Gentile nations) in a way that is effective, eternal and permanent. This is the Lamb of God which the grand progenitor of Israel (father Abraham) saw in the spirit, and of whom he prophesied when he said to his son Isaac, "God himself will provide the lamb for the burnt offering my son" (Gen. 22:8).Read further Genesis 22:13 and note that God immediately provided a ram (not a lamb) for Abraham for the sacrifice at that moment. Holy Scripture and other sources record that human beings provided animals to make sacrifice to their gods in both the ancient and modern world. But in this instance, Abraham stated that "God himself" (not Abraham) would provide "the lamb" for his own sacrifice. Like those of his peer group, Abraham who was earthly had on other occasions provided earthly lambs or animals for sacrifice for Yahweh. But on this occasion, in Genesis 22:8, he made a divine pronouncement that the divine God himself would provide the heavenly Lamb that would make the ultimate and grand sacrifice which would take away the sin of the world. This holy prophecy was confirmed in John 1:29, 36.

Dear reader, it is of blissful significance to note here in Genesis 22:13 a substitutionary sacrifice for the first time which Paul remanded the Gentile nations in all his epistles (Rom. 3:25; 1 Cor. 5:7; Eph. 5:2). As the ram was made the sacrifice and died instead of Isaac, so also Christ Jesus was made the ultimate sacrifice who died and gave his life as a ransom for many (Mark 10:45). The lamb which Abraham saw in the spirit is the substitutionary "Lamb of God", Christ Jesus, who came at "the right time."

Paul in his letter to the Romans stated, "You see, at just the right time, when we were still powerless, Christ died for the ungodly. Very rarely will anyone die for a righteous man, though for a good man someone might possibly dare to die, But God demonstrates his own love for us in this: while we were still sinners, Christ died for us" (Rom. 5:6–8). Dear believer in the precious and holy name of Christ Jesus, please do not allow the trials and temporary difficulties you are facing currently (which only you know best) to distract you from focusing on the Lord and saviour Christ Jesus. Be assured that as Christ Jesus came into this world to take away the sins of the world (including your own) "at the right time", so Christ Jesus will set you free from all your problems at the appropriate time of his chosen.

"Christ our Passover Lamb of God" is very familiar text in the New Testament. Here it suffices to cite Paul's first letter to the Corinthians, where he stated, "Get rid of the old yeast that you may be a new batch without yeast, as you really are. For Christ, our Passover lamb, has been sacrificed" (1 Cor. 5:7). In his death on the cross, Christ Jesus fulfilled the true meaning of the original or the first Jewish sacrifice of the Passover lamb (Isa. 53:7). Christ Jesus, who is the Lamb of God, was crucified on the cross for the sin of the world as the Passover lamb.

After the destruction of the second temple in Jerusalem by imperial Rome in 70 AD, all slaughtering of victim animals and birds in ritual ceremonies totally ceased. But the Passover continued as a family festival, as it had been in the earliest first night of the original Passover in Egypt as recorded in Exodus 12. The process of the parting of the ways between Christianity and Judaism made it possible for the Christian church and the Jewish synagogue to eventually go their separate ways. One of the most significant differences that triggered the separation between the church and the synagogue is the Lord's Supper or Holy Communion or Eucharist, which came to replace the Jewish ordinance of the Passover, just as the Christian baptism came to replace the Jewish circumcision in the Christian community.

Spurgeon, in his exuberance, spoke about the Passover and said:

> It was only one Passover that set them all free. I would
> have you, beloved, particularly remember one thing: that
> great as this emigration was, and enormous as were the
> multitudes that left Egypt, it was only one Passover that
> set them all free. They did not want two celebrations of
> the supper; they did not need two angels to fly through
> Egypt; it was not necessary to have two deliverances:
> but all in one night, all by the paschal lamb, all by the
> Passover supper, they were saved. One agonising sacrifice,
> one death on Calvary, one blood sweat on Gethsemane,
> one shriek of "It is finished" consummated all the work
> of redemption.

Spurgeon concluded, "I love it when I think it saves one sinner, but oh!
To think of the multitude of sinners that it saves."[5]

This "once and for all" Passover sacrifice is complete once for all, and
it is incomparable to the perpetual and ineffective daily sacrifice prescribed
in the Old Testament. In Romans 3:25, Paul pencilled these words: "God
presented him [Christ Jesus] as a sacrifice of atonement, through faith in
his blood. He did this to demonstrate his justice, because in his forbearance
he had left the sins committed beforehand unpunished." This sacrifice
of Christ Jesus is the sacrifice that satisfied the righteous wrath of God.
Without this appeasement (propitiation), all people would have been justly
destined for eternal punishment. The believer's faith is anchored firm and
secured upon the blood of Christ Jesus alone. The dogma of the Christian
saving faith looks and focuses on Christ Jesus in his divine and precious
blood which he shed and died before his ultimate resurrection. The blood
of Christ Jesus is the most important heavenly invisible emblem of the
Christian faith. It is also perceptible as wine on every Holy Communion
table in every denomination of the Christian faith.

Christ Jesus knows that his own blood is very precious, special, and
priceless, and he values it more than any earthly treasure. The body and

---

[5] Charles Haddon Spurgeon, *Spurgeon's Commentary on the Bible*, ed. Robert
Backhouse (London, 1997), 11–12.

the blood of Christ Jesus are the life of life and the salvation of salvation for those who believe in him – and for that glorious reason, Christ Jesus made an absolute statement: "I tell you the truth, unless you can eat the flesh of the Son of Man and drink his blood, you have no life in you. Whoever eats my flesh and drinks my blood has eternal life, and I will raise him up at the last day. For my flesh is real food and my blood is real drink" (John 6:53–55). Christ Jesus' flesh and blood point to us as the crucified and sovereign God and the source of our eternal salvation both in the present and the eschatological age. Christ Jesus esteems his body and blood to the extent that he replaced them with the Passover and commanded his disciples to make sure that they give a pre-eminent place to them.

After the Passover meal which he had with his disciples as his last supper, he said to them, "This is my body which is for you; do this in remembrance of me." In the same way, after supper he took the cup, saying, 'This cup is the new covenant in my blood; do this, whenever you drink it, in remembrance of me" (1 Cor. 11:23–25). It is noteworthy to state here that it is ironic that the "last supper" command of Christ Jesus to his Jewish disciples became the beginning of one of the supplications which made a distinctive mark between observances of the Mosaic command of the Passover in Judaism and Christ Jesus' command of the Holy Communion in Christianity. Here I cite that wonderful song from the Sacred Songs and Solos (SSS 379): "Have you been to Jesus for the cleansing power? Are you washed in the blood of the Lamb? Are you fully trusting in His grace this hour? Are you washed in the blood of the Lamb? Are you washed in the soul-cleansing blood of the Lamb? Are your garments spotless? Are they white as snow?"

Dear brother or sister, it is impossible to answer these soul-searching, probing questions on your behalf. It is only you who know your personal relationship with the Lamb of God. It is only you who know whether your sins are washed away by the precious blood of the Lamb, and it is only you who can affirm that you are walking daily by the saviour's side. And it is the same you who can vouchsafe that you are resting each moment in the crucified Christ Jesus. If you are not quite sure of your relationship with the Lamb of God, I implore you in the name of Christ Jesus to seek the Holy Spirit first and foremost to help and lead you to develop that divine relationship; and also talk to someone in the Lord to help you.

Jesus who was fully God and fully man knew that he would die on the cross and make the final sacrifice, and that was why he said "And as Moses in the wilderness lifted up the bronze image of a serpent on a pole, even so I must be lifted upon a pole so that anyone who believe in me will have eternal life" (John 3:14–15). He made a similar statement on the same subject with regards to his death and declared: "But I, when I am lifted up from the earth, will draw all men to myself" (John 12:32). In both passages, Christ Jesus told his Jewish audience in absolute terms of his sacrifice on the cross which would bring salvation to both the Jews and all the Gentile world. Christ Jesus was made the final and ultimate sacrifice for sin, offering himself (of his own volition) as a holy whole burnt offering on the cross of his passion.

## THE CROSS: DEMONSTRATION OF GOD'S LOVE

One of the central aspects of the New Testament understanding of the meaning of the cross of Christ Jesus relates to the demonstration of the love of God for humanity. Augustine of Hippo of Africa, one of the great patristic prolific apologetic writers of his generation, stated: "One of the motivations underlying the mission of Christ Jesus is the demonstration of the love of God towards humanity."[6]

In the Old Testament, I note that Mosaic Law stipulates rigid, rigorous, and endless sacrifices; transgressions and curses are imposed upon humanity. On the other hand, New Testament dogma is based on God's love, mercy, grace, blessings, and forgiveness that lead to salvation and eternal life which are from Christ Jesus. Christ Jesus underscored this heavenly love and said that God the Father loved the world so much he sent God the Son in order to save humanity from sin. All those who believe in God the Son shall not perish in condemnation in eternal and perpetual darkness, but will receive grace and mercy and have heavenly eternal life by his death on the cross and resurrection.

In John 15:13, Christ Jesus said, "Greater love has no-one than this that he lay down his life for his friends." Christ Jesus did not just say this to his disciples verbally, but he made his words of "laying down his life for

---

[6] Augustine, 2003.

his friends" good when he voluntarily went to the cross and died for his friends – not only for the first Jewish disciples but also all the subsequent believers who believe in his name through the ages who he loves. This is love the world expected since the fall of the first humankind. Christ's manifestation of the love of God on the cross is awesome and more glorious than the love which Paul described in 1 Corinthians 13. Christ Jesus instructed all his followers to continue to love each other with that same love which he exercised when he laid down his life on the cross for all those who are truly his friends (1 John 3:16).

Christ Jesus' love on the cross has infinite value; it has heavenly substitutionary character; and it has glorious redemptive power of both present and eschatological saving grace. That Christ Jesus "laid down his life" for all believers in him does not just mean that he only physically died for their benefit. Importantly, he died in their stead. He even experienced the torment of hell on the cross to the extent that God the Father seemed to have abandoned him.

Still on the same subject of the God's love, Paul wrote to the Church in Rome and stressed: "And hope does not disappoint us, because God has poured out his love into our hearts by the Holy Spirit, whom he has given us" (Rom. 5:5). [Paul] continued and said, "But God demonstrates his own love for us in this: while we were still sinners, Christ died for us" (Rom. 5:8). The powerful statement Paul made that "God has poured out his love" explains God's mystical love which he displayed in Christ Jesus on the cross. This love of God in Christ Jesus is not sprinkled or showered but poured down in torrents which rained very hard and heavily. The love of God that was poured out through Christ Jesus is stronger and more effective than the curse which was poured out upon the earth "on that day when all the springs of the great deep burst forth, and when the floodgates of the heaven were opened", which brought death, destruction, and eternal death to the world except Noah and his household and all the animals and birds that were in the Ark (Genesis 7). God's anger which was poured out brought curses, destruction, and physical and spiritual death to all humanity; God's love which was poured out through Christ Jesus brings kindness, mercy, blessings, physical and spiritual life, and eschatological salvation.

This theme of "the love of God" is one of the most important subjects to Paul, who remanded his readers in his epistles to all the Gentile churches, including the church in Ephesus. Here Paul stated: "Because of his great love for us, God, who is rich in mercy, made us alive with Christ even when we were dead in transgression – it is by grace you have been saved. And God raised us up with Christ and seated us with him in the heavenly realms in Christ Jesus" (Eph. 2:4–6).

This "great love" which God blissfully lavished on the cross through Christ Jesus is the greatest love the world has ever known. It transcends all earthly domains and pervades even the heavenly realms, it dotes on unimaginable scale, and is beyond human comprehension. This great love of God comes with the greatest affection, and it is full of God's heavenly treasures, even eternal salvation through Christ Jesus. God's great love makes it possible for believers in Christ Jesus to become beloved children of God.

This great love of God through Christ Jesus becomes the greatest divine riches in mercy, kindness, and grace; and the beloved children of God through Christ Jesus are far more beloved than the beloved one in the Songs of Songs. It is humanly impossible to give a full and satisfactory description and explanation of this great love, but I can conclude here that the only theologically valid interpretation of the cross of Christ Jesus is that it represents the unmeritorious and unwarranted love toward humankind of both God Almighty the Creator of the universe who is God the Father and Christ Jesus the saviour of the world who is God the Son.

## THE CROSS: FORGIVENESS OF SIN

To start this section, it may be useful to explain *sin* and *sinner*. In order to explore these words in detail, I put forward the following questions: What is sin? Who is a sinner? What is the real meaning of forgiveness?

The Bible uses a wide variety of terms in both the Old and New Testaments to express the idea of sin.[7] Sin is mentioned hundreds of times in the Bible, starting with the original sin when Adam and Eve ate of the tree of knowledge. Adam and Eve were made for the presence and

---

[7] Douglas, 1116–1119.

fellowship of God; but because of sin, they dreaded an encounter with God their maker. Sin, shame, and fear became their dominant emotions (Gen. 2:25, 3:7, 10). The effect of the fall of Adam and Eve extended to the physical cosmos, and God in his anger pronounced "cursed is the ground because of you" (Gen. 3:17). Sin is rebellion against God, and defiance of his holy authority and rule (Isa. 1:28). It is deliberate perversion or twisting (Isa. 24:1; Lam. 3:9). Sin is concrete wrongdoing – the violation of God's law (John 8:46; Jas. 1:15: 1 John 1:8). In Romans 5–8, Paul personifies sin as a ruling principle in human life (5:12; 6:12; 7:17, 20; 8:2).

One particular category of sinners that crops up frequently in the gospels is the tax or toll collector. Tax collectors were labelled as sinners and hated as collaborators with Rome. They were widely regarded as dishonest and rapacious; thus they were labelled as sinners not just by the Pharisees but by the ordinary people of the land, making them almost the moral equivalent of lepers.[8] However, despite the general perception of the people of the land in Palestine that tax collectors were sinners, Christ Jesus welcomed them into table-fellowship with himself.[9] The other category of sinners that is mentioned in the synoptic tradition are prostitutes.

What did Christ Jesus offer to these sinners? The simple answer is forgiveness. But like many other theological terms which have become standard in later Christian vocabulary, forgiveness needs further exploration if I am to locate Jesus within his historical mystery mission in the land in Palestine.

Centuries of Christians' usage of *forgiveness* have accustomed readers of the New Testament to think of it as primarily a divine gift to an individual person, which can be received at any time. It is, in that sense, abstract and ahistorical. However, it may burst upon one's consciousness with fresh delight in particular historical situations. On this basis, analyses of Christ Jesus' forgiveness have tended to focus on the piety (the sense of forgiveness) or the abstract theology (the fact of forgiveness or the belief in it) of Christ Jesus' hearers and/or the early Church.[10]

---

[8] N. T. Wright, *Jesus and the Victory of God*, (London, 1996) 266.

[9] Mark 2:15; Matt. 9:10, 11:19, 21:31; Luke 5:29, 7:29, 34.

[10] Wright, 268.

## Forgiveness: Old Testament Perspective

It may be of help to give a summary of the meaning of forgiveness in both the Old and New Testaments before I dive into the subject matter of the cross as the centre of absolution. There are different meanings of forgiveness in the Old Testament, but here I can only identify and discuss three. The first meaning is atonement, and it is used in connection with sacrifices. These two words, *atonement* and *sacrifice*, are predominate ones and the centre of Old Testament dogma, especially in Mosaic Law, which relates to different sacrifices and offerings for sins.

The significance of the doctrine of atonement and sacrifice cannot be overemphasised. They are eternally and sacredly presented in almost every book of the scripture in the Old Testament, and the same transcendental divinity has been transferred into the New Testament teachings that form the nucleus of the proclamation of the gospel by Christ Jesus and the Apostles (especially Paul) upon which the Christian faith and belief stand.

Forgiveness of sins is another way of saying "return from exile." The connection of forgiveness of sins and return from exile is loud and clear when we read some of the texts. The prophets at the time of the exile saw Israel's exile precisely as the result of, or the punishment for, her sins.[11] It should be clear from this that if astonishing, unbelievable things were to happen and Israel were to be brought back from exile, this would mean that her sins were being punished no more; in other words, Israel's sins were forgiven.

In this context, the writer of Lamentations stated the matter as clearly and boldly as one can understand: "O Daughter of Zion, your punishment will end; he will not prolong your exile, But O Daughter of Edom, he will punish your sin and expose your wickedness" (Lam. 4:22). This is to say that Israel was sent to exile in a foreign land because of her sins, and the prophet said that her exile would soon come to an end because Israel's sin had been fully paid by the punishment she had received in exile.

From the moment Adam and Eve disobeyed and offended God, humankind has been making endless and hopeless sacrifices in order to atone (make amends for sins or wrongdoing) and reconcile with God. Adam and Eve were punished for their sin (disobedience against God)

---

[11] See particularly Jeremiah, Ezekiel, and Isaiah 40–55.

and were expelled from the Garden of Eden (sent into exile). In the same manner, each time the people of Israel sinned against God (disobedience to God's law, especially worship of foreign gods), they were expelled from their promised land and sent for punishment in a foreign land.

The book of Job describes sacrificial procedures before Mosaic Law. The writer of the book of Job stated: "[Job's] sons used to take turns holding feasts in their homes, and they would invite their three sisters to eat and drink with them. When a period of feasting had run its course, Job would send and have them purified. Early in the morning he would sacrifice a burnt offering for each of them, thinking 'perhaps my children have sinned and cursed God in their hearts.' This was Job's regular custom" (Job 1:4–5). Here it is possible to note that the primary purpose of Job's sacrifice of burnt offerings on behalf of his children was to make atonement for any sin they might have committed and ask God for forgiveness and reconciliation.

Before the ceremonial laws of Moses and the Aaronic priesthood were introduced, the father of the household acted as the priest. In the Old Testament, "atonement" which brought reconciliation was the divine act of grace whereby Yahweh drew to himself those who were once alienated from him. It is God himself who devised this means of atonement because of his willingness to forgive sin. Because of its divine importance, he asked Moses to "make an atonement cover" with all the details in Exodus 25:17–22. The atonement cover in the Tabernacle was a masterpiece of art which demonstrated God's throne and signified his great grace and mighty mercy towards his helpless creatures. The atonement cover was an awesome and sacred place to the almighty Creator God, and because of this, the Lord said to Moses, "Tell your brother Aaron not to come whenever he chooses into the Most Holy Place behind the curtain in front of the atonement cover on the Ark, or else he will die, because I appear in the cloud over the atonement cover" (Lev. 16:2). This atonement cover of sacrifice in the Old Testament is the same which Paul attributed to Christ Jesus in Romans 3:25.

The second meaning of *forgiveness* in the Old Testament is "lift" and "carry", which presents a vivid picture of sin being lifted from the sinner and carried right away. This meaning of forgiveness indicates that God totally removes the sin from the sinner as if the sinner had not committed any sin before. God in his own righteousness swore by himself and promised his people of Israel and declared, "I, even I, am he who blots out your transgressions, for my own sake; and remembers your sins no more" (Isa. 43:25). Earlier, in Isaiah 1:18, God had already invited his people to himself for forgiveness of their sin and said to them, "Come now, let us reason together' says the Lord. 'Though your sins are like scarlet, they shall be as white as snow; though they are red as crimson, they shall be like wool." God's unconditional and total forgiveness includes even the murderers whose hands are stained with human blood. The guilty sinner here becomes an innocent saint ("crimson" has turn to "white as snow"). Here I can understand a powerful figurative description of the result of God's unilateral and unconditional forgiveness.

God also declared to his people, "I have swept away your offences like a cloud, your sins like the morning mist. Return to me, for I have redeemed you" (Isa. 44:22). It is wonderful to note here that God used his holy broom to sweep and remove every one of our sins, and they disappeared and are seen no more, like the morning mist that must give way before the divine strong ray of the sun. God wants us to return to him in our original perfect (before the fall of Adam and Eve) sinless condition because he has redeemed (set us free from sins) and has totally forgiven us our sins and has restored us to himself. This is the forgiveness of all forgiveness and the redemption of all redemption. This forgiveness becomes possible by the divine will of God alone because it is only the forgiving God who plans, initiates, and implements forgiveness of the sins of humankind. God declared and confirmed his absolution of sin and said, "For I will forgive their wickedness and will remember their sin no more" (Jer. 31:43b).

God's forgiveness is being received with gratitude and accepted with awe and wonder because the sin of human beings merits nothing less than eternal punishment and condemnation. God's pardon of sin is his awesome astounding grace, which he bestows on humans exclusively at his own prerogative. The psalmist realised that if God does not exercise his own authority for remission of sin, no human can stand before him. The Psalmist stated, "If you, O Lord, kept a record of sin, O Lord, who could stand? But with you there is forgiveness, therefore you are feared" (Ps. 130:3–4).

It is necessary to state here that the "fear of God" is not the negative connotation of distress or alarm caused by impending danger that is lurking, but on the contrary, it gives a positive confidence to honour, worship, trust, and serve God in spirit and in truth as the only true God who is all and in all. If God were not willing to exonerate humans from sin, descendants of Adam could only flee from him in terror and would have been perpetually separated from him.

God's condemnation of sin is possible because he is a God of grace. A very instructive and inspirational passage for the whole of the Old Testament understanding of God's forgiveness is Exodus 34:6, which records: "And he passed in front of Moses, proclaiming, 'The Lord, the Lord, the compassionate and gracious God, slow to anger, abounding in love and faithfulness.'" The Lord's proclamation of the meaning and implications of his name in these verses became a classic exposition that was frequently recalled elsewhere in the rest of the Old Testament.[12] Daniel echoed the same theme of acquittal of sin by God and stated: "The Lord our God is merciful and forgiving, even though we have rebelled against him" (Dan. 9:9). The thought of forgiveness is conveyed in most graphic imagery by David who stated, "As far as the east is from the west, so far has [God] removed our transgressions from us" (Ps. 103:12). Isaiah spoke of God as casting all Isaiah's sins behind God's back (Isa. 38:17). Our God is a God of amnesty of sins who not only puts our sins out of sight, but also puts them out of reach and out of existence.

There are many other texts in the Old Testament which I am not able to cite and analyse. There are also many other such vivid and graphic words of emphasis that tell the completeness of God's remission of sins which I have not covered. But here it suffices to conclude that when God forgives the sins of human beings, they are dealt with thoroughly once and for all; and God sees them no more.

## Forgiveness: New Testament Perspective

Forgiveness lies at the heart of Christianity. The one and only prayer which Christ Jesus taught his disciples, sacredly called "The Lord's Prayer" (Matt. 6:13–14; Luke 11:4) is the most important and commonly cited prayer

[12] Num. 14:18; Neh. 9:17; Ps. 86:15, 103:8, 145:8: Joel 12:13; Jonah 4:2.

in most Christian worship in every denomination. In this prayer, Christ Jesus instructed his disciples to ask for forgiveness of their sins from God the Father while praying; and also said that there should be a reciprocal process of forgiveness among human beings.[13]

Christ Jesus finished the teaching of "The Lord's Prayer" in Matthew 6:13, but he went on to put emphasis on the importance and the principle of forgiveness in 6:14–15, stating: "Your heavenly Father will forgive you if you forgive those who sin against you; but if you refuse to forgive them, he will not forgive you." Jesus taught this divine truth on other occasions (Matt. 16:35; Mark 11:25). This prayer has become a format for all believers who cite it during their private worship and also in formal public worship in churches and other appropriate places and occasions. Jesus spoke here of daily forgiveness, which is necessary to restore broken communication between God and humans as well as between human beings.

Exoneration of sin by God in the New Testament means "to deal graciously with", "to send away", and "to release", which is used in Luke 6: 37: "forgive, and you will be forgiven." The axiom of forgiveness is made crystal clear here in the sense that a readiness to forgive others is part of the indication that we have truly repented wholeheartedly.[14]

Remission of sin by God was and is still a key aspect of Jesus' activity. Jesus claimed the power to forgive sins, and he was confronted and challenged about this with the question, "Who can forgive sins but God alone?" This confrontation happened in the incident of the healing of the paralysed man lowered through the roof on a stretcher. Jesus performed the miracle expressly and explained "that you may know that the Son of man has authority on earth to forgive sins." Jesus said to the paralysed man, "I tell you, get up, take your mat and go home.' He got up, took his mat and walked out in full view of them all" (Mark 2:5–12).

Before I make further analysis of forgiveness, it may be necessary to cite Harrington's comment on the healing of the paralytic and forgiveness.[15] He raised the following main points:

---

[13] *Christianity: the Complete Guide*, ed. John Bowden (London, 2005), 470.
[14] Douglas, 390–391.
[15] Daniel J. Harrington, "The Gospel According to Mark", in *The New Jerome Bible Commentary*, ed. Raymond E. Brown, Joseph A. Fitzmyer, and Roland E. Murphy (London, 2013), 601–602.

- To show that Jesus is powerful in both words and deeds, Christ Jesus' power to forgive sins is confirmed by his power to heal the paralysed man. Harrington stated that this incident shows a good example for the early Christians as proof for their claims about forgiveness of sins through Jesus.

- Jesus said to the paralytic, "Son, your sins are forgiven." The address "son" is affectionate. The authoritative declaration of the forgiveness of sins may not have been what the paralytic and his friends wanted to hear. Dear reader, please learn to wait patiently for what you want from Christ Jesus, which may not be given to you in the first instance, but continue to wait and focus on him, because it must come to you eventually at the right time without delay.

- The scribes thought Jesus blasphemed because according to several Old Testament passages,[16] the only one who forgives sins is God. According to the reasoning of the scribes (they did not say it directly; see Mark 2:6, 8), Jesus' claim to forgive sins would thus be regarded as blasphemy. This indeed constituted an implicit claim to be divine (God) authority, which the teachers of Mosaic Law and the Pharisees contested and accused Jesus of; but it is something perfectly acceptable to the disciples and the early Christians who read Mark's Gospel, which is also the faith of present Christians who believe that Christ Jesus is Lord and God who can and does forgive sin.

- It is surely easier to say that a man's sins are forgiven (for which there is no empirical test) than to say that a paralytic should get up and walk (for which there would be an immediate empirical test and proof with the practical act to walking).

- In the composite account in Mark 2:1–12, the healing function is the sign for the validity of Jesus' declaration about forgiveness.

- Jesus heals by word alone, a fact that confirms the authority of his words about forgiveness.

- In the Marcin context, the object of the crowd's amazement included both Jesus' healing power and his claim to forgive sins.

---

[16] Exod. 34:6–7; Isa. 43:25, 44:22.

It is paramount to understand that the person of Christ Jesus is not separate from his work. Forgiveness by or through Christ Jesus means real and divine forgiveness arising from all that he is and all that he does. Who Christ Jesus is, *is* what he does, which is salvation. Christ Jesus is the saviour of the world who brings salvation to all who believe in his name.

Christ Jesus' authority, the power to forgive sins, and the grace of salvation are firmly attached to the cross because he died on the cross for atonement. Forgiveness rests basically on the atoning work of Christ Jesus on the cross. This atoning work is an act of sheer divine grace because "[Christ Jesus] is faithful and just" and will continue to forgive us our sins (1 John 1:9). For a person to receive this free and full forgiveness, there is need for a total and wholehearted repentance. Repentance and forgiveness (although each comes from different source: human and divine) are inseparably interwoven. Without repentance of sins by the human (sinner), there is no forgiveness of sins from Christ Jesus, who is divine and a forgiver of sin. Of this viewpoint, I cite John the Baptist as an example, who preached "a baptism of repentance for the forgiveness of sins" (Matt. 3:11, Mark 1:4, Luke 3:3). Christ Jesus himself commanded that "repentance and forgiveness of sins" should be preached in his name (Mark 1:15; Luke 13:3, 24:47).

John the Baptist applied two key words in his baptismal ministry: repentance and forgiveness. Repentance involves voluntary, swift, and deliberate turning from sin to righteousness, and John's emphasis on repentance takes me to memory lane to a similar preaching in the Old Testament by prophets such as Hosea (3:4–5). As stated above, God always grants forgiveness when humans repent of their sins. Repentance includes wholehearted sorrow for sin and determination to live a holy life, which leads to forgiveness of sins of the penitent person from sin's penalty because of the death of Christ Jesus on the cross and his resurrection.

Repentance and forgiveness of sins were the main theme of Peter when he first addressed the crowd on the day of Pentecost, which inaugurated Peter as the leader of the early Jewish Church and established and laid the foundation of Christianity. Peter's answer to the intrigue question from the crowd ("Brothers, what shall we do?") who were "cut to the heart" (which reflects both belief in Christ Jesus and regret over rejection of Christ Jesus) was "repent and be baptised, every one of you, in the name of Jesus Christ for the forgiveness of your sins" (Acts 2:38). Peter's prescription for the question "what shall we do" encapsulates the basic Christian message in four main points: repentance, baptism, forgiveness, and the gift of the Holy Spirit. Israel had to repent (Acts 5:31), but so too did the pagan Gentile world (Acts 17:30).

The double package "repentance and baptism" is associated with the forgiveness of sins (Luke 3:3). Baptism is now "in the name of Christ Jesus" (not mentioned in John's baptism) and will be followed or accompanied by the gift of the Holy Spirit.[17] This is the promise that dominated Peter's speech. This speech is not restricted to only the apostolic elite; it is as universal as the need for repentance.

The final line of Joel 2:32 embellished and was cross-referenced to Isaiah 57:19, which highlights the universality of God's promise to the polyglot Jerusalem crowd. The verse of the scene on the day of Pentecost dramatically highlights the sermon's positive result: "Those who accepted his message were baptised, and about three thousand were added to their number that day" (Acts 2:41). This marked the first step in the Church's exponential growth from the small, inward-looking group described in Chapter 1 to a significant movement with a worldwide impact (Acts 26:26).

Paul explained forgiveness as God's passing over of sins done in earlier days. Paul stated: "God presented [Jesus Christ] as a sacrifice of atonement, through faith in his blood. [God] did this to demonstrate his justice, because in his forbearance he had left the sins committed beforehand unpunished" (Rom. 3:25). This "sacrifice of atonement" is a sacrifice that satisfies the righteous wrath of God; and without this appeasement (propitiation), all the people on earth are justly destined for eternal punishment.[18]

John the Apostle commented on this divine sacrifice of the atonement and stated: "[Jesus Christ] is the atoning sacrifice for our sins, and not only for ours; but also for the sins of the whole world" (1 John 2:2). It is necessary to state here that God's holiness demands punishment for humans' sin; but God out of his own heavenly love (John 3:16; 1 John 4:10) sent his son to make substitutionary atonement for the believers' sins. In this way, the Father's wrath is propitiated (satisfied, appeased), and his wrath against the sinner has been turned away and directed towards Christ

---

[17] Loveday Alexander, "Acts", in *The Oxford Bible Commentary*, 1032.
[18] NIV Study Bible, 1675.

Jesus. Forgiveness through Christ Jesus' atoning sacrifice is not limited to one particular group of people; rather, it has a worldwide application.

The writer of the Gospel of Luke recorded that Christ Jesus was in-between two "criminals" (who were sinners) while on the cross. This is Luke's account: "Two other men, both criminals, were also led out with [Jesus] to be executed. When they came to the place called the Skull, there they crucified him along with the criminals – one on his right, the other on his left" (Luke 23:32–33). Here on the cross among sinners I see Christ Jesus the suffering God who was in indescribable agony yet showed himself as the sovereign God who pleads for forgiveness of sins with the Father. While on the cross, [Christ Jesus] said, "Father forgive them, for they do not know what they are doing" (Luke 23:34). This is Godself pleading for forgiveness on the cross for those who were putting him to death by the cruellest method. According to Karris, Luke has sayings of Jesus in each main section of the crucifixion narrative (Luke 23:28–31, 43, 46). The inclusion of a saying here on the cross confirmed Luke's artistry. Jesus' prayer on the cross is part and parcel of Luke's theology of a rejected prophet and of a Jesus who taught and practiced forgiveness of enemies (Luke 6:27–28; 17:4).

Christ Jesus, who had come to call sinners to repentance (Luke 5:32), continued that ministry to the end of his physical earthly life as he prayed to his Father for forgiveness even on the cross. Jesus as the suffering God showed his divine nature as the sovereign God who pronounces forgiveness and compassion. I am on holy ground to postulate here that Christ Jesus is the same God who appeared to Moses on that holy ground and identified himself as "I Am Who I Am" (Exod. 3:14). This is the name by which God wished to be known and worshipped in Israel. This name expressed his character as the dependable and faithful God who desires the full trust of his people. Jesus knew that he was "I Am Who I Am" and applied the phrase to himself. In so doing, he claimed to be God and risked being stoned for blasphemy (John 8:58).

Dear beloved reader whose sins are forgiven by Christ Jesus himself, be assured that [Christ Jesus] is the same God who appeared to Moses on that holy Mount Sinai as recorded by Moses himself: "Then the Lord came down in the cloud and stood there with [Moses] and proclaimed his name, the Lord. And he passed in front of Moses, proclaiming, 'The Lord, the Lord, the compassionate and gracious God, slow to anger, abounding in love and faithfulness'" (Exod. 34:5–6). The Lord's proclamation of the meaning and implications of his name in these verses became a classic exposition that was frequently recalled elsewhere in the Old Testament. The forgiving Christ Jesus himself in his physical lifetime on earth showed and expressed the character of "I Am Who I Am" as a dependable and faithful God who desires the ultimate and full trust of all those who believe in him.

As Lord God, Christ Jesus proclaimed forgiveness on the cross and showed compassion, grace, kindness, divine love, and faithfulness. It is Christ Jesus' loving kindness and mercy for his people, and his faithfulness to his Father, which led him to die on the cross. Christ Jesus showed a divine character of compassion, grace, and slowness to anger even on the cross where he was supposed to be angry with those who were killing him in the cruellest way. But understand the divine mindset of Christ Jesus, dear faithful child of God. Please note that Christ Jesus who is the suffering God on the cross is also the sovereign God who has the power to "call fire down from heaven to destroy" all those who were responsible for his trial and execution (Luke 9:54). And of course, Christ Jesus also has the authority to call on his Father, who would have at once put at his disposal more than twelve legions of angels which would have been an overwhelming celestial force to defeat the Roman soldiers without going to the cross (Matt. 26:53). But note that because of our innumerable sins, the most powerful omnipotent God became the most feeble and powerless human being on the cross; yet he had the divine character to proclaim forgiveness as "I Am Who I Am".

The themes of God's forgiveness and compassion have echoed as classic through the ages in the Old Testament upon which the Israelites relied, especially in times of national crisis when they had to wholeheartedly depend on Yahweh.[19] In fact, the main purpose of the book of Jonah is to display God's forgiveness of sinners (both to the Jewish prophet Jonah and the Gentile people of Nineveh). Paul in his epistle to the Ephesians stated: "In him [Christ] we have redemption through his blood the forgiveness of sins, in accordance with the riches of God's grace" (Eph. 1:7).

---

[19] Num. 14:18; Neh. 9:17 ; Ps. 86:15, 103:8, 145:8; Joel 2:13; Jonah 4:2.

The Ephesians in the lifetime of Paul were very familiar with the Greco-Roman practice of redemption. Paul used the word *redemption* because the Ephesians were familiar with and understood the practice and principles of redemption whereby slaves were freed by payment of a ransom. Paul compared the ransom necessary to free slaves with the ransom necessary to free sinners from the bondage of sin and the resulting curse imposed by Mosaic Law. Paul asserted that this is possible because of the death of Christ Jesus, the blood he shed on the cross, and his eventual resurrection from the dead. Paul's letter to the Ephesians is very clear. He told them the whole of God's purpose from the beginning of creation which focuses on Christ Jesus. Through the death of Christ Jesus, personal liberation (redemption), and forgiveness for all wrong done had been genuinely experienced by all who believed in him.

It is paramount to note that Christ Jesus himself is the one in whom the blessings of heaven and the spirit are to be known in the here, now, and then. Dear beloved reader, it is vital to know that the very word *Christianity* denotes a life of eternity both presently and eschatologically, and not least, that Christ Jesus in a real divine sense constitutes the hope for the world and the final reconciliation between God and human beings. All these are made possible because of the free gift of forgiveness he offers to all who believe in him.[20] Redemption and forgiveness have been made possible because of the death of Christ Jesus on the cross of Calvary and his ultimate resurrection, into which Christians are now incorporated through baptism. Paul used such phrases in Romans 1:5–7 as "adopted children", "the Beloved", "good pleasure", and "forgiveness of transgressions", and he later referred to "being sealed with the spirit" (Rom. 1:13), which suggest baptismal traditions. To associate forgiveness with baptism is consonant with the early first-century Jewish-dominated Christian tradition, as Paul himself "got up and was baptised, and after taking some food, he regained his strength." Following baptism, "At once [Paul] began to preach in the synagogue that Jesus is the Son of God" (Acts 9:18b–20).

Repentance, baptism, and forgiveness – the mini trinity – were the key words of Peter's address to the crowd on the day of Pentecost when the foundation of the Church was established as stated above. Just to recapitulate, Luke recorded that at the end of Peter's address to the crowd,

---

[20] James D. G. Dunn, "Ephesians", in *The Oxford Bible Commentary*, 1168.

"When the people heard this, they were cut to the heart and said to Peter and the other Apostles, 'Brothers, what shall we do?' Peter replied, 'Repent and be baptised, every one of you, in the name of Jesus Christ for the forgiveness of your sins. And you will receive the gift of the Holy Spirit" (Acts 2:37–38).

Repentance is important in the message of the forerunner of Christ Jesus, John the Baptist (Mark 1:4, Luke 3:3), in the preaching of Christ Jesus (Mark 1:15, Luke 13:3), and in the instruction Christ Jesus gave to his disciples shortly before his ascension (Luke 24:47). Baptism was also important to John the Baptiser (Mark 1:4), in the last command Christ Jesus gave to his disciples (Matt. 28:18–19), and in the preaching recorded in Acts 8:12, 18:8, where it is associated with belief.

I analyse the third word, *forgiveness*, and cite the full phrase as it applies here, which is "for the forgiveness of your sins". It is paramount to know that baptism on its own does not affect forgiveness. Rather, forgiveness comes through that which is symbolised by baptism (Rom. 6:3–4). It is necessary to take note that both forgiveness and the Holy Spirit are gifts from Christ Jesus. The promise of the indwelling gift of the Holy Spirit is given to all Christians (Rom. 8:9–11; 1 Cor. 12:13).[21]

It is necessary once again to go back to Peter's reply: "Repent and be baptised every one of you, in the name of Jesus Christ for the forgiveness of your sins" (Acts 2:38). To be baptised "in the name of Jesus Christ" in this context, there is no contradiction of the fuller formula given in Matthew 28:19, which is "baptising them in the name of the Father and of the Son and of the Holy Spirit", which is prescribed as a command by Christ Jesus himself. In Acts, the abbreviated form emphasises the distinctive quality of this baptism, for Jesus is now included in a way that he was not in John's baptism (Acts 19:4–5).

Before I bring this section on the cross and forgiveness of sins to a close, it is vital to state that sin is a spiritual heavy and unbearable burden on all sinners in all the world. That spiritual load can only be taken off from the sinner by Christ Jesus because of his precious blood, which he shed on the cross of Calvary. It is only when the sinner comes to the cross of Christ with a sincere and broken heart that the spiritual burden is loosened up in toto from the burdened sinner.

---

[21] NIV Study Bible, 1614.

John Bunyan was born in 1628 in the English village in Elstow near Bedford. He saw in his dream a man called Christian whose burden of sin was loosened at the foot of the cross of Christ Jesus. I present the record of Bunyan's dream in the following paragraphs:

Now I saw in my dream, that the highway up which Christian was to go, was fenced on either side with a wall, and that wall was called Salvation. Up this way, therefore, did burdened Christian run, but not without great difficulty, because of the load on his back.

He ran thus till he came at a place somewhat ascending; and upon that place stood a cross, and a little below, in the bottom, a sepulchre. So I saw in my dream, that just as Christian came up with the cross, his burden loosed from off his shoulders, and fell from off his back, and began to tumble, and so continued to do till it came to the mouth of the sepulchre, where it fell in, and I saw it no more.

Then was Christian glad and lightsome, and said with a merry heart, He hath given me rest by his sorrow, and life by his death. Then he stood still a while, to look and wonder; for it was very surprising to him that the sight of the cross should thus ease him of his burden. He looked therefore, and looked again, even till the springs that were in his head sent the waters down his cheeks. Now as he stood looking and weeping, behold three shining Ones came to him, and saluted him with "Peace be to thee". So the first said to him, "Thy sins be forgiven thee", the second stripped him of his rags, and clothed him with change of raiment, the third also set a mark in his forehead, and gave him a roll with a seal upon it, which he bid him look on as he ran, and that he should give it in at the celestial gate: so they went their way. Then Christian gave three leaps for joy, and went on singing.

Thus far did I come laden with my sin,

Nor could aught ease the grief that I was in,

Till I came hither. What a place is this!
Must here be the beginning of my bliss?
Must here the burden fall from off my back?
Must here the strings that bound it to me crack?
Blest cross! Blest sepulchre! Blest rather be
The Man that there was put to shame for me![22]

## THE CROSS AND RECONCILIATION

The main focus in this section is to draw your attention to the significance of the cross which is the centre for reconciliation because of the sacrificial blood of Christ Jesus which was shed on the Calvary cross. There are four important New Testament Pauline passages which treat the work of Christ Jesus under the figure of reconciliation.[23] I will analyse these texts and other appropriate scriptures to explain that the cross of Christ Jesus is the crux for propitiation between God and humankind.

*Reconciliation* means doing away with enmity and bridging over a quarrel. It is an appeasement which implies that two parties that were formerly hostile to one another are being united or in reunion because of a new understanding between the two parties. All the Holy Scriptures, both in the Old and the New Testaments, state bluntly that sinners are "enemies of God and are hostile to him" (1 Sam. 15:23, Isa. 59:2–3, Rom. 5:10, Col. 1:21, Jas. 4:4). The way to overcome enmity is to take away the cause of the quarrel. In the course of taking away the quarrel, we may apologise for the hasty word, we may pay the money that is due, and we may make that reparation or restitution which is appropriate.[24] The point I am establishing here is that in every case, the way to reconciliation lies through an effective grappling with the core root cause of the enmity.

Dear reader, believe without an iota of doubt that Christ Jesus died on the cross to put away our sins (the core and main root and the cause of enmity between God and humankind) once and for all. In this way,

---

[22] John Bunyan, *The Pilgrim's Progress: The Classic Allegory of the Christian Life* (Buckingham, 2010), 57–59.

[23] Rom. 5:10, 2 Cor. 5:18–20, Eph. 2:11, Col. 1:19.

[24] Douglas, 1012–1013.

he dealt with the cause of enmity between God and humankind. Christ Jesus put our sins out of the way, out of sight, and beyond reach. He made the way wide open for humanity to re-establish the original friendly relationship between God the Father Creator and his creatures before the loss of Paradise. It is this process which is divinely described by the term *reconciliation*.

There is no New Testament scripture which indicates that Christ Jesus reconciles God to human beings. On the other hand, all the texts in the New Testament stress that mankind is being reconciled to God. What does this tell us? The fact is that it was the act of the disobedience of the first human beings (Adam and Eve) which brought sin and separated mankind from God (Gen. 3:1–7), and it is the acts of obedience and righteousness of Christ Jesus (especially on the cross) which brought about the reconciliation between God and humanity. God never moved away from human beings and did not need to go back to them. It was human beings (Adam and Eve) who ran away from God because of sin, and for that reason, it is human beings who need to go back to God and ask for forgiveness of sin. This is the grand work of Christ Jesus, the greatest reconciler between God and human beings.

Paul explained this in his epistle to the Romans in summation and stated: "Death through Adam, life through Christ" (Rom. 5:12–20). Reconciliation of mankind to God in some sense was effected outside human beings before it happened within mankind. In other words, humanity did not do anything to reconcile themselves to God. In his epistle to the Ephesians, Paul bluntly stated this: "For it is by grace you have been saved [reconciled to God] through faith – and this is not from yourselves, it is the gift of God – not by works, so that no-one can boast" (Eph. 2:8–9). That is to say, humankind is being reconciled to God through the death of Christ Jesus on the cross because of God's grace, kindness, unmerited favour, forgiveness, and everlasting love. Reconciliation which leads to salvation is not by work or the effort of the reconciled; it is all from God as gratis, which is pure and holy. Paul reiterated this point emphatically and said "so that no-one can boast". In other words, no-one (except the Creator God) can take credit for his or her own salvation.

In summation, Ephesians 2:1–10 is captioned "once dead, now alive with Christ Jesus."[25] This passage is God's grand scheme as it affects humanity. Please note the summary of 2:8–10 with dependence on Pauline vocabulary, which includes *grace, faith, works,* and *boasting*. The text primarily speaks of salvation of the believer as a result of the reconciliation brought about because of the death of Christ Jesus on the cross, which is a divine gift of God. Please note that the dichotomy is no longer faith versus works (Rom. 3:28) but now between God's grace and human good deeds. These human good deeds are unattainable by "observing the Mosaic laws" (Rom. 3:20, 28). Such a legalistic approach to salvation is consistently condemned in both the Old and New Testament scriptures.

Ephesians 2:1–10 is where one of the most forceful statements in the Bible is made regarding the human condition apart from God's grace and the way in which that grace operates for salvation.[26] The answer to lives dominated by human weakness and self-indulgence is the recognition which leads to salvation given by grace, through faith (2:8). It may be useful to state here that by "works", Paul seemed to mean any product of carnal human effort. The main emphasis here is that reconciliation which brings about salvation is wholly, totally, and solely a divine gift from God the Father. There is no scope of any kind of boasting in oneself, but total reliance and dependence on the Creator God Almighty (2:9). According to Dunn, this is the "turned-in-upon-oneself-ness" of the old life (2:3) which has been given a new focus and orientation. The outcome is a complete contrast to the old way. This is a new creation of the template of Christ Jesus, which is "good works" that God had made humankind for since the creation of the world (Rom. 3:10; 4:24; 1 Cor. 3:10–15). This new creation in Christ Jesus makes a contrast between a life lived by grace – through faith in Christ Jesus – and a life determined by the desires of the flesh and mind of the old creation.

Reconciliation is a powerful image used by Paul and only by the Pauline text in the New Testament (2 Cor. 5:18–20). God reconciled us to himself. The imagery of reconciliation presupposes a state of estrangement or hostility between God and humankind. The idea that a dead man (even

---

[25] Paul J. Kobelski, "The Letter to the Ephesians", in *The New Jerome Bible Commentary*, 887.
[26] Dunn, 1169.

on a cross) can bring about reconciliation may in itself evoke the idea of martyr theology (as implied also in Rom. 5:6–8).

There are four notable features of reconciliation in 2 Corinthians 5:18–20 which I want to explain as follows:

1.  The first one is Paul's strong insistence that the reconciliation is between God and the world. It is the fundamental Creator/ creature relationship which has been restored here. Note that Christ Jesus who is God the Son is the medium of reconciliation between God Almighty who is God the Father and humankind. Christ Jesus who is God the Son does not reconcile himself to the Almighty God who is the Father because Christ Jesus has and is always with his Father. On the other hand, God the Son reconciles humankind to God the Father who were once separated from God because of their original sins from Adam and Eve.

2.  The second thing to notice is Paul's equally strong insistence that God was wholly and solely involved in the act of the process of reconciliation which is "through Christ" (2 Cor. 5:18) and "in Christ" (5:19). This emphasis is equivalent to what is stated in Romans 3:25, not to mention 2 Corinthians 5:21. The image is not of God as an angry opponent having to be cajoled or entreated, but God the injured partner who is actively seeking reconciliation for mankind to come back to him.

3.  Another striking point is the correlated or alternative metaphor "not counting their transgressions against them". This strong image of forgiveness or choosing to ignore active hostility can be as effective as that of sacrifice for sins.

4.  Not the least but probably most significance is the confirmation that the message of reconciliation which is focused on the cross (2 Cor. 5:21) is the heart of the gospel.

This last point is also the crux of this section and probably one of the most resounding messages of this book. There is no iota of doubt that Christ Jesus is God the Son and the representative of God the Father in effecting divine reconciliation. Paul stated: "God was reconciling the world to himself in Christ" (2 Cor. 5:19). This is an equivocal and undeniable expression that God the Father himself is fully in God the Son who is

Christ Jesus in the reconciliation process on the cross and ultimately in the resurrection victory which brings reconciliation and salvation to humanity.

For the rest of this section, I will analyse some of the other reconciliation imagery by Paul in the New Testament. In Romans 5:10–11, Paul stated:

> For if, when we were God's enemies, we were reconciled to him through the death of his Son, how much more, having been reconciled, shall we be saved through his life! Not only is this so, but we also rejoice in God through our Lord Christ Jesus, through whom we have now received reconciliation.

I understand here that man is the enemy of God, not the reverse. Therefore, the hostility between God and man must be first and foremost removed from man if reconciliation is to be accomplished through Christ Jesus. It is God himself who took the self-determined initiative in bringing this holy pacification through and by the death of God the Son on the cross of misery. As stated earlier, to reconcile is "to put an end to hostility", and this is closely related to the term "justify", as the parallelism in Romans 5:9–10 indicates. Please note that in 5:9, there are three key words/phrases: "justify", "by his blood", and "shall we be saved". These are analogous to "reconciled", "through the death of his Son", and "shall we be saved" in 5:10 respectively.

Reconciliation has made it possible for the believer to be "saved through [Christ Jesus'] life". This is a special reference to the unending life and ministry of the resurrected Christ Jesus for his people (Heb. 7:25). Since the believers are being reconciled while they are still God's enemies, they are being saved because Christ Jesus lives forever; provided the saved person is perpetually living in the Lord Jesus Christ, he/she has everlasting life in heaven. It is necessary to observe in Romans 5:11 that the believer now receives reconciliation through the death of Christ Jesus on the cross. This reconciliation, like justification (Rom.5:1) is a present reality for all Christians, and it is something to be jubilant and rejoice about.

In Romans 5:10–11, the sinner is not just "weak" or "ungodly" but an "enemy" of God. Despite this, the death of Christ Jesus on the cross brings about the reconciliation of such an enemy; this is but another way of expressing the "peace" in Romans 5:1; for "reconciliation' is also the restoration of the estranged and alienated sinner to heavenly friendship and intimacy with God.[27]

Romans 5:1–11 states "God's reconciling love is the foundation for legitimate boasting in Christ Jesus". Here I identify two verbs that dominate this passage: *boast* and *reconcile*. Paul stated in Romans 4:2 that Abraham had no ground for boasting before God. Similarly, in Romans 3:2, Paul made the point that boasting is excluded (see also Rom. 2:17, 23). However, here in Romans 5, boasting is neither groundless nor excluded, because Paul boasts "in the hope of sharing the glory of God" (Romans 5:2), in "sufferings" (5:3), and "in God" (5:11). It is vital to note that the difference here, of course, is that Paul is not, as in 2 Corinthians 10:13–15, "boasting beyond limits" – claiming as his own achievement. It is perfectly proper to boast in what God has done, rather than in what one has done for God (Rom. 3: 24). The main focus and cardinal point here is that what God has done in Christ Jesus, in Romans 5:1–11, is to reconcile humanity with God.

I reiterate that *reconciliation* means return from alienation and the restoration of the relationship (which was broken because of the sins of humankind) between God and sinner. Reconciliation here puts the divine–human rift in deeply personal (as opposed to exclusively forensic) terms – an estrangement that yields only to the prevailing power of God's love (Rom. 5:8).[28] This state of reconciliation is described in verse 1 as "peace with God". Because reconciliation is achieved only from God's side and offered when most undeserved (5:8), the believer possesses security in the hope of eternal life (5:2, 5), and confidence in the midst of earthly trials (5:3–4).

## *Ministry of Reconciliation*

Another Pauline text which considers the work of Christ Jesus under the metaphor of reconciliation is 2 Corinthians 5:11–21. In this text, the theme is "the ministry of reconciliation". Paul stated:

---

[27] Joseph A. Fitzmyer, "Letter to the Romans", in *The New Jerome Bible Commentary*, 844.

[28] Craig C. Hill, "Romans", in *The Oxford Bible Commentary*, 1094–5.

All this is from God, who reconciled us to himself through Christ and gave us the ministry of reconciliation: that God was reconciling the world to himself in Christ, not counting men's sins against them. And he has committed to us the message of reconciliation. We are therefore Christ's ambassadors, as though God were making his appeal through us. We implore you on Christ's behalf. Be reconciled to God. (2 Corn. 5:8–28)

This is the motto of the Baptist Royal Ambassador. As a member, I repeated it several times in each and every meeting of the BRA but without much understanding.

Please note well that here, Paul has a new dimension of the word *reconciliation*. He adds the word *ministry* and formulates the all-important Christian catchphrase "the ministry of reconciliation". Paul stated that God takes the initiative in redemption, and he sustains and brings it to completion through the death of Christ Jesus on the cross and ultimate resurrection which has brought reconciliation and eventual salvation to all humankind who believe in Christ Jesus. Paul realised that God reconciled Paul to himself and therefore Paul was obliged to carry out the ministry of reconciliation in order to reconcile the unreconciled to God.

Those believers who are recipients of the divine reconciliation through the ministry of reconciliation by the Apostles and Paul have the privilege and obligation of being like them in a sense: the heralds and instruments in God's hands to minister reconciliation throughout the whole universe. This ministry of reconciliation is fundamental and is the focus of the Christian faith, doctrine, and belief. The ministry of reconciliation had already been commanded by Christ Jesus himself (the reconciler) in Matthew 28:16–20. Because of his resurrection and reconciliation power, Christ Jesus commanded the "eleven disciples" to "go and make disciples of all nations" (28:19), which is to say to reconcile humanity to God in all nations.

I have earlier stated above that reconciliation is another word for restoration or reinstatement. I note that Christ Jesus reinstated Peter and gave to him the ministry of reconciliation in John 21:15–23. Please understand here that it is Christ Jesus who took the initiative because of his divine love, kindness, mercy, and grace to reconcile Peter to himself. In this holy dialogue between Christ Jesus and Peter, Christ Jesus commanded Peter to carry out the ministry of reconciliation by telling him to "feed my lambs", "take care of my sheep", and "feed my sheep". I emphasise in this paragraph that every believer who has been reconciled to God is obliged to take the ministry of reconciliation in order to reconcile the unreconciled to God. I understand that each and every Christian is uniquely and individually reconciled to God; and because of this personal salvation, the believer in Christ Jesus is personally under obligation to be in this ministry of reconciliation irrespective of what the other believer does.

In order to proclaim the ministry of reconciliation strong and loud, I draw your attention to the dialogue between Jesus and Peter in the text mentioned above

> Peter turned and saw that the disciple whom Jesus loved was following them. (This was the one who had leaned back against Jesus at the supper and had said, "Lord who is going to betray you?") When Peter saw him, he asked, "Lord, what about him?" Jesus answered, "If I want him to remain alive until I return, what is that to you? You must follow me." (John 21:20–22).

"You must follow me." This is the divine command from the holy lips of Christ Jesus with regards to the ministry of reconciliation. By means of these words, the Lord Christ Jesus impressed upon Peter's mind the fact that curiosity about John's future must make way for obedience to the Lord's all-important commands: "Follow me", "Feed my lambs", "Take care of my sheep", and "Feed my sheep". Peter must not be so deeply interested in God's secret council (regarding John) that he fails to pay attention to God's revealed will. It is a lesson which every believer in every age should take to heart. There is work to be done. There are souls to be reached and won, and there is a task to be accomplished. Peter must rivet all his attention upon this. Peter must be ready to follow Christ Jesus, and as the shepherd of Jesus' sheep, he would give his life, just as the Master himself laid down his life for them (John 10:15, 17–18).

Some believers (even ministers of God) are always asking questions. They ask so many questions that their real mission in life fails to receive the proper amount of interest and energy.[29] "You must follow me" is the beatific charge issued by the wonderful, glorious, and greatest reconciler, Christ Jesus, to all believers through the ages to be engaged in the ministry of reconciliation in order to reconcile the unreconciled to himself. Nothing and absolutely nothing should prevent the believer in Christ Jesus from implementing the most important and supreme Christian obligation of the ministry of reconciliation. This mission of reconciliation can be carried out by any believer (pastors or priests and members of the church; theologians and laypeople; full or part-time workers in the Church in home and mission fields; and those in all professions in the body of Christ Jesus at all places and all times).

The third Pauline corpus which treats the work of Christ Jesus under the figure of reconciliation is Ephesians 2:11–22. Here, Paul talks about the salvation of both the Jews and the Gentiles because of the work of Christ Jesus and his power of reconciliation. God reconciles the Jews as well as the Gentiles to himself and then brings reconciliation between the Jews and Gentiles through the death of Christ Jesus on the cross. The emphasis here is that both the circumcised Jews, who are God's People of Israel and the promise of the Old Covenant, and the uncircumcised Gentiles, who were separated and excluded from citizenship in Israel and foreigners (but now were part of the New Covenant), are reconciled to God through the death of Christ Jesus and have been grafted together by one God who is the Creator of all.

The rite of circumcision was applied to all Jewish male babies, so this physical act ("done in the body by hands of men") was a clear mark of distinction between Jew and Gentile, in which Jewish people naturally took pride. But now the death of Christ Jesus on the cross – which brought reconciliation between God and humankind and among humanity – has made the mark of distinction between Jew and Gentile disappear. Now there is no "uncircumcised Philistine" (1 Sam. 17:26).

Paul was a true Jew in all aspects of life and a Hebrew of the Hebrews, and he was ceremoniously circumcised; yet he gave his verdict regarding circumcision when he stated: "A man is not a Jew if he is only one outwardly, nor is circumcision merely outward and physical. No, a man is a Jew if he is one inwardly, and circumcision is circumcision of the heart, by the spirit,

---

[29] William Hendriksen, *New Testament on John*, 491.

not by the written code. Such a man's praise is not from men, but from God" (Rom. 2:28–29). Here the indwelling of the Holy Spirit of God has displaced the human code of circumcision. The true sign of belonging to God is not an outward mark on the physical body, but the regenerating power of the Holy Spirit within the believer in Christ Jesus. This is what Paul meant by "circumcision of the heart".

This "circumcision of the heart" is also the original promise God made to the people of Israel through their chief lawgiver, Moses, who said: "The Lord your God will circumcise your hearts and the hearts of your descendants, so that you may love him with all your heart and with all your soul, and live" (Deut. 30:6). This grand promise of the "circumcision of the heart" has now been made possible for both Jews and Gentiles by the blood of Christ Jesus, which cleanses the hearts of both, and by his resurrection and reconciliation power.

The fourth and final Pauline corpus which treats the work of Christ Jesus under the figure of reconciliation is Col. 1:19–20. In this passage, Paul stated: "For God was pleased to have all his fullness dwell in him [Christ Jesus], and through him to reconcile to himself all things, whether things on earth or things in heaven, by making peace through his blood, shed on the cross." In this scripture, Paul gave a more spiritual understanding and insight of reconciliation. Firstly, for reconciliation to come to humankind through Christ Jesus, God unconditionally and without reservation poured out all his divine powers and attributes on Christ Jesus that made him fully God and fully man. Secondly, this supernatural holy power of God in Christ Jesus has made it possible for Christ Jesus not just to reconcile some people (probably the Jews) but more importantly all the people of the earth, including all the Gentile nations. This is what Paul meant when he said, "Through him to reconcile to himself all things".

However, to "reconcile to himself all things" does not mean that Christ Jesus by his death has saved or will save all people of the earth. The Bible speaks of an eternal hell and makes it loud and clear that only believers in Christ Jesus have been and will be saved. When Adam and Eve sinned, not only was the harmony between God and humankind destroyed, but disorder also came into creation (Rom. 8:19–22). When Christ Jesus died on the cross, he brought peace between God and man, and he restored harmony in the physical world – although the perfect and full realisation of the harmony will only be established in the second advent of Christ Jesus.

After his resurrection, Christ Jesus said to his disciples, "All power is given unto me in heaven and in earth. Therefore go and make disciples in all the nations." Christ Jesus' instruction of disciple-making is not confined within the boundary of Israel, but extends to every nook and corner of the Gentile world (Matt. 28:18–19). In fact, Mark made a fuller version of the same statement: "[Christ Jesus] said to them, 'Go into the world and preach the good news to all creation. Whoever believes and is baptised will be saved, but whoever does not believe will be condemned'" (Mark 16:15–16). Our main point here is that not all humankind in all the nations will be reconciled and be saved through the death and the resurrection of Christ Jesus. But the angelic gospel is that all those who believe in the Lord Christ Jesus in all the nations are being and will be reconciled and be saved.

The writer of the fourth Gospel made this crystal clear by stating: "Yet to all who received him, to those who believed in his name, he gave the right to become children of God – children born not of natural descent, nor of human decision or husband's will, but born of God" (John 1:12–13). The good news is that every believer in every nation who accepts Christ Jesus as saviour and Lord has the divine right to be a member of the universal family of God through the grace of God. Death and resurrection of Christ Jesus brought to us reconciliation between God and humankind in all the nations in all times and for all time.

## THE VICTORY OF THE CROSS

We cannot overemphasise the theological and the spiritual significance of the cross of Christ Jesus as the divine and only source of victory for Christians. This super-spiritual and mysterious victory of the cross has been recognised and believed through the ages of the apostolic period (AD 33–99), the patristic period (AD 100–700), the Middle Ages and the Renaissance (AD 700–1500), the Age of Reformation (AD 1500–1750), and the modern period (AD 1750 to date).[30]

---

[30] Alister E. McGrath, *Christian Theology* (Oxford, 2007), v.

You might have noticed that I have already discussed five aspects of the cross above. The main focus of this section is to analyse the victorious significance of the cross. Before I plunge into the subject matter, I will stop for a moment and explain the meaning of the word *victory*, because it will be useful (although initially it may seem too rudimentary and unnecessary) and will set the base for my reference in this section and in the rest of this book.

There are different definitions and explanations of the word *victory* in dictionaries and other academic textbooks. In summary, I state that victory is the position or state of having overcome an enemy or adversary in combat, battle, or war; that is, supremacy or superiority achieved as the result of armed conflict. However, victory is also ultimate success in any contest or struggle. This being the background, I now proceed to examine the Old Testament perspective of victory.

## Victory: Old Testament Perspective

The Old Testament panorama of victory is the primary biblical assertion that victory belongs to God. In Genesis 14, we read the story of how Abram and his men went to war to rescue his nephew Lot. Abram gained supremacy and was successful; he had victory over his enemies and saved Lot. This is confirmed in 14:17: "After Abram returned from defeating Kedorlaomer and the Kings allied with him, The King of Sodom came out to meet him in the valley of Shaveh (that is the King's valley)." Abram believed and realised that the battle is the Lord's and for that divine reason [Abram] gave Melchizedek, king of Salem, a tenth of everything (14:20b). Melchizedek, who also realised that victory in the battle belongs to God, had already said to Abram, "Blessed be Abram by God Most High, Creator of heaven and earth. And blessed be God Most High, who delivered your enemies into your hand" (14:19). In fact, it was the victory which God Most High gave to Abram that instigated and instituted the ordinance of tithing (which is not my interest of discussion in this book).

The writer of Hebrews stated that Melchizedeck means "king of righteousness"; and also, "king of Salem" means "king of peace". Without father or mother, without genealogy, without beginning of days or end of life, like the Son of God he remains a priest for ever (Heb. 7:2b–3). In fact, the whole of the seventh chapter of Hebrews talks about Christ's superior priestly order over both Aaron's and Melchizedeck's priestly orders.

That victory belongs to the God Most High was succinctly expressed by King David (the greatest warrior and the most successful winner of wars or battles in the whole history of Israel in Palestine), who had absolute confidence and unshakable faith in the Yahweh of Israel. King David wholeheartedly believed that his Lord and shepherd the almighty and most powerful God of Israel has the final and ultimate power to give victory to all his people who put their trust in him. It was this absolute faith and total reliance and dependence which led David to say to Goliath the Philistine:

> This day the Lord will hand you over to me, and I will strike you down and cut off your head. Today I will give the carcasses of the Philistine army to the birds of the air and the beast of the earth, and the whole world will know that there is a God in Israel. All those gathered here will know that it is not by sword or spear that the Lord saves, for the battle is the Lord's and he will give all of you into our hands. (1 Sam. 17:46–47)

The victory that David anticipated here would demonstrate to the world the existence and the power of Israel's God. Part of David's statement in 17:47, "the battle is the Lord's", has become an axiom phrase for the people of God both in the Old and New Testaments. It emphasises the point that victory exclusively belongs to Yahweh, Israel's God, and it is his to bestow at will. David's absolute expression that "the battle is the Lord's" was to indicate to both the Israelite and Philistine armies the error of placing trust in human devices for personal or national security.

The people of God in the Old Testament enter upon victory by the obedience of faith; that is to say, they experienced victory in God's victory. This victory in God's victory was expressed by Moses when he encouraged the fleeing Israelites and said to them, "Do not be afraid, stand firm and you will see the deliverance the Lord will bring to you today. The Egyptians you see today you will never see again. The Lord will fight for you; you need only to be still" (Exod. 14:13–14). Please note here that although Israel was "armed for battle" and "marching out boldly" (Exod. 13:18, 14:8), the victory would still be won by God alone.

For the remaining part in this section of the Old Testament perspective of victory, I will examine the victories of David, who believed that "the battle is the Lord's" and only Israel's God is the ultimate and divine source of victory. Instead of starting from the beginning of David's life, I will, ironically, start with the very last moment of his life as recorded in 2 Samuel 23:1: "These are the last words of David: the oracle of David son of Jesse, the oracle of the man exalted by the Most High, the man anointed by the God of Jacob, Israel's singer of songs". I start with this citation because it is a summation of both the spiritual devotion of David to Israel's God and David's physical and personal integrity and aggrandizement as "the man to whom God gave such wonderful successes", "the anointed of the God of Jacob", and "sweet psalmist of Israel". None of Israel's kings before or after him received such an ecclesiastical description as David in the entire Bible, because he believed "the battle is the Lord's".

In fact, most of the victory statements in the Old Testament are associated with David. I will cite just a few of these in order to buttress my point.

- "The Lord gave David victory wherever he went" (2 Sam. 8:6, 14) refers to David's conquests as listed in 8:1–14 and provides valuable historical insight into the extent of his power and kingdom. David's military leadership brought him phenomenal success and led to the establishment of what was virtually an empire.[31] The catalogue of victories, probably compiled from ancient fragments, is arranged thematically rather than chronologically. David's supremacy over the Philistines, although placed some time afterwards, was gained through a number of military victories because of his total dependence on Yahweh, God of Israel, who determines the outcome of every battle.

- David attributed all his victories in battle and in his songs of thanksgiving to the Almighty God of Israel: "[God] gives his King great victories, he shows unfailing kindness to his anointed, to David and his descendants forever" (2 Sam. 22:51, Ps.18:50). Please note that this song celebrates David's achievements due to God's marvellous works, which corresponds with Psalm 18. Using

---

[31]  Gwilym H. Jones, "1 and 2 Samuel", in the Oxford Bible Commentary, 219.

images of a place of refuge on a rock, it is claimed that God is David's refuge and thus when he calls on God's name, he is saved from all his enemies.

- In Psalm 20:5, David declares, "We will shout for joy when you are victorious and will lift up our banners in the name of our God." This Psalm is generally a prayer for the king that accompanied sacrifice before battle. The theme of the prayer in this Psalm is for God to grant victory to the king in battle. David says: "We (the assembled people of Israel) will shout for joy when you [God] are victorious." David acknowledged that it was not himself who was victorious in battle but God himself who win; and when God wins the battle, the people of God receive the blessings and are at peace. The people of Israel, the people of God, "shout for joy when God is victorious" because this reflects Israel's religious consciousness that praise must follow deliverance.

- Such praise was usually offered with thank-offerings and involved celebrating God's saving act in the presence of those assembled at the Jerusalem temple (Ps. 50:14–15, 23). The believer in the Lord Jesus Christ should always make thankful-offering in praise, but this becomes a self-imposed duty when Christ Jesus delivers the believer in specific circumstances or situations.

- Another Psalm attributed to David in this subject matter of victory is Psalm 21. Here David declares, "O Lord, the King rejoices in your strength. How great is his joy in the victories you gave. Through the victories you gave, his glory is great; you have bestowed on him splendour and majesty" (21:1, 5). This is another Psalm of praise for victories granted to King David which is linked with Psalm 20. In Psalm 21, the people's praise follows that of King David (21:1). In Psalm 20, the people's prayer was added to that of King David. In its general structure, Psalm 21 is framed by verses 1 and 13 ("Lord, in your strength" is in both verses) and is focused around 21:7, which proclaims the king's trust in the Lord and the security afforded him by God's unfailing love.[32]

- David's victories over his enemies (because "the battle is the Lord's") are recorded in detail in 2 Samuel 8:1–14, 10:1–19 and 1

---

[32] NIV Study Bible, 788.

Chron. 18:1–13, 19:1–19. These accounts of David's war victories serve to show the blessings of God on his reign as God keeps his promise to subdue David's enemies (1 Chron. 17:10).

It is not possible to cite and analyse all the scriptures in the Old Testament that are attributed to David's victories over his enemies. However, before I close my discussion of David's victories, I will cite some of David's songs of thanksgiving which he sang to the Lord when the Lord delivered him from the hand of all his enemies and from the hand of Saul. This particular citation is from Psalm 18, but I will concentrate on 18:50, in which David states, "He gives his King great victories; he shows unfailing kindness to his anointed, to David and his descendants for ever" (Ps. 18:50, 2 Sam. 22:51).

Please note that Psalm 18:46–50 make up a concluding doxology showing that David regarded himself as the Lord's chosen and anointed king (1 Sam. 16:13). In Psalm 18:50, David's final words recalled the Lord's covenant with him through the prophet Nathan (2 Sam. 7:8–16). The whole song is to be understood in the context of David's official capacity and the Lord's covenant with him. What is claimed in this grand and ultimate conclusion – as, indeed, in the whole psalm – has been and is being fulfilled in Christ Jesus, who came to Israel as David's great descendant and who is both David's son and Lord.[33]

"God's unfailing kindness to his anointed, to David and his descendants forever" is echoed in Psalm 89:3–4, which states: "You said 'I have made a covenant with my chosen one, I have sworn to David my servant, I will establish your line forever and make your throne firm through all generation'" This Psalm also refers to God's promise to King David in the same 2 Samuel 7:8–16 through the same prophet Nathan. Christian tradition has linked it with Christmas. God's covenant promise is fulfilled in Christ Jesus. Topology might find parallels between the king's humiliations (Psalm 89: 38–45) and Christ's humble birth, earthly mission, cruel death, and final glorious resurrection in triumph in the New Testament.

With this final comment on the victories of King David in the Old Testament, I proceed to the next section on "David's Son and Lord" who is Christ Jesus and analyse his victory on the cross in the New Testament.

---

[33] NIV Study Bible, 786.

## *Victory: New Testament Perspective*

In the preceding subsection, I discussed the Old Testament perspective of victory and mainly focused on David's great exploits and conquests, which Israel's Yahweh granted him because he believed that all his victories came through the victory of the God of Israel because "the battle is the Lord's." All that has been discussed above about King David's victories cluster in a unique and divine way on the cross of the Lord Christ Jesus, who is both David's son and Lord and the supreme and ultimate victor for God.

In the New Testament, Matthew traced the family tree of Jesus as proof of the relationship between Jesus and David by stating, "A record of the genealogy of Jesus Christ the Son of David, the Son of Abraham" (Matt. 1:1). The types of people mentioned in this genealogy reveal the broad scope of those who make up the people of God as well as the genealogy of Jesus. Note here that Matthew's first sentence is a summation of the genealogy of Christ Jesus with specific two names: David and Abraham. That is the reason I specifically discussed the victories of David in my Old Testament analysis; he was one of the most dominant characters in the Old Testament among the people of Israel's God. I also think of Abraham the father of faith and founder of God's people of Israel, who also had victory over his enemies because of the victory God granted him in Genesis 14.

Jesus is identified as the son of David, a popular Jewish title for the coming Messiah found several times in the New Testament. Both Matthew and Luke recorded that Mary and Joseph (who were not biological parents of Jesus) were descendants of David (Matt. 1:20; Luke 2:4, 5). Christ Jesus did not have the blood of both Mary and Joseph, because the "Holy Spirit" did not fuse with their blood. Matthew recorded the birth of Jesus and stated: "This is how the birth of Jesus came about: His mother Mary was pledged to be married to Joseph, but before they came together, she was found to be with a child through the Holy Spirit" (Matt. 1: 18). Luke gave a fuller account of the birth of Jesus Christ (Luke 1: 26-38). Regarding the purely divine birth of Jesus Christ by the "Holy Spirit", Luke stated: "The angel answered, "The Holy Spirit will come upon you, and the power of the Most High will overshadow you. So the holy one to be born will be called the son of God" (verse 35). It is of paramount importance to note that Mary was a surrogate mother who gave birth to Jesus Christ the Son of God on behalf of God the Father. In Syria, the Roman province in which Palestine was located, women of twelve years of age and older were required to pay a poll tax and therefore to register. Matthew by means of this genealogy and its sequel (the narrative of the virgin birth, 1:18–25) aimed to show that Jesus according to his human nature is indeed the legitimate seed of David in fulfilment of prophecy. From Joseph, his legal father, and thus from Joseph's ancestor, David, Jesus received his physical legitimate right to David's throne. From Mary (Matt.1:16) and via Mary, also from David, Jesus received David's flesh and blood figuratively. Yet neither to Joseph or to Mary belonged the glory. Joseph deserved no credit for his own birth as a descendant to David, and this is thoroughly due to the fact that Joseph had nothing whatsoever to do with the virgin or divine conception of Jesus. Mary simply knew that what happened in her womb was the work of the Holy Spirit. She willingly agreed to be "the humble maid of the Lord", carry the holy child of God in her virgin womb, and implemented the plan of God the Father to wrought salvation for the whole wide world. (Luke 1:34, 35, 38). The glory belongs to God alone. It is by grace that man is saved, through faith, and this is not of himself, it is the gift of God (Eph. 2:8).[34]

Matthew 1:1 can be titled "Book of the New Creation wrought by Christ Jesus". In this text, the title "Son of David" is the starting point for the genealogy of Jesus, of which David is the key figure. It is also explicated that Christ, the anointed one, fulfilled the promises made to David (2 Sam. 7:12–16, Isa. 11:19, Zech. 3:8). Jesus himself later acknowledged that he is "the Christ" (Matt. 16:13–20), and the title played an important part in his trial (Matt. 26:57–68).[35] The genealogy of Jesus Christ in Matthew 1:2–17 first shows the evidence for the title and confirms that Jesus is indeed a descendant of the royal family of David as stated earlier. Secondly, it makes Israel's history culminate in Christ Jesus, the Messiah who is the ultimate goal and fulfilment of the Old Testament biblical story. Thirdly, the genealogy helps to give the church its identity, which is the Christian community by virtue of its union with Christ Jesus and shares his divine heritage. His lineage is traced to the patriarch Abraham, who was himself a Gentile by birth, yet Genesis 12:3b promises that "all peoples on earth

---

[34] William Hendriksen, *New Testament on Matthew*, 111.
[35] Dale C. Allison, "Matthew", in *The Oxford Bible Commentary*, 848.

will be blessed through" him. It is fitting to say that soon after the birth of Christ Jesus, he was honoured by Gentile representatives, the magi (Matt. 2:1–12).

The victory of "Christ Jesus the Son of David, the Son of Abraham" charted in the New Testament is as much human as divine, because Christ Jesus was fully God and fully human during his earthly lifetime in Palestine. It is in this respect that the gospel narratives of the ministry of Christ Jesus provided the essential framework for an understanding of "the victory of the cross". This victory is achieved by the obedience of Christ Jesus to his Father (Matt. 4:11, Mark 1:12–13, Luke 4:1–13). These passages begin with the temptation of Jesus, which represents, so to speak, the opening engagement in a struggle destined to reach its culminating encounter in Gethsemane and on the cross (Matt. 26:36–46, Mark 14:42–42, Luke 22:40–46). The summation and significance of the temptation of Christ Jesus is that Adam, when tempted, failed. So Christ Jesus too must now be tempted in order that his victory over temptation and over the tempter would, for all those who believed in him, undo the result of Adam's failure.[36] The summary and main points of the temptation are as follows:

- Resist the devil by appealing to scripture, as Jesus did three times in succession.
- Rest assured that Christ Jesus, as his people's representative, has vicariously rendered the obedience which Adam, as mankind's representative, failed to render.
- Derive comfort from the fact that believers in Christ Jesus have a high priest (Christ Jesus) who, having himself been tempted, is able to help believers in all their temptation (Heb. 4:14–16).

Going back to the citation above on Gethsemane, where Christ Jesus prayed and kept watch, a great diversity of opinion has been expressed among commentators. I share the opinion of Hendriksen and say that the shepherd who has been asking the disciples to watch with him is now tenderly keeping vigil over them. His own victory having been won (by communion with his Father whom he loves and who loves him and that the Father's will be done, come what may), perfect peace has been restored to

---

[36] Hendriksen, 235.

his own heart. He has been strengthened through payer and communion with his heavenly Father.

Please note that surely, the three who were closest to him had failed him by all accounts and standards. But his kindness, mercy, and love never failed them, and the same is applicable to you, even to the end of the world. What can be observed sacredly here is one of the most touching pictures in the Gospel – and one, moreover, that is entirely in harmony with the sympathetic character of the saviour Christ Jesus that is beyond human description and comprehension. The tenderness, loving mercy, and kindness of the Prince of Peace is explicitly expressed by one of the eyewitnesses – the beloved disciple of Christ Jesus and one of the three who could not even watch with Christ Jesus at the most distressing moment of his master.

John recorded the incident of the arrest of Christ Jesus in the garden of Gethsemane in 18:1–11: "Jesus, knowing all that was going to happen to him, went out and asked [those who came to arrest him], 'Who is it you want?" (18:4). "And they said, 'Jesus of Nazareth.' 'I told you that I am he,' Jesus answered. 'If you are looking for me, then let these men go" (John 18:8). Please note the threefold repetition of "I am" in 18:5, 6, and 8, which emphasises the solemn words. Even at that final and critical moment of his earthly life, Christ Jesus gave priority to the safety and protection of his disciples and negotiated for their freedom before he voluntarily surrounded to the detachment of soldiers and some officials from the chief priests and Pharisees who came to arrest him. He commanded those who came to command and arrest him and said to them "Let these men go", and of course, they obeyed him.

This last scene in Gethsemane exhibits the divine power of the sovereign Christ Jesus and his omnipotence in all situations and circumstances and to assure those who believe in him that he is in absolute control of their life all the time. Christ Jesus cared for the disciples even as he was going to die. Dear beloved child of God, take heart and be assured that Christ Jesus' love and care for you now is not less than the tender care he had for his disciples two millennia or so ago. Christ Jesus the greatest high priest and king forever in the order of Melchizedek lovingly and carefully protects his disciples through the ages at all times, at all places.

One of the most unequivocal statements of victory in the entire New Testament is made by Christ Jesus himself. It is recorded by the writer of the fourth Gospel, who stated: "When he had received the drink, Jesus said, 'It is finished.' With that he bowed his head and gave up his spirit" (John 19:30). Apparently, this is the loud cry recorded in Matthew 17:50 and Mark 15:37. This is the grand and ultimate victorious statement proclaimed by the divine victor of both physical and spiritual battle – the mother of all battles in the past, present, and future. It surpasses all the victories of his ancestor David because David's victories were physical, temporal, and mainly for the Jewish nation. Christ Jesus died as a victor and had completed what he came to do, and that is to bring eternal victory to all believers in all the world through ages by his death on the cross and resurrection. As Christ Jesus himself saw it and concluded, the entire work of redemption (both active and passive obedience, which fulfilled the law and bore its curse) had been brought to final completion in him permanently.[37]

"It is finished" is Christ Jesus' last word of bravo – the cry of approval of his divine mystery mission. "It is finished" is a self-appraisal that Christ Jesus made to conclude that he has done the greatest work for humankind of all time and is personally satisfied. Christ Jesus himself divinely surveyed his mystery mission work on earth, gave holy approval, and put his celestial royal seal on every aspect of it. There is no better or more notable and knowledgeable person both on earth and in heaven than Christ Jesus himself to assess his salvation work, because he is both omnipotent and omniscient.

"It is finished", which means full completion and accomplishment (that is self-evaluation and satisfaction of God the Son), is in concurrence with an earlier similar self-satisfaction and absolute authoritative declaration of God the Father in Genesis in the story of the six days of creation. Please note that at the end of each day of creation, God the Father spent some time in order to make self-examination of his work of creation, and "God saw that it was good". Finally, "God saw all that he had made and it was very good. And there was evening, and there was morning – the sixth day" (Gen. 1:31). Everything God created is "very good", is the conclusion and verdict of the Creator God himself on all his work from the beginning to

---

[37] William Hendriksen, *New Testament on John*, 435.

the end of creation. The creation, as fashioned and ordered by God the Father, had no lingering traces of disorder and no dark and threatening forces arrayed against God or humankind.

God the Father, the Creator, made this grand and absolute declaration of his finished work of creation on the final (sixth) day of his creation and declared it to be "very good". Just like God the Father, God the Son – Christ Jesus who is the bringer of salvation – finished the work of salvation in the final moment of his earthly life mystery mission and shouted the victory work of salvation on the cross: "It is finished."

The shout of the salvation work of victory, "It is finished," did not end with Christ Jesus on the cross as "he bowed his head and gave up his spirit" (John 19:30) and after Joseph of Arimathea took down Jesus' body from the cross, "wrapped it in a linen cloth and placed it in a tomb cut in the rock, one in which no-one had yet been laid" (Luke 23:50–54). On the contrary, Jesus' shout of victory, "It is finished," finished and completed with his resurrection power on the third day, which brings re-enforcement and rejuvenation in an unlimited dimension and new direction. In fact, after his resurrection, Christ Jesus is more assertive and more powerful and more open about his mystery earthly mission than before his death.

By his risen power from the grave, Christ Jesus added heavenly vitality to his last word on the cross ("It is finished") in an exuberant manner with more vigour and new assurance and confidence. He commanded his disciples and all future disciples to follow and said to them:

All authority in heaven and on earth has been given to me. Therefore go and make disciples of all nations, baptising them in the name of the Father and of the Son and of the Holy Spirit, and teaching them to obey everything I have commanded you. And surely I am with you always, to the very end of the age. (Matt. 28:18–20)

As stated earlier, the finished work which Christ Jesus declared on the cross did not end with him in his grave after burial. His finished work on the cross is actually the beginning of his salvation work, which must start with the disciples through the ages. I note here that Christ Jesus is claiming all heavenly power and right to exercise and bring salvation to all nations. Note here that Christ Jesus said, "All authority in heaven and on earth has been given to me." I think that Christ Jesus was referring to a divine gift he received from God his Father as the "Resurrected Mediator" who wrought salvation for all humankind.[38] It is God the Father himself who has bestowed divine authority on Christ Jesus as the "Son of Man". This authority is that of the kingdom of God (2 Chron. 36:23, Dan. 7:14, Matt. 6:10).[39]

Please note that the resurrection marks the end of Christ Jesus' mystery ministry in earthly time and inaugurates the time of the post-Easter Church. This periscope both looks back and summarises Christ Jesus' ministry as a whole ("All I have commanded you") and looks forward to the time of the Church to outline a programme for the future ("go and make disciples of all nations"). In summation, this text functions to relate two periods of time which, although different, have the same Lord, the same mission, and the same work of salvation.[40]

I make my final statement on John's Gospel and say that it depicts the progress of Christ Jesus to the cross as a movement of victorious conquest. To be sure, here I can rightly interpret John 19:30 ("It is finished") in the light of John 16:33 ("Be of good cheer, I have overcome the world") as a divine announcement of triumph. It is from such perspective of assurance that I interpret the encounter with and defeat of evil that are so much a feature of the synoptic account of the mystery mission of Christ Jesus.

In the paragraphs above, I have analysed the victory of the cross as has been presented by the four Gospel writers and also cited the words from the holy lips of Christ Jesus himself who is the victor of all victories and has given to all his followers the victory of salvation. For the remaining part of this section, I will evaluate the theology of other New Testament writers (such as Paul) on the subject of the victory of the cross.

I start with the theology of Paul the Apostle in his first epistle to the Corinthian Church, which he wrote to them regarding the nature of the resurrection of the body. Paul stated:

[38] Hendriksen, *New Testament on Matthew*, 998.
[39] Benedict T. Viviano, "The Gospel According to Matthew," in *The New Jerome Bible Commentary*, 674.
[40] Allison, 885.

When the perishable has been clothed with the imperishable, and the mortal with immortality, then the saying that is written will come true: "Death has been swallowed up in victory." "Where, O death, is your victory? Where, O death, is your sting?" The sting of death is sin, and the power of sin is the law. But thanks be to God! He gives us the victory through our Lord Jesus Christ. (1 Cor. 15:54–57)

The original and full statement of 1 Corinthians 15:54 is taken from Isaiah 25:8. Paul emphatically stated here that "Death has been swallowed up in victory". Death the great swallower (Ps. 49:14) has been swallowed up (not will be swallowed in the future, but had already been swallowed up in the past tense) through the death of Christ Jesus on the cross on the first Good Friday when he announced the good news of victory that "It is finished."

Finally, when Christ Jesus was resurrected on the first Easter Sunday morning and declared, "All authority in heaven and on earth has been given to me," death which had been the victor from the time of Adam and Eve was now the victim, since the victory of Christ Jesus on the cross was accomplished. The final nail on death's coffin is the ultimate resurrection of the victorious conqueror of death – our Lord and saviour, Christ Jesus. That makes him the grandest and ultimate victor creation has ever seen.[41]

Take courage dear reader, for 1 Corinthians 15:54 contains eschatological promises for all believers in Christ Jesus. Note that 15:55 is an allusion to Hosea 13:14. In 1 Corinthians 15: 55-56, Paul employed his words to taunt death with its ultimate powerlessness. Believers can now shout a "holy jubilant hurrah" because they are granted victory over both the power of sin and eternal death (Rom. 8:37–39). This is the greatest free gift of love from God the Father, who sent his one and only son (Christ Jesus) that whoever believes in him shall not perish, but have eternal life (John 3: 16). Paul stated that victory through our Lord Jesus Christ (1 Cor. 15:57) is over the condemnation for sin that the law brought (15:56) and over death and the grave (15:54–55), through the death and resurrection of Christ Jesus (Rom. 4:25).[42]

---

[41] John Barclay, "1 Corinthians," in *The Oxford Bible Commentary*, 1132.
[42] NIV Study Bible, 1724.

The next Apostle I cite in the matter of holy triumph of the cross is the writer of the fourth Gospel: John, son of Zebedee (Mark 1:19–20), a member of the inner circle of the disciples of Christ Jesus and also the writer of the Book of Revelation. In his first general circular epistle sent to the churches scattered throughout the province in Asia (in modern Turkey), he stated, "For everyone born of God overcomes the world. This is the victory that has overcome the world, even our faith. Who is it that overcomes the world? Only he who believes that Jesus is the Son of God" (1 John 5:4–5).

Dear reader, may your heart bubble with joy and know that every Christian (of which you are surely one) is an overcomer, because you believe that Christ Jesus is the one and only Son of God who died on the cross and rose from the dead. Your faith in the Lord Christ Jesus serves as a spiritual automated transmission to have "the victory that has overcome the world". To overcome the world is to gain victory over its sinful pattern of life, which is another way of describing obedience to God. Such obedience is quite possible for all believers because they have been washed by the precious blood of the Lamb, and the Holy Spirit dwells within them and gives them divine strength now and forever. Here John speaks of two aspects of victory:

1. The initial victory of turning in faith from the world to God ("has overcome").This is first and most significant, but it is also the most difficult part of becoming a Christian.

2. The continuing day-by-day victory of Christian living ("overcomes"). This second aspect of the daily living of the believer needs to be committed to and controlled by the Holy Spirit who comforts and encourages the believer in everyday temptation and struggle.

I share the viewpoint of the Swedish theologian Gustav Aulen that the atonement (reconciliation) of Christ Jesus is both a divine conflict and victory. Aulen stated: "Christ—Christus victor fights against and triumphs over the evil powers of the world, the tyrants under which mankind is in bondage and suffering; and in Him [Christ] God reconciles the world to Himself."[43] The atonement is a divine victory of God. God the Father in

---

[43] Colin Gunton, *the Actuality of Atonement* (London, 1988), 54.

God the Son – Christ Jesus – overcomes the hostile powers which hold humankind in bondage after the fall of Adam and Eve. The cross of Christ Jesus is metaphorically conceived as a divine victory over the power of evil. Reconciliation through Christ Jesus is achieved because after his incarnation, mission, death, and resurrection, the powers of the evil one are taken away by God. Paul stated: "Having cancelled the written code, with its regulations, that was against us and that stood opposed to us; he took it away, nailing it to the cross. And having disarmed the powers and authorities, he made a public spectacle of them, triumphing over them by the cross" (Col. 2:15). Not only did God cancel out the accusations of the law against the sinners who believe in Christ Jesus, but he also conquered and disarmed the evil angels ("powers and authorities" – 1 Col. 1:16, Eph. 6:12) who entice people to follow asceticism and false teaching about Christ Jesus.

What Paul stated here paints a picture of conquered soldiers stripped of their clothes as well as their weapons to symbolise their total abasement and defeat. The understanding of "Christ Jesus triumphing over them" literally means "leading them in a triumphal procession". This is a strong and powerful metaphor which Paul recalled to be meaningful to those of his generation where a Roman general leading his captive through the streets of his city for all the citizens to see was evidence of his complete victory (2 Cor. 2:14). Note that Christ Jesus triumphing over the devil and his cohort is also seen in Matt. 12:29, Luke 10:18, and Rom. 16:20. The victory of Christ Jesus can be viewed as an earthly one as well as heavenly. The victory of Christ Jesus is seen to continue in the life of the Christian so that Paul could say "In all things we are more than conquerors through him who loved us" (Rom. 8:37), while the Johannine author conceived the victory as earthly in the life of the Christian community and stated, "For everyone born of God overcome the world. This is the victory that has overcome the world, even our faith" (1 John 5:4).

In this book, I am not attempting to load all of the weight of the victory and salvation of Christ Jesus wholly and solely on the cross – unlike Moltmann, who stated that "the cross is the test of everything in Christianity and … the 'cross alone' and nothing else, is its test, since 'the cross refutes everything, and excludes the syncretistic elements in

Christianity.'" Moltmann asserted that "Christian faith stands and falls with the knowledge of the crucified Christ Jesus on the cross".[44]

In contrast, I am putting forward a balanced biblical, Christological, and soteriological viewpoint that the ultimate and grand victory of Christ Jesus on the cross is linked with Christ's incarnation, lifetime mystery mission, death on the cross, and of course ultimate resurrection on the first Easter Sunday morning, which is a full, true, and complete narrative story of both present and eschatological victory and salvation. I believe that both the Old Testament and New Testament support my viewpoint, either by using the language of victory or recording events that can be so interpreted in connection with all aspects of Christ Jesus' story. This includes his incarnation, temptation, earthly mission, and final obedience to his Father, which motivated him to go the cross.

## THE CROSS: SOURCE OF CHRISTIANITY

The cross as the grand and divine source of Christianity and the faith of the Christian community is the final discussion of the theological meaning of the cross and its pre-eminence in both Christology and soteriology. The main biblical text for this motif is John 12:32–33, where Christ Jesus himself declared: "But I, when I am lifted up from the earth, will draw all men to myself." John explained this statement of Christ Jesus: "[Jesus] said this to show the kind of death he was going to die." The writer of the fourth gospel recorded a similar statement which Christ Jesus made earlier: "Just as Moses lifted up the snake in the desert, so the Son of man must be lifted up, that everyone who believes in him may have eternal life" (3 John 14:15).

It is noticeable that in both texts, Christ Jesus pointed to his impending and inevitable death by crucifixion and made reference to Numbers 21:8–9. It is necessary to understand in this passage that in response to the Israelites' confession of sin against God and Moses (21:7), God directed Moses to make a copper image of a snake and set it upon a pole for all to see, so that anyone who had been bitten could look at it and live. God always made good on his promise by healing those who looked to it and

---

[44] Jurgen Moltmann, *The Crucified God* (London, 2001), 1, 62.

trusted the means God had provided. This is the typological use by Christ Jesus of the incident in John 3:14–15, 12:32–33. The cross is the supreme exaltation of Christ Jesus. As God honoured and fulfilled the promise he made to Moses and healed all those who were bitten by the snake as they trusted and put their faith by focusing on the copper image of the snake, so also God heals all humankind who are laden with a load of sin and look upon Christ Jesus, who died and shed his precious blood on the cross that washes away or "takes away the sin of the world!" (John 1:29).

Dear child of God, understand, know, and rejoice that the cross of Christ Jesus is incommensurable and incomparable to the copper image of the snake which Moses made. The cross of Christ Jesus is much holier and more precious than the copper image of the snake. The copper image of the snake was earthly and of temporary measure to heal those bitten by the snake, as all those who were physically healed died and perished in the wilderness. The cross of Christ Jesus is heavenly, designed for both physical and spiritual healing which brings present and eschatological salvation. The healing from the copper image of the snake was only for the desert-wandering Jews, and it did not lead them to trust and understand Yahweh better in the rest of their journey to the Promised Land. The cross of Christ Jesus draws all people from all nations to God, making them children of God, and walks with him in their daily life. I have enumerated in the preceding sections the dogma and the doctrine of the cross, so it suffices to state here that through the death on the cross, Christ Jesus draws humankind to himself without regard to nationality, ethnic affiliation, or status.

The three synoptic gospel writers recorded a similar incident (with minor variations) about the curtain of the temple which was torn from top to bottom; this occurred while Christ Jesus was still on the cross.[45] Here I focus on two verses in Matthew 27: "At that moment the curtain of the Temple was torn in two from top to bottom. The earth shook and the rock split" (27:51). When the centurion and those with him who were guarding Jesus saw the earthquake and all that had happened, they were terrified and exclaimed "surely he was the Son of God!" (27:54). I am on holy ground to say that these two verses give us the key to unlock this figurative statement of Christ Jesus: "But I, when I am lifted up from the earth, will draw all

---

[45] Matt. 27:51–54, Mark 15:38–39, Luke 23:45–48.

men to myself" (John 12:32). The two verses cited also pave the way for the beginning of the fulfilment of Jesus' statement to "draw all men to himself". In the following paragraphs, I will analyse the mysterious tear of the curtain in the temple in Jerusalem and the great confession of the Gentile centurion, both of which happened at the death of Christ Jesus.

## The Jerusalem Temple Curtain

Before I examine the tearing of the curtain in the temple which occurred few minutes before the death of Christ Jesus, it may be helpful to give a bird's-eye view of the temple. This temple was Herod's temple (20 BC to 70 AD) rebuilt by King Herod the Great and referred to as the second temple in Judaism. The second temple was an important Jewish holy temple during the earthly ministry of Christ Jesus and stood on the Temple Mount in Jerusalem between 516 BC and 70 AD. It replaced Solomon's temple (the first temple), which was destroyed by the Neo-Babylonian Empire in 586 BC when Jerusalem was conquered and a portion of the population of the kingdom of Judah was taken into exile in Babylon.

The second temple itself was later completely destroyed. In 66 AD, the Jewish population rebelled against the Roman Empire and took temporary control of Judah and Jerusalem. After four years, in 70 AD, Roman legions under Titus retook and subsequently destroyed most parts of Jerusalem and totally destroyed the Second Temple.

## Death of Christ Jesus

The curtain of the temple being "torn in two from top to bottom" occurred while Christ Jesus was dying on the cross. I state that the tearing of this curtain in the Jerusalem temple is very significant in fulfilment of Christ Jesus' confident and absolute declaration: "But I, when I am lifted up from the earth, will draw all men to myself." I believe that the tearing of the curtain in two from top to bottom opened up and broke the demarcation within the temple structure even among the Jewish people and more significantly between the only Jewish nation of God and the rest of the Gentile nations of the ungodly.

I assume that Matthew referred to the inner curtain in the temple that separated the holy place from the most holy place. I will make further analysis of the tearing of the curtain later, but here it suffices to state that the torn curtain signifies that Christ Jesus' death on the cross has made it possible for all first-century believers and all subsequent believers (including the Jews) who did not have direct access to Yahweh to go directly to the presence of the Lord God Almighty, their Creator (Heb. 9:1–14, 10:14–22).

I share the viewpoint of Hendriksen, who said that it is natural to think of this curtain as the inner one, the veil which separated the holy place from the holy of holies. This inner curtain is the one described in Exodus 26:31–33, 36:35, and 2 Chr. 3:14. As pictured in these passages, strands of blue, purple, and scarlet were interwoven into a white linen fabric in such a manner that these colours formed a mass of cherubim, the guardian angel of God's holiness, symbolically as it were barring the way into the holy of holies.[46]

At the moment of the death of Christ Jesus, this curtain in the Herodian temple was suddenly sliced in two from top to bottom. According to Hendriksen, the tear happened at three o'clock, when priests must have been busy in the temple. The perplexing question is how did the tearing of the curtain come about? I am sure that it did not happen through natural wear and tear of the cloth, if that were the case, there would probably have been rents all over, and the tearing would more likely have been from the bottom up. I also do not think that Matthew was trying to convey the idea that this splitting in two of the curtain was caused by the earthquake. Had that been his intention, he would have mentioned the earthquake phenomenon before the incident of the tearing of the curtain. The tearing of the curtain is clearly nothing less than a divine intervention – a divine miracle wrought by God the Father, father of God the Son, who was dying on the cross. The symbolic significance of this miracle is made clear by two considerations: it occurred exactly at the moment when Jesus died, and as explained in Heb. 10:19, 20, through the death of Christ Jesus, symbolised by the tearing of the curtain, the way into the holy of holies – that is, heaven – is opened to all those who take refuge in him.

Other theologians said that the precise identification of the "veil" of the temple is uncertain. They indicated that two possible curtains could be intended: that which stood at the entrance to the holy of holies,

[46] Hendriksen, 974.

symbolically preventing God from being seen by human beings, and the temple as a whole, with the tearing of the veil a symbol of the destruction of the temple and the end of the Jewish cult (Mark 11:16–19, 13:2, 14:58). In the first text (Mark 11:17), Christ Jesus said, "Is it not written: "My house will be called a house of prayer for all nations?"[47] Christ Jesus cited Isaiah 56:7b, which assured godly non-Jews that they would be allowed to worship God in the temple in Jerusalem. By allowing the court of the Gentiles in the temple to become a noisy, smelly marketplace, the Jewish religious leaders were interfering with the provision made by God for the Gentile nations.

Whatever differences of opinion exist on this tearing of the curtain, I am sure that the event enables everyone (including all Jews) to see God now without any barrier. In particular, the tearing of the curtain in the Jerusalem temple enables the Gentile Roman centurion to see Jesus beyond his disfigurement, humiliation, and shameful degradation. As a result of the tearing of the curtain, for the first time in Marks's story, a human being (not even a Jew, but a cruel and brutal Roman commander from a Gentile nation) now comes to the realisation that Christ Jesus is indeed and truly the "Son of God".

## Death of Christ Jesus: Centurion Confession

Matthew gave this account of the centurion: "When the Centurion and those with him who were guarding Jesus saw the earthquake and all that had happened, they were terrified, and exclaimed, "surely he was the Son of God" (Matt. 27:54). Matthew had earlier presented the faith of a centurion and his authority as a Roman military officer in charge of one hundred soldiers. This centurion wanted Christ Jesus to heal his servant (Matt. 8:5–13). In Luke's account (7:1–5), Jewish elders and friends of the centurion came to Jesus on his behalf, but Matthew did not mention these intermediaries. I do not want to speculate whether the centurion who wanted Jesus to heal his servant was the same one who declared Jesus the "Son of God".

That being the summation of the centurion as the background in the Gospel, I now turn to my main point of discussion, which is the confession of the centurion who proclaimed Christ Jesus as the "Son of God" who died

---

[47] C. M. Tuckett, "Mark," in *The Oxford Bible Commentary*, 920.

on the cross. What did the confession of the centurion mean for himself, and how did this divine revelation bring about the ultimate fulfilment of Jesus' statement about drawing all people to himself? Matthew had already used one of the titles of Jesus ("Son of God") in his story of the temptation of Jesus, when "the tempter came to him [Christ Jesus] and said 'if you are the Son of God, tell these stones to become bread'" (Matt. 4:3). Theologians are divided in opinion and are not sure of the precise meaning of "If you are the Son of God", but here I present my opinion in line with my belief. The tempter (Satan) knows and acknowledges Christ Jesus as "Son of God"; that is why Satan spontaneously and instantly used the title "Son of God" for Christ Jesus. On this occasion, the tempter probably meant to say, "Since you are God's son and that is what the Father told you at your baptism" (Matt. 3:17) and "Furthermore, that is what you also believe, because you have heard from your mother Mary what the angel Gabriel said to her concerning you that 'You [Mary] will be with a child and give birth to a son, and you are to give to him the name Jesus. He will be great and will be called the Son of the Most High. The Lord will give him the throne of his father David'" (Luke 1:31–32).

Note that the title "the Son of the Most High" has two divine meanings: the divine Son of God and the Messiah born in time. The messiahship is clearly referred to in Luke 1:32b–33, and "Most High" is a title frequently used of God in both the Old and the New Testaments.[48] Satan knows the meaning and its significance in the scriptures more than human beings, and with that knowledge, he tempted Jesus to make use of his majestic dignity and power and no longer be tortured by hunger.

Beloved child of God, please do not stop here with the deceptive and malign statement of Satan the tempter, but proceed to the divine biblical axiomatic answer from the holy lips of our Lord Christ Jesus: "It is written: 'Man does not live on bread alone, but on every word that comes from the mouth of God'" (Matt. 4:4). Dear child of God, take courage and comfort, and be assured that just as the Almighty God gave the Israelites manna in a supernatural way on which they relied for the rest of their wilderness journey for forty years (Deut. 8:3), so also you should rely on the Lord and saviour Christ Jesus wholeheartedly for the rest of your earthly journey for both your spiritual and physical food.

---

[48] Luke 1:35, 76; 6:35; 8:28; Gen. 14:19; 2 Sam. 22:14; Ps. 7:10.

Take example and have a divine lesson from Christ Jesus, who totally relied on his Father instead of his own miraculous power for the provision of his material needs. Satan is sure that Christ Jesus is the Son of God, and he is aware that you are also God's child washed and saved by the blood of the Lamb. Be assured that you are a child of God through faith in Christ Jesus (Gal. 3:26). Perhaps at this very moment in time, you are in a difficult situation. Whatever that may be, stand assured that Christ Jesus who overcame Satan the tempter is with you in your current circumstances, and he will enable you to overcome all your trials and temptations. You will triumph and be victorious, just as Christ Jesus had victory over satanic power during both his temptation in the wilderness and his final trial on the cross.

Once again, I will like to go backwards to the motif of "Son of God" as has been proclaimed by the Roman centurion. The NIV Study Bible explains that the proclamation of "Son of God" by the centurion cannot determine precisely whether the centurion made a full Christian confession or whether he was only acknowledging that, since the gods had so obviously acted to vindicate this judicial victim, Jesus must be one especially favoured by them. But in view of the ridicule voiced by the Jews (Matt. 27:40), it seems probably that Matthew intended the former.[49]

My understanding of the text and especially the title "Son of God" is that the centurion and his hundred soldiers made a full and heartfelt confession which was probably made by the first Gentile Christian believer. Whether this is correct or not, I am certain that the synoptic writers saw in the declaration of the centurion a vindication of Jesus. Since the centurion was the Roman official in charge of the crucifixion process, his testimony was viewed as a very significant fact that confirmed the purpose and truth of the gospel that God sent his one and only son who came to the world and died on the cross in order to save humanity from their sins.

I understand that the confession of the centurion made it possible for the first time in Mark's story for a human being to come to the realisation that Jesus is truly the "Son of God" (Mark 15:33–39). But this has not given us a satisfactory and spiritual understanding of the interpretation of the heavenly meaning of "Son of God". At one level, the interpretation may be provided in 15:38. From my analysis of the feature

---

[49] NIV Study Bible, 1458.

151

of the Jerusalem temple, I concluded above that the curtain was the one veiling the holy of holies; when this was torn in two from top to bottom, the barrier separating God from the Jewish men and women, but most importantly God from the Gentiles was ripped apart. Now God himself could be seen by both the Jews and Gentiles without any physical or spiritual demarcation. The divine truth here is that Mark's scene vividly and dramatically presents Jesus the Son of God as the very representation of God himself. However, I understand that there is a vital corollary in all this, for the context of the confession in 15:39 is not only 15:38, but the whole scene itself, including 15:37.

Dear child of God who has been redeemed by the precious blood of the Lamb of God, please stop for a moment and pray for an inner and deeper spiritual understanding of the confession of the Gentile centurion. How could a Roman commander who was in charge of the execution of a Jewish criminal see and observe the death of the same so-called rebellious man hanging on a shameful cross, make a turnaround in the opposite positive direction, and say that this same person is the Son of God? If Mark intended in 15:38 to claim that Jesus as Son of God represented God (which I assume and believe he is saying), then Mark's story also vividly and violently not only says something about what it means to be "Son of God", it also says something about God himself. I observe here that the confession of the centurion who identified Christ Jesus on the cross is not only about Christology; its significance is the totality of Christian theology, which is the gospel of soteriology.

God is to be seen most clearly and starkly in the abandonment, weakness, and powerlessness of the crucified Christ Jesus on the cross. The German prisoner of World War II and theologian Jurgen Moltmann expressed a similar opinion in his book *The Crucified God*. Moltmann believed that God suffered in Jesus on the cross as Jesus cried out of his abandonment, "My God, my God why have you forsaken me?" (Matt. 27:45, Mark 15:34). According to Moltmann, through his abandonment by God on the cross, the crucified Christ Jesus brings God to those who are abandoned by God. Through his suffering on the cross, he brings salvation to those who suffer. Through his death on the cross, he brings eternal life to those who are dying. And therefore the tempted, rejected, suffering, and dying Christ Jesus came to be the centre of the religion of the oppressed and the piety of the lost.[50]

Legend has it that the Gentile Roman centurion became a Christian. That is very likely true. Matthew recorded the centurion's statement as: "Surely he was the Son of God!" (27:54). Mark recorded it as "Surely this man was the Son of God!" (15:39). Luke stated: "The Centurion, seeing what had happened, praised God and said, 'Surely this was a righteous man" (23:47). What is the difference between "Son of God" and "righteous man"? Here I think there is no difference among the Synoptic writers, as they are all essentially saying the same thing about the confession of the centurion who has come to the realisation of the divinity of Christ Jesus. In other words, "Son of God" and "a righteous man" would have been virtually equivalent.

Matthew recorded that the confession was not only made by the Centurion but also by those hundred soldiers who were with him. According to Matthew: "When the centurion and those with him who were guarding Jesus saw the earthquake and all that had happened, they were terrified, and exclaimed, "Surely he was the Son of God!" (Matt. 27:54). I postulate here that while Christ Jesus' body was still on the cross, the first Gentile Roman soldiers believed in him and probably later formed or established the first Christian Church in Rome. It is true that the soldiers had mocked Jesus (Luke 23:36). But that was before "the earthquake and all that had happened" (Matt. 27:54). After seeing what happened, the soldiers who had crucified Jesus changed their minds.

I notice that the centurion and the soldiers heard all the insults and mockeries of the passers by – the chief priests, teachers of the law, and elders who said to him, "If you are the Son of God", "He saved others", "He trusts in God", "I am the Son of God". But when the centurion and his hundred soldiers saw the earthquake and all that happened, they disregarded the contempt of the scorners and esteemed and realised (I suppose spiritually) that the one hanging on the cross was truly "The Son of God" and worthy of their praise and the praise of all believers through the ages. Probably they believed that if Christ Jesus had saved others, if he trusted in God, and if he was the Son of God as had been confessed by his opponents and mockers, he could save them, help them to put their trust

---

[50] Moltmann, 44.

in God, and make them sons of the living God. Probably they believed that the things they desired spiritually would not have been given to them because they were not the direct seed of Abraham, like Christ Jesus himself. But they looked at him upon the cross and saw him as who he was as the Son of God, and what he did as the bringer of salvation to them and the whole wide world.

The centurion and his hundred soldiers looked at Jesus on the cross and saw salvation in him. The Holy Spirit prompted their hearts to believe that he could bring salvation to them. Paul later stated: "That if you confess with your mouth, 'Jesus is Lord,' and believe in your heart that God raised him from the dead, you will be saved. For it is with your heart that you believe and are justified, and it is with your mouth that you confess and are saved. As the scripture says 'anyone who trust in him will never be put to shame." For there is no difference between Jew and Gentile. The same Lord is Lord of all and richly blesses all who call him, for "Everyone who calls on the name of the Lord will be saved" (Rom. 9:10–13). Dear beloved child of God, be encouraged and note that the centurion and his soldiers did not just observe the unusual natural phenomenon and feel mystified; they apparently confessed in their hearts that Christ Jesus was the Son of God, and they probably became the first Gentile Christians.

In order to make sure that I am on holy ground with regards to what has been said above, I will buttress my viewpoint with the account of the writer of the fourth Gospel with regards to the death of Jesus. John stated:

> Now it was the day of Preparation and the next day was to be a special Sabbath. Because the Jews did not want the bodies left on the cross during the Sabbath, they asked Pilate to have the legs broken and the bodies taken down. The soldiers therefore came and broke the legs of the first man who had been crucified with Jesus, and then those of the other. But when they came to Jesus and found that he was already dead, they did not break his legs. Instead, one of the soldiers pierced Jesus' side with a spear, bringing a sudden flow of blood and water. (John 19:31–34)

The piercing of Jesus' side was probably to make doubly sure that he was really and completely dead, but perhaps the action in John 19:34 could be an act of brutality (see Isa. 53:5, Zech. 12:10, Ps. 22:16). But quite different from the intended evil, John also explained that "these things happened so that the scripture would be fulfilled.' Not one of his bone will be broken" (John 19:36; see also Exod. 12:46, Num. 49:12, Ps. 34:20, and 1 Cor. 5:7). My main interest in the citation of the above is John 19:34, which states, "Instead, one of the soldiers pierced Jesus' side with a spear, bringing a sudden flow of blood and water." In the following paragraphs, I will explain the significance of this sudden "flow of the blood and water".

I am of the same opinion as Hendriksen, who stated that in order to insure that not the slightest possibility would exist that any life had remained in the body of Jesus, one of the soldiers with his lance or spear pierces the side of Jesus. If the spear was held in the right hand, as it probably was, it was in all likelihood the left side of Jesus that was pierced. John enlarged upon the significance of the blood and water and devoted no less than four verses to it. He must have had a purpose in doing so. It is altogether probable that he was trying to tell his readers that Christ, the Son of God, actually died (according to his human nature). The death of Jesus was not a mere semblance; it was real. The Apostle was there himself and saw the "blood and water" flowing from the side of the Lord.[51]

Legend says that the Roman soldier who pierced the precious side of Jesus had a defective eye, and as he punctured Jesus' side, the "sudden flow of the blood and water" from the riven side of the greatest healer poured on the face of the soldier and touched his defective eye. What was the expected result? If you do believe that Christ Jesus was and is still the greatest divine healer, know for sure that the eye of the soldier (whatever the defect may have been) was instantaneously made whole and restored.

Dear reader, if you believe in this miraculous healing power of the "blood and water" on the eye of the Roman soldier, you will agree that this would have added to the faith of the centurion and all the soldiers who participated in the execution of Christ Jesus and also saw this phenomenon. I have no doubt that the centurion and his soldiers became the first Gentile Christians.

---

[51] William Hendriksen, *New Testament on John*, 439.

I propose here that John 19:34 influenced the life of Augustus M. Toplady (1740–1778) and occupied his mind. He recognised the spiritual significance of the "blood and the water" to the effects of Christ Jesus' atonement when he wrote:

Rock of ages, cleft for me,
Let me hide myself in Thee,
Let the water and blood
From Thy riven side which flowed
Be of Sin the double cure,
Cleanse me from its guilt and power.[52]

Christ Jesus is the greatest divine healer the world has ever seen and known. His miraculous healing recorded in the New Testament surpasses all the healing of the Old Testament prophets put together. These miracles of Jesus are innumerable, to the extent that the writer of the fourth Gospel summarised them in his last final statement: "Jesus did many other things as well. If every one of them were written down, I suppose that even the whole world would not have room for the books that would be written" (John 21:25).

Elisha was one of the Old Testament great prophets who had Yahweh's healing power. Here I will draw analogy between the "bones" of Elisha and the "blood and water" which flowed from the "riven side" of the Lord and saviour, Christ Jesus (as both wrought healing after their death). The writer of 2 Kings narrated a legendary story of the prophet Elisha and stated that "Elisha died and was buried. Now Moabite raiders used to enter the country every spring. Once while some Israelites were burying a man, suddenly they saw a band of raiders, so they threw the man's body into Elisha's tomb. When the body touched Elisha's bones, the man came to life and stood up on his feet" (2 Kings 13:20–21). The hasty burial of the man's body in Elisha's grave resulted in resurrection.

I do believe that this is a real and divine true story of holy wonder which glorifies Elisha's miraculous healing power, which had defied death even in his own grave, as it had done during his lifetime (2 Kings 4:18–37).[53] I understand that the life-giving power of the God of Elisha presented as

---

[52] Elsie Houghton, *Christian Hymn-Writers* (Wales, 1982), 160.
[53] Walter Dietrich, "1 and 2 Kings", in *The Oxford Bible Commentary*, 256.

a prophet of Yahweh is demonstrated once again in this last reference to Elisha. Furthermore, it can be noticed that even in death, as so often in life, Elisha continued to be the conduit of Yahweh's life-giving powers. In 2 Kings 4:8–37, we read the account of the Shunammite woman's son's restoration to life by Elisha. I do believe that this story is true and trustworthy and that I am sure to be on holy ground.

The New Testament writers recorded a few occasions when Christ Jesus raised people from death. For instance, the widow's son and Lazarus (Luke 7:11–17 and John 11:1–44) and the restoration to life of Jairus's daughter (Matt. 9:18–26, Mark 5:22–43, and Luke 8:41–56). The miracles of Elisha and Christ Jesus may be similar at face value, but I note that the miracle Christ performed was more miraculous than that of Elisha, because the widow's son and Lazarus were in worse condition than the son of the Shunammite woman.

Christ Jesus performed many and various types of healing, especially the restoration of the eyes of the blind.[54] Restoration of sight to the blind is another indication of what Christ Jesus (God the Son) does to bring salvation and what Yahweh (God the Father) had promised through the prophet Isaiah: "Then will the eyes of the blind be opened and the ears of the deaf unstopped. Then will the lame leap like a deer, and mute tongue shout for joy. Water will gush forth in the wilderness and streams in the desert" (Isa. 35:5–6).

Dear beloved child of God, take courage, believe, and trust in the saviour, the greatest healer of all time, our Lord and saviour Christ Jesus, who performs miraculous healing of all sorts of sicknesses and diseases as recorded in all the four Gospels. Both physical and spiritual healing are incorporated in Christ Jesus' ministry and were signs as well as the confirmation and the fulfilment of the messianic age. Restoration of sight to the blind underlines the fact that God's compassionate mercy and power are available for all followers of Christ Jesus who in the midst of difficult circumstance recognise their inadequacy and call for God's help. In the case of the healing of a blind man at Bethsaida (Mark 8:22–26), Mark probably intended to illuminate and illustrate Christian discipleship. That is to say the reinstallation of sight to the blind man symbolises the new life and salvation that is available to those who follow Christ Jesus.

---

[54] Matt. 9:27–31, 20:29–34; Mark 8:22–26, 10:46–52; and Luke 18:35–43.

It is striking to note that all the healings which Christ Jesus performed among the blind that are recorded in details in the gospels are not identical or alike. In other words, Christ Jesus gave sight to the blind men individually and personally which was unique according to their situations and circumstances. This shows that in his love and divine wisdom, Christ Jesus deals with his people on an individual basis in order to bring salvation. The heart of Christ Jesus goes out to the needy not as a group of family, ethnic, nationals, or any sort, but to each one in particular and in special circumstance. That is the reason his treatment of individual cases was never and will never be a mere duplication of what had been done before. To be certain of this principle of individualism of physical healing (which is applicable to spiritual healing as well), explore and compare some of the recordings in the New Testament.

You may be pondering of my intention with the summary I have presented above of Christ Jesus' healing power to restore the sight of the blind. Please note that I have presented an apologia to support the evidence given earlier regarding the "blood and water" which flowed from the riven side of Christ Jesus after his death on the cross that brought restoration to the eye of the Roman soldier who pierced him with his spear. As stated above, Christ Jesus' restoration of the sight of the blind man at Bethsaida symbolised new life and salvation vis-à-vis the "blood and water" which flowed from the wounded side of Chris Jesus and brought physical restoration to the eye of the Gentile Roman soldier.

I have already cited the phenomenal story of the resurrection of the dead man when his body touched the bones of the great prophet Elisha. I state here that the resurrection of that man was merely physical and temporal; it probably did not lead to eternal life or salvation. On the other hand, I believe that the Roman soldier whose eye was restored had permanent healing and instantaneous salvation, as well as eschatological eternal life because he acknowledged Christ Jesus as the Son of the living God. I am standing on holy and firm ground to say that if the bones of the prophet Elisha did wonders to bring back to life the dead man (which is scripturally correct and true as cited above), be assured and believe that the blood and water which gushed out from the divine and precious side of God the Son (who is God himself) does even more miracles, because

Christ Jesus is more and far greater than Elisha and all the prophets of the Old Testament, including Elijah who was the master of Elisha.

All the Old Testament prophets waited and wanted to see the Messiah in order to witness and observe his earthly ministry and miraculous healing power. Christ Jesus, the Messiah, said to his disciples privately, "Blessed are the eyes that see what you see. For I tell you that many prophets and Kings wanted to see what you see but did not see it, and to hear what you hear but did not hear it" (Luke 10:23–24). After his resurrection, Christ Jesus unequivocally said to his disciples that everything written in the Old Testament is pointing to him, as he said to them, "This is what I told you while I was still with you: everything must be fulfilled that is written about me in the Law of Moses, the prophets and the Psalms" (Luke 24:44). This statement of Christ Jesus is the summation of the Old Testament. The law of Moses, the prophets, and the psalms form the three main parts of the Hebrew Old Testament (Psalms was the first book of the third section, called the Writings), indicating that Christ (the Messiah) was foretold in the whole Old Testament.[55] Peter reiterated a similar statement when he addressed the crowd on the day of Pentecost and said:

> Indeed, all the prophets from Samuel on, as many as have spoken, have foretold these days. And you are heirs of the prophets and the covenant God made with your fathers. He said to Abraham, "through your offspring all peoples on earth will be blessed." When God raised up his servant, he sent him first to you to bless you by turning each of you from your wicked ways. (Acts 3:24–26)

The emphasis is that Christ is the fulfilment of prophecies made relative to Abraham, Moses, and David (Acts 3:24). Christ was foretold in Samuel's declarations concerning David. Samuel anointed David to be King in Israel and spoke of the establishment of David's kingdom (1 Sam. 16:13, 13:14, 15:28, 28:17). Nathan's prophecy to David was ultimately messianic (2 Sam. 7:12–16). Christ was to bring blessing to all people as promised to Abraham. Luke had interest on the motif of the supremacy of Christ Jesus over and above all the Old Testament prophets as he recorded

---

[55] NIV Study Bible, 1557.

it both in his gospel and Acts of the Apostles. On the same subject matter, Luke referred to the speech by Peter at the house of Cornelius. In that speech, Peter made his conclusion remark and said: "All the prophets testify about him that everyone who believes in him receives forgiveness of sins through his name" (Acts 10:43).

All the Mosaic laws or ordinances, prophecies, and miracles in the Old Testament awaited final fulfilment in the Messiah who is Christ Jesus. As stated earlier, all the healing miracles which were performed by the prophets in the Old Testament were for physical disabilities, but the healing and the restoration power of Christ Jesus goes beyond the physical and penetrates into the disability of all disabilities, which is spiritual disability cause by sin. It is only the prophet of all prophets who heals physically as well as spiritually, and this includes forgiveness of sins. It is only Christ Jesus (God the Son) who does the work of forgiveness of sin as God; and he authoritatively declared, "But that you may know that the Son of Man has authority on earth to forgive sins" (Mark 2 7–10; Luke 5:21–24).

Let me once again bring to the fore the centurion and his soldiers. I notice that they mocked Jesus (Matt. 27:27–31; Mark 15:16–20) and sinned against him. But all these things took place before they "saw the earthquake and all that happened and were terrified and exclaimed, "Surely he was the Son of God!" (Matt. 27:54). I state here that as soon as they acknowledged Christ Jesus as the "Son of God", their sins were forgiven and at that moment, the soldier with an eye defect received physical and spiritual healing that brought salvation to the Gentile Roman soldiers at the crucifixion.

I go further to the motif of salvation of the Roman soldiers and hypothesise that probably they were among the first Gentile Christians who went to Rome at the completion of military service in Palestine and established the Church in Rome. My understanding (mainly from the New Testament, without historic input) is that there is no definite and accurate information about the establishment of the Christian church in Rome in the New Testament. When Paul wrote his letter to the Christians in Rome (probably in the early spring AD 57), the recipients of the epistle were not individual Christians in Rome but rather the Christian Church as a corporate body. In order words, about the AD 57, there was an established and well-functioning church in Rome. A group of theologians who commented on the establishment of the Church in Rome stated that "of the origin of this important Church we know little, and it is perhaps useless to conjecture".[56] It might have been established by converts from the day of Pentecost who returned to their Roman homes rejoicing in their newfound faith. Although some Romans are mentioned in Acts 2, there is no indication that any of these were converted to Christianity on that day.

Please note that I am not attempting to write the history of the establishment of the church in Rome; this is not, in any case, the aim of this section. The main focus in the last few paragraphs above is to draw a link between Christ's death on the cross and the probability of the establishment of the Church in Rome by the centurion and his soldiers. I have already postulated above that the Roman soldiers were probably the first Gentile converts to Christianity because of all that happened and what they observed during the crucifixion of Christ Jesus.

To keep this discussion alive, I bring in another person, Simon of Cyrene, who probably also became one of the first Gentile Christians. Simon of Cyrene, like the soldiers, observed all the wonderful events and experienced the natural phenomena which took place while Christ Jesus was on the cross. All the synoptic writers mention Simon of Cyrene who helped Jesus carry his cross.[57] Here I cite Mark and present his account: "A certain man from Cyrene Simon the father of Alexander and Rufus, was passing by on his way in from the country, and they forced him to carry the cross" (Mark 15:21). Cyrene was an important city in current Libya in North Africa that had a large Jewish population. My meticulous investigation has shown that Simon was a Jew who was born in Cyrene. Whether he was in Jerusalem as a pilgrim to celebrate the Passover or as a permanent resident is uncertain.[58]

In order to buttress my point about the cross which is the source of Christianity, and how it probably connects to Simon the Cyrenian, I join Hendriksen and make the following reconstruction – which, though not certain, is however probable. Simon, a Jew, has come to Jerusalem to attend

---

[56] Douglas, 1035.
[57] Matt. 27:32; Mark. 15:21; Luke. 23:26.
[58] Daniel J. Harrington, "The Gospel According to Mark", in *The New Jerome Bible Commentary*, 628.

one of the great festivals (in this case the Passover), as was the custom of many Jews, including those from Cyrene (Acts 2:10). According to Luke, there was even a Cyrenian synagogue. Now on this particular Friday, returning to the city from a visit to the country, Simon was pressed into service by the soldiers who were leading Christ Jesus to Calvary and were coming through the gate out of the city. Perhaps Simon was initially reluctant, but he finally carried Christ's cross and arrived at the final and ultimate destination of Calvary.[59]

At this point of the narration, I believe that Simon did not just hand over the cross of Christ to the centurion and his soldiers and go on his way in a hurry to Jerusalem in order to carry on his scheduled business of the day. I propose that Simon was prompted by the Holy Spirit to stay behind and join the Roman centurion and his soldiers who were executing the crucifixion, and the chief priest, the teachers of the law, and the elders who mocked Christ Jesus and wanted to see and make sure that he truly and really died and was buried. I believe that Simon did not in any way participate in the mocking by those who passed, the Jewish leaders, and the criminal who was crucified alongside Christ Jesus. I believe Simon stood at a distance and observed the way and manner in which Christ Jesus took control of his own death and conducted himself throughout his dying moments on the cross. Simon probably had a special interest in the Son of God, particularly his willingness to forgive those who were crucifying him, as he pleaded "Father, forgive them, for they do not know what they are doing" (Luke 23:34).

Franklin and other theologians thought that Jesus' prayer on the cross for forgiveness of his executioners and persecutors was textually defective. Because of this and other related reasons, many manuscripts of diverse origin omit Jesus' prayer for forgiveness, which is unique to Luke.[60] On the other hand, Karris and other theologians of similar mind who commented on this prayer of Jesus for forgiveness gave a statement that supports my viewpoint in this matter. Karris said that internal evidence weighs heavily for Jesus' prayer of forgiveness and the authenticity of the record in Luke's Gospel. He emphasised that the language and thought are all Lucan. He cited passages such as Luke 10:21, 11:2, 22:42, and 23:46, in which

---

[59] William Hendriksen, *New Testament Commentary on Mark*, 648.
[60] Eric Franklin, "Luke", in *The Oxford Bible Commentary*, 957.

Christ Jesus addresses the Father and prays for forgiveness of those who are crucifying him because of their ignorance. According to Karris, Luke balanced Stephen's prayer (Acts 7:60) with that of Jesus.

Luke has sayings of Jesus in each main section of the crucifixion narrative (Luke 23:28–31, 43, 46). The inclusion of a saying here conforms Luke's artistry. Jesus' prayer is part and parcel of Luke's theology of the rejected prophet and of Christ Jesus who taught and practiced forgiveness of enemies (Luke 6:27–28, 17:4). Jesus, who had come to call sinners to repentance (Luke 5:32), continued that to the very end of his ministry, even on the cross as he prayed to his Father. On the other hand, Karris suggested that Jesus' prayer could have been deleted by later copyists because it conflicted with their interpretation of Luke 22:28–31; because they felt that the destruction of Jerusalem and its temple in AD 70 showed that Jesus' prayer was ineffective; or because of anti-Jewish sentiment.[61]

In support of the positive affirmation of Jesus' prayer for forgiveness and its authenticity as presented above, I will add another comment by Hendriksen, who shared a similar positive viewpoint on the prayer of Jesus for forgiveness on the cross. Hendriksen stated that Jesus' prayer for forgiveness – "Father, forgive them, for they do not know what they are doing" (Luke 23:34) – in all probability is the first of "The Seven Words on the Cross". Hendriksen called it deplorable that so much opposition has been raised against this first saying. Some would exclude it entirely, and others would try to tone it down. The reasoning of some who oppose it are as follows: those who killed Jesus were reprobates, and God does not in any sense bless reprobates. Therefore, Jesus could not have asked that they be forgiven. Besides, the verb used here (forgive) has a very wide meaning (this, by the way, is true). The conclusion is that Jesus must have meant "Father, hold back your wrath; do not immediately pour out the full measure of your fury".

Hendriksen analysed the true meaning of the earnest supplication of Christ Jesus on the cross as follows:

1. "Forgive them" means exactly that. It means, "Blot out their transgression completely. In your sovereign grace cause them to repent truly, so that they can be and will be pardoned fully."

[61] Robert J. Karris, "The Gospel According to Luke", in *The New Jerome Bible Commentary*, 719.

2. Hendriksen emphatically said that this meaning is clear from the fact that the grammatical construction is exactly the same as in Luke 11:4, "And forgive us our sins," and in Luke 17:3, "If he repents, forgive him."

3. It is even conceivable that he who insisted so strongly that his followers must forgive every debtor and that they must even love their enemies should exemplify this virtue himself.

4. Stephen, at death's portal, was clearly an imitation of the dying Christ Jesus on the cross. Stephen prayed, "Lord, do not hold this sin against them" (Acts 7:60). Here Stephen was giving us the truest interpretation of Christ's supplication, "Father forgive them."

5. Hendriksen said, "Take special note of the word Father; that there is divine trust and love in it". Here we are reminded of "though he slays me, yet will I hope in him" (Job 13:15).

6. It is marvellous beyond words that Jesus, in his earnest intercession for his torturers, even presented to the Father a special plea, an argument as it were, for the granting of his petition, namely, "For they do not know what they are doing."

7. Hendriksen said that by offering this prayer, Jesus fulfilled the prophecy of Isaiah: "for he bore the sin of many and made intercession for the transgressors" (Isa. 53:12). See also Jeremiah 7:16, 27:18; Isaiah 59:16; and Hebrews 7:25.

Hendriksen concluded that it was indeed true that the Roman soldiers certainly did not know what they were doing. But even the members of the Sanhedrin (the Jewish council), though they must have known that what they were doing was wrong and wicked, did not comprehend the extent of that wickedness, especially in the writings and prophecies of the Old Testament.[62]

The final point here is the obvious question: did God the Father hear and answer the prayer of God the Son who was dying on the cross? The answer is probably yes, because history records that the fall of Jerusalem and the total destruction of the second temple did not occur immediately after the death of Christ Jesus. For a period of about forty years, the gospel

---

[62] William Hendriksen, *New Testament Commentary on Luke*, 1027–1028.

of salvation which Christ Jesus brings that is full and free was proclaimed to the Jews. Not only that, but many Jews were actually led to Israel's Yahweh. On the day of Pentecost, three thousand were converted to the Lord (Acts 2:31, 42), and a little later, a thousand more, which increased the number of believers to about five thousand (Acts 4:4). The word of the Lord spread, and the number of disciples in Jerusalem increased rapidly.

A large number of priests became obedient to the faith (Acts 6:7). This "large number of priests", though involved by lineage and life service in the priestly observances of the old covenant, accepted the preaching of the Apostles, which proclaimed the sacrifice of Christ Jesus. His sacrifice made the old sacrifices as prescribed by Moses unnecessary (Heb. 8:13, 10:1–4, 11–14), and the priests became obedient to the faith in Christ Jesus. It is important to note that although the whole people of Israel did not turn to Yahweh, many families and individuals converted to the Lord formed the early first century Jewish Christian community.

Finally, I go back to my hypothesis that the Cyrenian Simon and the Gentile Roman centurion and his soldiers became the first converts to Christianity, and that together they established the Church in Rome. It is possible that, like the centurion and those with him who were carrying out the death sentence of Christ Jesus, Simon saw the earthquake and all that happened, heard Christ Jesus' prayer for forgiveness, saw how he finally died, and was terrified and exclaimed, "Surely he was the Son of God" (Mark 15:39). I think this incident of the death of Christ Jesus on the cross left such an indelible impression on Simon that he probably became a Christian.

Documentary evidence shows that Simon and his family subsequently lived in Rome. He might have been living there before, but in any case, he was a Cyrenian by birth. Among the early Christians, there were many Cyrenians (Acts 11:19, 13:1). You may notice that of the four Gospel writers, only Mark who wrote specifically to the Romans mentioned "Simon, the father of Alexander and Rufus" (Mark 15:21). The reference is very brief, but they are referred to in such a way as to suggest that they were known by those to whom he wrote.[63] In other words, Mark did not waste time on his reference to Alexander and Rufus because he assumed as if to say, "You know these people who are with you in Rome and you are

---

[63] NIV Study Bible, 1498.

well acquainted with their active role and commitment in the Church". Paul in his letter to the Romans (16:13) wrote, "Greet Rufus, chosen in the Lord, and his mother, who has been a mother to me too". Evidently, the mother of Rufus who was the wife of Simon had rendered some motherly service to Paul in his Christian mission.

The conclusion is that if the above reconstruction is factual, then the service which Simon rendered, though initially forced, turned out to be a genuine blessing for himself, his family, and many others and for many generations (to the present and future) as the Church in Rome became the one and only universal Roman Catholic Church which held together the Christian faith and its religion for more than one and a half millennia, and still represents the Christian community at the global level and in interfaith dialogue with other religions worldwide.

Finally, I bring this chapter to a close by stating that the cross of our Lord and saviour Christ Jesus is the gravitational force which pulls people from every tribe, tongue, and nation from east to west and from north to south and brings them all to Christ Jesus who is the centre and focal point of the Christian faith. I state that the cross:

- was a death-trap (although temporary) for Christ Jesus but is now a source of freedom and eternal life for all believers through the ages;
- was an emblem of sacrilege and shame for Christ Jesus but now represents a holy and divine logo of piety and reverence to Christ Jesus and the universal Christian community;
- is now a channel of blessing to the condemned and the reprobate humans who receive free and absolute forgiveness from the divine saviour our Lord Christ Jesus;
- is now the medium where the victimised seed of Adam becomes victorious because of the victory of Christ Jesus who is the divine seed of the universal Almighty God;
- is now a means by which Christ Jesus freely and unreservedly gives divine love and affection to all who were in antipathy and hostility with God;
- was a symbol of shame to the Jews as well as to the Gentiles but now has become a mark of honour, distinction, and glory for Christ Jesus and to all Christians worldwide.

And now, dear beloved child of Christ, join Isaac Watts (1674–1748) and "survey the wondrous cross."[64] Also, have the desire of George Bennard (1873–1958) to "Cling to the old rugged cross on a hill far away and exchange it some day for a crown." Finally, have the same faith as Fanny J. Crosby (1820–1925) and cry out "Jesus, keep me near the Cross" and draw "nearer, nearer blessed Lord, to the cross where Thou has died".

---

[64] Houghton, 54.

.

# PART TWO

# SOURCE OF SALVATION: RESURRECTION

# Chapter 8

# INTRODUCTION

In Chapter 1 of this book, I stated that the birth, mission, death, and resurrection of Christ Jesus are the divine quadruplet foundation upon which the Church of Christ is laid. I have analysed the first three (birth, mission, and death) in various chapters in Part One. My main task in this Part Two is to critically examine the fourth heavenly constituent which brings salvation to its perfect and holy completion: resurrection.

For the past twenty years or so, I have prayerfully thought about the resurrection and developed a divine interest in the power of the resurrection phenomenon and the work of salvation because of what has been said about them by teachers in Sunday school, preachers in fellowship and worship centres, theologians who have written innumerable books on the subject matter, and other Christian as well as non-Christian channels of communication where such issues have been discussed. Since the resurrection of our Lord and saviour Christ Jesus on the first Easter Sunday, different opinions, dogma, and theories have been postulated about the terms *resurrection* and *salvation* which have brought eternal life in Christ Jesus through his death on the cross. These controversies will continue till the second advent of Christ Jesus himself, who will unfold to us the mystery of his salvation which is ultimately wrought in his resurrection.

There are varied and diverse opinions among writers on the resurrection event and the work of salvation. As a matter of fact, it is this realisation of the disjunction that has instigated the title of this second part of the book: "Source of Salvation: Resurrection". Here, I will critically analyse the resurrection phenomenon that wrought the work of salvation. The resurrection of our Lord Christ Jesus is one of the main sources and fountains of salvation. My main hypothesis in this part of the book is "no resurrection, no salvation". The two main terms in this Part Two are *resurrection* and *salvation*, which are among the most important Christian doctrines in the whole of the New Testament. Their significance in Christian faith and belief are of prime magnitude and cannot be overemphasised. They are the bulwarks of the Christian religion to the point that if they are removed from the New Testament, Christianity as a religion would flatly collapse, crumble, and fade away like most of the religions of the ancient world.

## RATIONALE: RESURRECTION

Here I present my religious reasons for my endeavour to put forward my faith and believe in the resurrection phenomenon which I believe will help you to have an inner and deeper spiritual understanding of the subject matter. I believe that the doctrines of resurrection and salvation are very important and significant in Christianity. They pull and draw other dogmas of the Christian faith, belief, and teaching that are grounded and steadfast on the rock of Christ Jesus and cannot be moved. It is vital to state unequivocally that if the doctrines of the resurrection event and the work of salvation (like the birth, mission, and death) are removed from Christian fidelity, belief, and education, Christianity would disappear totally, annihilated like the second temple of Judaism from where it started. The work of salvation is embedded in the event of the resurrection, and both are interwoven and inseparable in the Christian religion.

The work of salvation is accomplished through the birth, mission, death, and resurrection of Christ Jesus. In order words, the finished work of salvation in Christ Jesus emanates from the power of the resurrection and all the other elements. The message of the resurrection story and the grace of salvation are the bulwarks, steppingstones, and cornerstones of the preaching of Peter, the Apostles, and Paul after the first Good Friday and the first Easter Sunday. The first divine gospel, which was proclaimed by the angel to the women who were looking for the body of Christ Jesus by his grave, is that "He is not here; he has risen, just as he said. Come and see the place where he lay." (Matt. 28:6, Mark 16:6, Luke 24:6).

In order to make the resurrection doubly sure, the angel encouraged the women to go closer to the tomb to convince themselves that everything was orderly and that no disciple had been there to remove the body, nor had an enemy pillaged the tomb. In either case, the bandages would no longer have been present. The women, Peter, and John, who all went to the tomb that same morning, must have seen that the Lord, restored from death to life, had himself removed the bandages; provided for himself a garment such as was worn by the living; calmly and majestically put everything in its place in the tomb; and departed from the tomb gloriously alive.[1]

Notice that Christ Jesus' resurrection was the work of the triune God. God the Father raised God the Son from the dead, and God the Holy Spirit prompted the angel to speak to the women. God the Son divinely took back the life which he had laid down. Dear believer who is waiting for the eschatological resurrection, be assured that these three are, and will always be, one because of their inter-Trinitarian divine relationship that is undividable and inseparable. The resurrection is the final, necessary end – the ultimate and grand successful conclusion of Christ Jesus' earthly mission. Without it, Christ Jesus' birth, mission, death, and the whole of his earthly missionary activities are vacant and thrown into oblivion, and his opponents exonerated. Thanks be to God, with the resurrection Christ Jesus is vindicated and venerated as Lord and God, confirming his earthly salvation and authority and bringing ignominious defeat to all his opponents, including the devil himself.[2]

The resurrection is both phenomenon and mystical. That is to say that the resurrected body of Christ Jesus is a phenomenal experience for the Apostles and the first-century Jewish Christians who saw the risen Christ Jesus in a period of about forty days and observed all the post-resurrection activities of the risen Lord. This is a mystery to those who did not witness that resurrection phenomenon and yet believe that they have been raised to life from death and will rise again to an eternal life like him through

[1] William Hendriksen, *New Testament Commentary on Matthew* (Guilford, 1976), 990–991.
[2] Dale C. Allison, "Matthew", in *The Oxford Bible Commentary*, ed. John Barton and John Muddiman (Oxford, 2011), 885.

their sacrament of baptism. Salvation, which is eternal life in Christ Jesus, is a mystery that has never been physically observed or experienced by any living human. It is only by faith that Christians believe that they are saved, and this is indeed true to all believers through all the ages who believe in the saving grace of Christ Jesus.

The one and only reason for someone to become a Christian is grounded on the present and eschatological hope of eternal life in Christ Jesus. According to Augustine, this has only been made possible through the resurrection of Christ Jesus as the culmination of his work of salvation. The resurrection from the dead by Christ Jesus is the very centre of eschatological transformation, the dividing line between time and eternity. So the expectation of the resurrection is the distinctive faith of Christians, the hope that marks off Christian doctrine from pagan wisdom. The resurrection is the only vision of lasting happiness promised to Christians (Ps. 36:1, 9). If faith in the resurrection of the dead is taken away, all Christian teaching perishes. Eschatological hope is not simply for everlasting life, but for a life that would eventually include this visible flesh in some transformed glorious state. The main ground for this Christian hope is the resurrection of Christ Jesus as the culmination of his work of salvation.[3]

The Apostles and the first Jewish Christians who observed the post-resurrected body of Christ Jesus regarded the resurrection as the most significant event and experience once for all. They could not avoid or keep silent about the resurrection, and it became one of the main themes in all their preaching. In fact, the proclamation of the resurrection of Christ Jesus by the Apostles identified, distinguished, and isolated them from the rest of the different sects of Judaism in the second temple, which signalled and triggered the early beginning of the "partings of the ways between Judaism and Christianity". It was the same proclamation of the resurrection of Christ Jesus by the Apostles that also set them off from all other teachings of the ancient world.[4]

The first speech or preaching by Peter after the resurrection was based on the phenomenon of the resurrection of Christ Jesus. Peter addressed

---

[3] Allen D. Fitzgerald, *Augustine through the Ages: An Encyclopaedia* (Cambridge, 1999), 772.
[4] James D. G. Dunn, *The Partings of the Way between Christianity and Judaism and their Significance for the Character of Christianity* (London, 2006), xi.

the dumbfounded crowd on the day of Pentecost and said to them, "But God raised [Christ Jesus] up, having freed him from death because it was impossible for [Christ Jesus] to be held in its power" (Acts 2:24). With many other words, Peter warned them, and he pleaded with them, "Save yourselves from this corrupt generation" (Acts 2:40). The key phrases in Peter's message are "raised him up" and "save yourselves", which imply resurrection and salvation respectively.

My main point here is that resurrection and salvation are interwoven and inseparable. They are the principal themes that run through the New Testament. Peter's speech on the day of Pentecost attested to the resurrection of Christ Jesus which effectively wiped away the reproach of the death of Christ Jesus on the cross. The main focal point here is that Peter mentioned the resurrection and put emphasis on it at the very first day of the beginning of the Christian faith. Peter must tell his audience that God the Father did not abandon God the Son on the cross and in the grave. God the Father loosed Christ Jesus from the power of death which could not hold him. Peter saw, ate, and had dialogue with the resurrected and living Christ Jesus.[5]

Paul's epistles were recognised by many first-century readers as divinely inspired. They were the first canonised Holy Scriptures and sacred writings in the New Testament. This is evident from the fact that these letters were preserved and that churches continued to follow the instructions and directions which Paul pointed out.[6] Paul's scriptures and sacred writings contain some of the earliest testimonies of the resurrection story of Christ Jesus.

Paul in all his corpora clearly regarded the resurrection story and the work of salvation as of primary importance. Some members of the Church in Corinth cast doubts on the resurrection and argued that there was no resurrection of the physical body. Paul was very perplexed and spiritually concerned about this false contention, and he tried to correct the misconception in his epistle to the Church in 1 Corinthians 15:12–19. Here, Paul emphatically, forcefully, systematically, and logically presented the facts of the resurrection of Christ Jesus as follows:

---

[5] Matthew Henry, *Matthew Henry's Commentary on the Whole Bible* (Peabody, Massachusetts, 2008), 1653.

[6] Edward P. Blair, *The World Illustrated Bible Handbook* (London, 1987), 33.

1. "But if it is preached that Christ has been raised from the death, how can some of you say that there is no resurrection of the dead?" (15:12).
2. "If there is no resurrection of the dead, then not even Christ has been raised" (15:13).
3. "And if Christ has not been raised, our preaching is useless and so is your faith" (15:14).
4. "More than that, we are then found to be false witnesses about God, for we have testified about God that he raised Christ from the dead. But he did not raise him if in fact the dead are not raised" (15:15).
5. "For if the dead are not raised, then Christ has not been raised either" (15:16).
6. "And if Christ has not been raised, your faith is futile; you are still in your sins" (15:17).
7. "Then those also who have fallen asleep in Christ are lost" (15:18).
8. "If only for this life we have hope in Christ, we are to be pitied more than all men" (15:19). Hope in this life is not a complete salvation, because salvation wrought by Christ Jesus is for both the present age and the age to come in the eternal life with Christ Jesus in his heavenly kingdom. The resurrection is seen as a present reality as well as an eschatological hope for all believers who are expecting an eternal life of salvation where Christ Jesus is the royal king in his glory and splendour in his kingdom. So Paul brought his presentation to its divine final point and said,
9. "But Christ has indeed been raised from the dead, the first fruits of those who have fallen asleep" (15:20).

Hallelujah! Praises and glory and power and honour and majesty belong to the living and sovereign King and eternal saviour our Lord and God Christ Jesus who reigns on the heavenly throne now and evermore. In this citation, Paul's categorical conclusion on the resurrection of Christ Jesus is based on evidence he has set as a proof in 1 Corinthains15: 3–8, and concluded in verses 20 -22. Note that Paul presented Christ Jesus metaphorically as "first fruits", which is the first sheaf of the harvest given to the Lord (Lev. 23:10–11, 17, 20) as a token that all the harvest belonged to the Lord and would be dedicated to him through dedicated lives. So Christ Jesus who has been raised is the guarantee of the resurrection of all God's redeemed people (1 Thess. 4:13–18).[7] Please note that Paul did not just pass the good news of the resurrection to the Corinthians because of what he read about it or what he heard from the Apostles (like Peter and John). He confirmed to the Corinthians of the resurrection of Christ Jesus because Paul himself had seen the risen Lord, who appeared to him.

All Christians from the apostolic age to the present era believe that Christ Jesus has transformed their lives and given them salvation for now and then. This transition to the new life has only been made possible through the death of Christ Jesus on the cross on the first Good Friday and his resurrection on the first Easter Sunday morning, which delivers us from eternal death and darkness into his glorious, eternal life and light.

## PERIOD OF ENLIGHTENMENT: RESURRECTION

It may be worthwhile to summarise the term *Enlightenment*, which refers to a long period between 1650 and 1850 (also known as the modern period) that is one of the great turning points in human history. Groups of free-thinkers in the West, particularly in France, emerged and grouped knowledge in an exercise of critical reason. Enlightenment ideas were also employed to defend particularly Christian doctrines and to modify Christian belief along lines more amenable to the spirit of the age. Modern Christian apologetics is very much the product of Christian responses to Enlightenment critique, but equally, many anti-religious concepts and movements – such as materialism, socialism and atheistic humanism – have their roots in this period.[8]

The resurrection of Christ Jesus has been a bone of contention since the biblical period. More than two millennia after Christ Jesus' resurrection, disagreement rages on, and this trend will continue until the second advent of Christ Jesus himself, who alone will unveil the mystery of his power of resurrection and work of salvation. This confusion and commotion regarding the resurrection and salvation is the plan and work of the antichrist, which is

---

[7] NIV Study Bible, 1722.
[8] *Christianity: the Complete Guide*, ed. John Bowden (London, 2005), 373.

the main motif of the epistles which John the Evangelist wrote to his readers, warning them against a conventional eschatological scheme that was very familiar to the recipients (1 John 2:18, 2:22, 4:3; 2 John 7).

*Antichrist* is any person who opposes Christ Jesus and his work of salvation and who is an opponent or an alternative Christ. John the Evangelist was the "beloved one" of Christ Jesus who wrote against the antichrists (who existed even in the lifetime of John), stating: "Dear children, this is the last hour and as you have heard that the antichrist is coming, even now many antichrists have come. This is how we know it is the last hour" (1 John 2:18). John assumed that his readers knew that great enemies of God and his people would arise before the second advent of Christ Jesus. That person is called *antichrist* who is "the man of lawlessness" (2 Thess. 2:3) and "the beast" (Rev. 13:1–10). But prior to the beast, there will be many antichrists. The following is an outline of some aspects of their character:

- They deny the incarnation (1 John 4:2; 2 John 7) and dismiss the divinity of Christ Jesus (1 John 2:22).
- They deny the Father and the Son (1 John 2:22).
- They do not acknowledge the Father and the Son (1 John 2:23).
- They are liars (1 John 2:22) and deceivers (2 John 7).
- They are many (1 John 2:18).
- In John's days, they left the Church because they had nothing in common with the true believers in Christ Jesus (1 John 2:19). The antichrists who were referred to in John's letters were the early Gnostics.[9]

In the case of the enlightenment period, the main issue which the antichrists raised was whether Christ Jesus indeed arose from the dead. In other words, they denied the resurrection phenomenon, and by doing that they tried to put the whole good news of the birth, mission, death, resurrection, and salvation of Christ Jesus into dispute and jeopardy. In regards to the subject of resurrection, this period saw an enormous development of intense opposition or sceptical ideas and ideologies towards the resurrection event. In the following paragraphs, I will present some of the theologians of the Enlightenment era and summarise their opinions on the resurrection phenomenon.

---

[9] NIV Study Bible, 1869.

I start with the eighteenth-century Enlightenment author Gotthold Ephraim Lessing. Lessing was one of the anti-religious critics of his time and was very sceptical of the resurrection. He concluded that the resurrection was "non-event". He stated that there was no similar event of the first century resurrection story which could be compared to the Enlightenment era of his generation.[10] I will make my critical analysis later, but it suffices to state here that Lessing did not have the Christian faith which is based on belief. I totally disagree with him and reject his idea of the resurrection "non-event". I will forcefully and rigorously put forward my reasons of disagreement in my discussion later in Chapter 11.

Another critic of the resurrection in the Enlightenment period was David Friedrich Strauss, who regarded the resurrection as a "myth". He concluded that the resurrection of Christ Jesus was not in the physical body which the disciples saw; this was a figment of their imagination that was re-conceived in the minds of the disciples as well as the Gospel writers.[11] Strauss stated: "In this scientific age, it is impossible to believe in a miracle. As a result, belief in an object resurrection of Jesus is no longer possible." His conclusion is that the resurrection is to be regarded as a mythical event, pure and simple.[12]

Rudolf Bultmann of the same Enlightenment period had a similar view to both Lessing and Strauss. I utterly and totally disagree with all these, and later in Part Two I will present compelling evidence to dismiss their negative views of the resurrection. Other theologians of the Enlightenment period also made negative comments on the resurrection and discarded it as a "mythical event". Their main point was that technological development and scientific discoveries are more practically acceptable and reliable than a first-century story of resurrection. These are but one of the paradigms of Enlightenment theorists who were sceptical of the resurrection event.

These negative conceptions of theologians of the eighteenth-century Enlightenment era are in direct conflict and opposition to the faith and belief of the fourth-century classic theologian Augustine of Hippo. Augustine totally and wholeheartedly believed in the physical bodily

---

[10] Alister E. McGrath, *Christian Theology: An Introduction* (4th edn, Oxford, 2007), 320.
[11] McGrath, 321.
[12] McGrath, 332.

resurrection of Christ Jesus. His unshakable faith in the resurrection of the living Christ Jesus has edified the body of Christ through the ages. Augustine stated: "Thus the one purpose of Jesus' post resurrection appearances was that we might believe in the resurrection of the dead". I will expatiate upon this later in subsequent places in this book.

This faith of Augustine in the resurrection is in harmony with all the New Testament writers, including Paul, the theologian, who stated: "But Christ has indeed been raised from the dead" (1 Cor. 15:20). Human logic of the Enlightenment period of theologians gives way to the passion of the Apostle proclaiming conviction that transcends reason and experience.[13]

Paul the Apostle's statement strongly demonstrates the pivotal significance of the resurrection of Christ Jesus within the scheme of salvation. Paul's categorical affirmation and conclusion on the evidence of the resurrection is based on the post-resurrection appearances of Christ Jesus to Peter, the eleven disciples, more than five hundred disciples at the same time, James, and finally to Paul himself, who saw and heard from the resurrected Christ Jesus.[14] These opinions support my viewpoint of the inseparability of the event of the resurrection and the work of salvation. Resurrection of Christ Jesus is the guarantee of the resurrection of all God's redeemed people.

It is obvious that the above paragraphs show the divine divide between the doubting Thomases and the believing Abrahams, and this is just the tip of the iceberg. In subsequent parts of this book, critical analyses will be made on both the cynical and credulous theories of the resurrection which the believer in Christ Jesus has obtained presently and also is waiting for the eschatological final fulfilment of the age to come.

Dear beloved child of God, please be encouraged to proceed to the following chapters in order to understand and make spiritual gain and heavenly bliss of this mystery of the resurrection of our Christ Jesus, who wrought salvation for you in this earthly city presently as well as your eschatological salvation which is waiting for you in the city of God where you will be with the Lord forever.

---

[13] Jerome Murphy-O'Connor, "'The First Letter to the Corinthians", in *The Jerome Bible Commentary*, ed. Raymond E. Brown, Joseph A. Fitzmyer, and Roland E. Murphy (London, 2013), 812.

[14] John Barclay, "1 Corinthians", in *The Oxford Bible Commentary*, 1131.

Chapter 9

# THE RESURRECTION AND ITS SIGNIFICANCE

The purpose of this chapter is to examine the significance of the resurrection of Christ Jesus in the dogma of the Christian religion and what it means to individual Christians. In order to achieve this, I will discuss other related ancillary topics, such as Old Testament perspective of the resurrection, the main concept of the resurrection in the New Testament, and the divine link between the resurrections, and believers in Christ Jesus. I intend to religiously bring to the fore the importance of the resurrection in Christian faith and belief.

## RESURRECTION: OLD TESTAMENT PERSPECTIVE

Relatively speaking, the word *resurrection* is scanty in the Old Testament. That is not to say that it is not there. There is resurrection in the Old Testament, but not very renowned. The people of the Old Testament were very practical and mainly concentrated on the task of living out the present life in the service of God. They had little time to spare for speculation about the life to come. Moreover, it is necessary to understand that they lived on the other side of Christ Jesus' resurrection, which gives the doctrine its basis. Sometimes the people in the Old Testament used the idea of resurrection to express national hope of the rebirth of the nation (e.g. Ezek. 37).[1]

The first Old Testament scripture which alludes to resurrection is the book of Job. I will focus on 19:25–27 where Job stated, "I know that my Redeemer lives, and that in the end he will stand upon the earth. And after my skin has been destroyed, yet in my flesh I will see God; I myself will see him with my own eyes – I, and not another. How my heart yearns within me!" There is no iota of doubt that this is Job's personal confession or affirmation of faith in the resurrection of the dead.

Because of the staunch confession of faith in the resurrection, the cited scripture above in Job has been appropriated by generations of Christians, especially through the medium of Handel's *Messiah*. But this tradition celebrates redemption from guilt and judgement; Job had something else in mind. Although in other contexts he desired a defender (Prov. 23:11) as an advocate in heaven who would plead with God on his behalf (Job 9:33–34, 16:18–21), in Job 19:25–27 the redeemer Job seemed to declare was none other than the Creator God himself.[2] Notice that the dominant phrases in this expression of Job in the resurrection are "my redeemer" and "I will see God." Job was sure in his faith that physical death was not the end of his earthly existence, and for that reason he would stand in the presence of his redeemer in his resurrected body after his physical death sometime in the future. He was certain that a heavenly figure (Christ) would help him arise (resurrect) from death.

Note that the word *redeemer* was derived from Jewish family law. The redeemer is the avenger of blood, the nearest male relative who vindicates a wronged member of the family. The redeemer also redeemed property that had been sold because of economic distress, recovered stolen property, bought back a family member reduced to slavery, and married a childless widow to perpetuate the dead husband's name.[3] Please read the short story in the book of Ruth. As an episode in the ancestry of David, the book of Ruth sheds light on the importance, principles, and role of the redeemer in Israel's secular society. Boaz was a "close relative who was one of the kinsman-redeemer" who was related to Elimelech, the husband of Naomi.

---

[1] J. D. Douglas, *New Bible Dictionary: Second Edition* (Leicester, 1994), 1020.
[2] NIV Study Bible, 738.
[3] James L. Grenshaw, "Job", in *The Oxford Bible Commentary*, 343.

Elimelech and Naomi had two sons, Mahlon and Kilion, and both of them died in the land of Moab. Naomi and Ruth returned to Bethlehem, and Boaz married Ruth – the wife of Kilion, son of Elimelech – as "kinsman-redeemer" in order to perpetuate the name of Kilion.

There are three possible meanings of the phrase "I know that my redeemer lives":

1. A heavenly figure, likely the witness (Job 16:18–21), would champion Job's course after his death.
2. A heavenly figure would enable Job to arise from the dead, or as a disembodied shade Job would witness his vindication.
3. Job 19: 25–26a may refer to vindication after Job's death, but what he most desires (Job 19: 26b–27) is that this event occur prior to his demise.

Other scripture passages in the Old Testament which allude to the resurrection phenomenon include Psalms 10 and 49:14–15; Isaiah 26:19; and Daniel 12:2 and 13. Dear reader, I strongly recommend and encourage you to read these passages and any other Old Testament corpus that will help you to have an in-depth understanding of the mystery of the resurrection.

In the following paragraphs, I will examine what is undoubtedly one of the plainest and most explicit statements on resurrection: Daniel 12:2, which states "Multitudes who sleep in the dust of the earth will awake: Some to everlasting life, others to shame and everlasting contempt", and 13, "As for you, go your way till the end. You will rest, and then at the end of the days you will rise to receive your allotted inheritance." It is imperative to notice that this passage is one of the clearest and most unambiguous affirmations of the resurrection in the whole of the Old Testament. It is the only Old Testament scripture that gives a definite reference to the resurrection of both the righteous people of God who will resurrect to eternal salvation in the kingdom of their God in the City of Yahweh and also the wicked children of the devil that will resurrect to "everlasting contempt" to spend eternity in perpetual darkness. The phrase "everlasting life" occurs only in this citing in the entire Old Testament. There is a striking parallel between Daniel 12:2 and John 5:24–30, where Christ Jesus made a similar statement regarding the eschatological resurrection and eternal life.

In order to buttress my point here, I cite Davies, who shared a similar opinion and stated: "The resurrection is explicitly affirmed only here in the whole of the OT, though belief in it subsequently spread, until it finally became orthodox Jewish doctrine." Davies suggested that both the righteous and the wicked will resurrect and face justice. Among those to live forever are the "wise" who have a special place because they are religious leaders. Davies concluded that Daniel was promised an eschatological resurrection along with his successors of believers in the resurrection of Christ Jesus.[4]

# CHRIST THE REDEEMER

Before I bring this Old Testament perspective of the resurrection to a close and turn to the New Testament viewpoint of the resurrection, I once again reiterate the heartfelt cry of Job: "I know that my Redeemer lives." The famous statue "Christ the Redeemer" overlooks the city of Rio de Janeiro in Brazil. The statue is a model of Christ with his arms extended so that his body forms the shape of a cross. Brazilian architect Heitor da Silva Costa designed the figure. He imagined that the city's residents would see it as the first image to emerge from the darkness at dawn. At dusk, he hoped the city dwellers would view the setting sun as a halo behind the statue's head.[5]

There is spiritual value in keeping our eyes on our redeemer each day and every moment during the good times as well as the difficult periods. As Job suffered, he said: "I know that my Redeemer lives and [Christ Jesus] shall stand at last on the earth." (Job 19:25). Job's wholehearted cry points us to Christ Jesus who is our redeemer-king and living saviour who will visit the earth again one day at his second advent (1 Thess. 4:6–18). Let us keep our eyes focused intently on Christ Jesus, bearing in our minds and hearts that we have been rescued from our sins. Christ Jesus "gave Himself for us, that He might redeem us from every lawless deed and purify for himself His own special people" (Tim. 2:14). If you have accepted Christ Jesus as your personal Lord and saviour, you have every reason to trust

---

[4] P. R. Davies, "Daniel", in *The Oxford Bible Commentary*, 570.
[5] "Tuesday 30 June, 2015", *Our Daily Bread* (Lancashire, 2015).

and obey him. Whatever situation and circumstance you may be going true right now, continue to hope and focus on him and look forward to enjoying eternal life with Christ the Redeemer.

Dear child of the redeemer, be assured that the redeemer Job believed in (in about the second millennia, 2000–1000 BC) who "shall stand at last on the earth" physically actually and really stood on the same earth more than two millennia ago in full fulfilment of Job's prophecy. The name of this redeemer is Christ Jesus, the son of the Most High Living God, the Son of Man, David's son as well as David's Lord, who condescended himself and incarnated onto the earth and was born by virgin Mary. Christ Jesus physically lived, walked, and worked for the kingdom of his Father, willingly went to the cross and died, and ultimately rose from the dead by the power of his Father. His statue overlooks the city of Rio de Janeiro in Brazil, but his real person stands in the centre of the heavenly kingdom of his Father and overlooks the whole universe in each and every passing moment, and he has been there before the beginning and the foundation of Brazil and before the statue of Christ the Redeemer was erected.

Be assured, his real holy spirit in all its glorious form is at the centre of your life and taking control of your daily life in every situation and circumstance in which you find yourself. His presence will be perpetual until you disembark from this earth ship and drop this physical body and put on a new spiritual garment in his heavenly kingdom. Then you will see him as he is in real divine personality and spend eternity with him. It is likely that the statue of "Christ the Redeemer" may crumble sometime someday, but Christ Jesus himself will continue to be the focus of worship perpetually in the eternal kingdom of his Father, which will stand forever.

## RESURRECTION: NEW TESTAMENT PERSPECTIVE

In the New Testament, on three occasions Christ Jesus brought back people from the dead (the daughter of Jairus, the son of the widow of Nain, and Lazarus). These, however, were not to be thought of as resurrection so much as resuscitation. There is no indication in the New Testament of what any of these people did other than came back to the life that they had left. The Apostle Paul stated explicitly that Christ Jesus is "the first fruits of those who have fallen asleep" (1 Cor. 15:20). These miracles of bringing back the dead to life which Christ Jesus performed divinely clearly show that Christ Jesus is the master and controller of death.[6]

In order to analyse this important Christian doctrine in the New Testament, it will be necessary to cite what Christ Jesus himself said: "I am the resurrection and the life. Those who believe in me, even though they die, will live, and everyone who lives and believes in me will never die" (John 11:25–26). This preliminary statement, which came from the divine lips of Christ Jesus who is the bringer and giver of "resurrection" and "life", is the summation of this book. Take note that firstly, Christ Jesus himself is the resurrection, and secondly, he is also the life of life (salvation). In other words, both the resurrection and the life are divinely engraved indelibly in Christ Jesus. It is his own resurrection from the dead which brings life, immortal life, or eternal life of salvation. In him is the fountain of life and source of salvation that flow to every believer in him.

Christ Jesus declared himself as "I am" in the first of a series of seven self-descriptions (John 6:35). Note that "I am" is the short form of "I Am Who I Am". This is the name Yahweh revealed to Moses in that first and terrifying encounter with God in the mysterious burning but not consumed bush. God said to Moses, "I Am Who I Am, this is what you are to say to the Israelites: I Am has sent me to you" (Exod. 3:14). "I Am Who I Am," expresses God's character as the dependable and faithful God who desires the full trust of his people. Jesus applied the phrase to himself, and in so doing, he claimed to be God and risked being stoned for blasphemy (John 8:58–59). In the context of the resurrection, Christ Jesus applied "I am" to indicate that he is both Israel's God and the resurrection and life. In some ways, these are identified with him in his earthly ministry, and his nature is such that final death is impossible for him and all those who put their trust in him. Christ Jesus is life (John 14:6, Acts 3:15, Heb. 7:16). Not only that, he conveys life to all believers so that death will never triumph over them (1 Cor. 15:54–57).[7]

It is imperative to note that the dialogue between Christ Jesus and Martha in John 11:23–26 is built on an important understanding of the doctrine of resurrection. Martha thought that Jesus was speaking about

---

[6] Douglas, 1020–1021.
[7] NIV Study Bible, 1580.

the resurrection at the end of time in the future, but Jesus asserted that he himself is the resurrection and the life, so much so that very soon Lazarus would be raised to life, at that moment of their dialogue and not in the distant future. Christ Jesus will help all those who believe in him to overcome their own physical and spiritual death. Christ Jesus is the resurrection and the life; the resurrection and the life is Christ Jesus. Both the resurrection and the life are rooted in himself.[8],[9]

Note the order of Christ Jesus' presentation: first resurrection and then life. Resurrection opens the celestial gate that leads to immortal life of salvation in Christ Jesus. Christ Jesus is resurrection and life in person (John 1: 3–4), the full blessed life of God. All the glorious attributes of God the Father – omniscience, omnipotence, omni-powerfulness, holiness, kindness, love, mercy, and many more – are all in Christ Jesus. He is also the main source or fountain from whom all God's blessings flow for all believers' glorious resurrection and everlasting life. Because he lives, all believers live and shall live. If you remove him from your daily life, there will be nothing left in you except physical and spiritual death; but if you put him in the centre of your heart, mind, and soul, both physical and spiritual resurrection and total life in all its fullness is guaranteed and assured by him.[10]

## RESURRECTION: SIGNIFICANCE

The doctrine of resurrection is one of the most important pillars upon which the foundation of the Church of Christ Jesus had been laid, and it is of primary importance in Christian faith and belief. Christ Jesus said "I am the resurrection." In steadfast heavenly hope, Christ Jesus predicted on several occasions his own death by crucifixion and resurrection after three days.[11] Generally, the texts cited in the footnote are some of the Holy Scriptures in the New Testament in which Christ Jesus predicted

---

[8]  Rom. 6:8, 9; 1 Cor. 15:20, 57; Col. 1:18; 1 Thess. 4:16.
[9]  Rene Kieffer, "John", *The Oxford Bible Commentary*, 1580.
[10]  William Hendriksen, *New Testament on John*, 150.
[11]  Matt. 16:21, 17:23, 20:17–19; Mark 8:31–39, 9:3, 10:33–34; Luke 9:22–27, 12:50, 17:25, 18:31–33.

his death and ultimate resurrection; but Christ's death has been predicted and or prefigured centuries before in the Old Testament (Ps. 22, Isa. 53, Zech. 13:7).

Matthew recorded the prediction of Christ Jesus' death in his third and final account of the prediction of the passion and the resurrection (Matt. 20:17–19), stating, "Now as Jesus was going up to Jerusalem, he took the twelve disciples aside and said to them, "We are going up to Jerusalem, and the Son of Man will be betrayed to the chief priests and the teachers of the law. They will condemn him to death and will turn him over to the Gentiles to be mocked and flogged and crucified. On the third day he will be raised to life." Observe the messianic meaning of the "Son of Man" from the divine lips of the Son of Man who is Christ Jesus himself. It is the most common and preferred title for himself which he used about eighty-one times or so in his earthly lifetime ministry in the Gospels and it has never been used by anyone but Christ Jesus alone.

In Daniel 7:13–14, the Son of Man is pictured as a heavenly figure who in the end times is entrusted by God his Father (the Ancient of Days) with "authority, glory and sovereign power; all peoples, nations men of every language worshipped him. His dominion is an everlasting dominion that will not pass way, and his kingdom is one that will never be destroyed". Christ Jesus' use of "Son of Man" as a messianic title is evident by his use here (Matt. 20:18), in juxtaposition to Peter's use of the title "Christ" (Matt. 16:16).[12].

Matthew recorded three main predictions of the death and resurrection of Christ Jesus.[13] Note that as the second prediction added certain particulars to the first, so the third announcement is more detailed than those that preceded it. In the final prediction, you can observe that not only was the Sanhedrin going to cause Jesus to suffer – as even the very first prediction had already declared – and not only was he going to be delivered over to that body, which action had been stipulated in the second announcement, but also:

- this highest court of the Jews (Sanhedrin) would condemn Christ Jesus to death, and after condemning him to death
- would hand him over to the Gentiles, with the result that

[12] NIV Study Bible, 1480
[13] 16:21, 17:22–23; 20:17–19.

- they, in turn would mock (according to Mark 10:34, "mock and spit upon") and scourge him, and that
- his death would be by crucifixion.

The climax of the third prediction is glorious, just as in the first two predictions: "and on the third day he shall be raised up" (resurrection which is our topic here).[14]

Observe that the last prediction is a detailed passion prediction that summarises the major events subsequent to Gethsemane. This scripture passage moves the story forward by taking Christ Jesus closer to Jerusalem and by forecasting for a third time and so emphasising upcoming events. As compared with the earlier passion predictions (Matt. 16:21, 17:22–23), the condemnation to death, deliverance to Gentiles, mocking, scourging, and crucifixion are new. Also take note that as Christ Jesus neared the end of his earthly mission, its shape became plainer. Also plainer is Christ Jesus' foreknowledge – which is not vague but exact and explicitly clear – of what was going to happen to him.

Observe that this passage is surrounded by two sizeable paragraphs having to do with eschatological rewards. But Matthew16: 17–19 are not about a disruptive foreign body; rather, they illustrate 19:30–20:16 in that Christ Jesus is the last (in his sufferings and death) who will be the first (when God exalts him).

Christ Jesus' prediction of his own death and ultimate triumph over death by resurrection is crucial to the Christian faith. It means that Christ Jesus was in full control of his own destiny and situation. It shows that he laid down his own life on the cross of his own accord and died, but also took back his life in his resurrected power to live forever.

In the following paragraphs, I will consult Paul the Apostle and theologian and seek his opinion about the significance of the resurrection of Christ Jesus. In Part One of this book, I cited several Pauline corpora and explained the importance and emphasis he placed on the crucified Christ Jesus on the cross. As the cross of Christ Jesus stands at the centre of Paul's theology, so also does the resurrection of Christ Jesus. The summation of Paul's theology is that Christ Jesus crucified is also he whom God raised from the dead. Understand that the significance of the

---

[14] Hendriksen, 742

crucified God cannot be grasped in isolation of the resurrected Lord and God who is Christ Jesus the saviour. Without the resurrection, the cross would be a cause for despair; and without the cross, the resurrection would be an escape from reality. Unless one died the death of all, the all would have little to celebrate in the resurrection of the one, other than to rejoice in his personal vindication.[15]

The resurrection of Christ Jesus is vital and occupies central ground in Paul's theology, to the extent that he stated it in the prelude of his epistle to the Romans: "And who through the spirit of holiness was declared with power to be the Son of God, by his resurrection from the dead: Jesus Christ our Lord" (Rom. 1:4). Here Paul put emphasis on the early Christian doctrine of faith and belief that Christ Jesus was appointed or designated Son of God at the resurrection. Christ Jesus is declared with power, and the main point is to put emphasis on Christ Jesus' exalted status because of his power of resurrection from the dead.[16] Paul attributed supremacy to Christ Jesus over King David and stated: "Regarding his Son, who as to his human nature was a descendant of David, and who through the spirit of holiness was declared with power to be the Son of God by his resurrection from the dead: Jesus Christ our Lord" (Rom. 1:3–4). The resurrected Son of God Jesus Christ is more powerful and holier than his ancestor King David.

Take note of the phrase "with power to be the Son of God", which does not express the inner-Trinitarian relationship of God the Father, God the Son, and God the Holy Spirit, but rather lays emphasis on the unique relationship of God the Son – Christ Jesus – to God the Father in the salvific process. For Paul, the resurrection makes a difference in that process. Just as the early Church looked on the resurrection as the event in Christ Jesus' existence by which he became "Lord" and "Messiah" to them (Acts 2:36), or earlier as Thomas declared, "My Lord and My God" (John 20:28) and applied to him apropos of it "you are my Son; today I have become your Father" (Ps. 2:7), so for Paul Christ Jesus was endowed

---

[15] James D. G. Dunn, *The Theology of Paul the Apostle* (London, 2008), 235.
[16] Craig C. Hill, "Romans", *The Oxford Bible Commentary*, 1088.

with a power of vivification at the resurrection (Philem. 3:10) and became of "vivifying Spirit" (1 Cor. 15:45).[17]

Matthew started his gospel with a summary of the genealogy of Jesus as follows: "A record of the genealogy of Jesus Christ the son of David, the son of Abraham" (Matt. 1:1). Here Matthew identified Jesus Christ as a descendant of Abraham from whom the Jewish nation was established and through whom "all people on earth will be blessed" (Gen. 12:3). Paul used this citation in his epistle to the Romans and emphasised the salvific work of Christ Jesus:

> Therefore, the promise comes by faith, so that it may be by grace and may be guaranteed to all Abraham's off-spring - not only to those who are of the law but also to those who are of the faith of Abraham. He is the father of us all. As it is written: "I have made you a father of many nations". He is our father in the sight of God, in whom he believed-the God who gives life to the dead and calls things that are not as though they were. (Rom. 4:16–17)

It is important to note that in this citation, Paul brought together "those who are of the law" and "those who are of the faith of Abraham" who are Jewish Christians and Gentile Christians, respectively. Paul alluded to the resurrection of Christ Jesus by saying that God gives life to the dead. As God the Father raised the physically dead Christ Jesus his son, so also Christ Jesus raises all those who are physically and spiritually dead who believe in him.

Paul emphasised the resurrection of the crucified Christ Jesus by saying that Abraham believed in "the God who gives life to the dead" (Rom. 4:17). Observe here that the first century Christians (both Jews and Gentiles) believed in God "who raised Jesus our Lord from the dead" (Rom. 4:24). The patristic father Abraham was justified because he believed in a God who brought life from the dead, so also all humankind is justified by believing in him "who raised Jesus our Lord from the dead".[18]

---

[17] Joseph A. Fitzmyer, "The Letter to the Romans", in *The New Jerome Bible Commentary*, 833.
[18] NIV Study Bible, 1677.

I present further analysis of the significance of the resurrection of Christ Jesus in the Pauline corpus in the following passages from Romans, in which Paul stated:

> We are therefore buried with him through baptism into death in order that, just as Christ was raised from the dead through the glory of the Father, we too may live a new life. If we have been united with him like this in his death, we will certainly also be united with him in his resurrection. (6:4–5)

> Now if we died with Christ, we believe that we will also live with him. For we know that since Christ was raised from dead, he cannot die again, death no longer has mastery over him. (6:8–9)

In these four verses, Paul made figurative statements and compares baptism, death, and resurrection. It is not my intention to discuss the ritual significance of baptism in the Christian dogma here. My main point is that baptism depicts graphically what happens as a result of the Christian's union with Christ, which comes with faith. Through faith, the Christian is united with Christ Jesus, just as through natural birth, all the people of the earth are united with Adam. As all humankind fell into sin and became subject to death by the deed of father Adam, so also all Christians now have died and been raised again (resurrected) with Christ Jesus. This is what baptism symbolises.

This analogy of baptism, death, and resurrection is emphasised in 6:8–9. I stand on holy ground when stating that as death is followed by resurrection in the experience of Christ Jesus, so the believer who dies with Christ Jesus is raised (resurrected) to a new quality of both moral and spiritual life on this earthly city now. Resurrection in the sense of a new birth is already a fact, and it is increasingly exerting its influence in the believer's new life.

Paul took the motif of death and resurrection to a different dimension and made an illustration from the institution of marriage in Romans 7:1–8 and concluded in 7:4: "So, my brothers, you also died to the law through the body of Christ, that you might belong to another, to him who was raised from the dead, in order that we might bear fruit to God". Observe that Paul drew his conclusion from the principle he stated in 7:1 and illustrated in 7:2–3. The Christian dies to sin and the law, but rises in righteousness with the resurrected body of Christ Jesus. The purpose of this union is to produce the fruit of holiness.

Understand that the "other man" is the glorified risen Christ Jesus, who as Lord and saviour takes control of every aspect of the believer now and then.[19] It is for that reason Paul stated "thanks be to God – through Jesus Christ our Lord!" (Romans 7:25). Jesus Christ becomes our Lord now and forever because he rose from the dead and is alive. Jesus Christ our Lord lives through his resurrection power. So also we live and shall live through our resurrection in the resurrection of Christ Jesus, our eternal Lord and God.

I continue with the significance of the resurrection by examining another Pauline scripture, Romans 8:11, 34: "And if the spirit of him who raised Jesus from the dead is living in you, he who raised Jesus from the dead will also give life to your mortal bodies through his spirit, who lives in you" (8:11). Paul continued with his logical presentation on the subject matter and stated: "Who is he that condemns? Christ Jesus, who died-more than that, who was raised to life-is at the right hand of God and is also interceding for us" (8:34).

Observe the significance of the resurrection in the two verses cited above and understand the following:

- The resurrection of the body is guaranteed to believers by the indwelling Holy Spirit, whose presence is evidenced by a spirit-controlled life.
- This spirit-controlled life in turn provides assurance that the believer's resurrection is certain even now.
- Because of his resurrection power, Christ Jesus is alive and seated at the right hand of God his Father now, as you read this book.
- It is the resurrection that has given him the divine position of power and authority in the city of God the Father.
- He is reigning in his resurrected power in the kingdom of his Abba Father and now interceding for all believers in him who are in this earthly city, but looking forward and journeying towards the city of God to be with the saviour forever.

---

[19] Fitzmyer, 850.

"The spirit of him who raised Jesus from the dead" is the spirit of the Father, to whom the efficiency of the resurrection is attributed. The power vivifying the believer is thus traced to its ultimate source, for the spirit is the manifestation of the Father's presence and power in the world since the resurrection of Christ Jesus and through it. The power of the resurrection will also give life to the believer's mortal body. This future tense expresses the role of the vivifying spirit in the eschatological resurrection of the believer. At his resurrection, Christ Jesus became the Father's glory both on earth and in heaven, and that is the principle of the raising believer.[20]

Paul juxtaposed the resurrection and the salvation in almost equal terms and stated "that if you confess with your mouth, 'Jesus is Lord' and believe in your heart that God raised him from the dead, you will be saved" (Rom. 10:9). "God raised [Christ Jesus] from the dead" is the bedrock truth of the Christian doctrine and the central thrust of apostolic preaching and teaching. Those who believe in the resurrection of Christ Jesus are already being saved in this earthly city and will finally be saved and be with the saviour, Christ Jesus, in the City of God.[21] Note here that Paul, as already shown elsewhere, laid emphasis upon the activity of God the Father in the resurrection of Christ Jesus, God the Son.

There are numerous other Pauline corpora which point to the momentousness of the resurrection in the Christian faith and dogma; but you will appreciate that it is impossible to meticulously examine each and every passage of the scriptures on the subject matter. However, before I bring this chapter to a close and turn my attention to the next chapter on the Christological significance of the resurrection, I bring to the fore Paul's verdict on the significance of the resurrection. He wittingly used an Old Testament agrarian term to make his final conclusion, saying, "But Christ has indeed been raised from the dead, the first fruits of those who have fallen asleep" (1 Cor. 15:20).

Observe here that Paul metaphorically compared the resurrection of Christ Jesus to "first fruits". The first fruits represent the first sheaf of the Jewish harvest which was set aside to be given to the Lord (Lev. 23:10–11, 17, 20) as a token that all the harvest belongs to the Lord and would be dedicated to him through dedicated lives. The first sheaf

---

[20] Fitzmyer, 853.
[21] NIV Study Bible, 1687.

is the most important and significant part of the harvest and must be dedicated to Yahweh God of Israel. But the resurrection of Christ Jesus is an unparalleled sacrifice, and the resurrection is beyond mortal imagination and comprehension. Christ Jesus who had been raised is the grand guarantee as well as the guarantor of the resurrection of all God's redeemed people (1 Thess. 4:13–18).

Paul established the truth of the resurrection of the dead, the holy dead, the dead in Christ Jesus, because Christ Jesus is indeed "the first fruit of those that sleep". Christ Jesus has truly risen himself, and he has risen in this very quality and character, as the first fruit – but not that material earthly first fruit of the Jewish harvest which was perishable. On the contrary, it is imperishable heavenly first fruit in the spiritual realm, and Christ Jesus reigns forever. As Christ Jesus has assuredly risen, so in his resurrection there is much given that the Jewish harvest in general should be accepted and blessed by the offering and acceptance of the first fruits.[22]

The resurrection of Christ Jesus is imperatively important in its divine sense because his resurrection stands as guarantee (himself being the guarantor) of all the resurrection of all believers in him. It is the resurrection of Christ Jesus that brought the work of salvation to its final and ultimate blissful and unblemished completion. One of the most important and common characteristics of the preaching of the Apostles (Peter and Paul) is the emphasis they placed on the resurrection of Christ Jesus. The Apostles witnessed the resurrection phenomenon of the risen Christ Jesus which assured them that all believers in him would in due course be raised also. The Apostles observed the Lord's Day (Sunday), a weekly memorial of the resurrection observed in place of the Sabbath Day (Saturday). On the Lord's Day, the Apostles celebrated the Holy Communion of thanksgiving (Eucharist), a thankful commemoration of the resurrection of Christ Jesus, which replaced the Passover celebration. Another sacrament of the Apostles is the baptism of believers, a reminder that all believers are buried with Christ Jesus and are also resurrected with him (1 Cor. 2:12). The teaching of the Apostles of "the risen Lord" Christ Jesus brought a sharp division between the Apostles and the rest of the Jewish teachers and strict observance of Mosaic Law in second-temple Judaism. The teaching and

---

[22] Matthew Henry, *Matthew Henry's Commentary on the Whole Bible* (Peabody, Massachusetts, 2008), 1819.

Dr Ibim Alfred

preaching of the resurrection also set the Apostles apart from all the other teachers of the ancient world.[23]

Finally, I state here that the significance of the resurrection of Christ Jesus is of first magnitude with divine blessings to all believers in him. The impact of the resurrection of Christ Jesus has brought about a radical revision in the earliest Christian understanding of how God the Father interacted with his world. The transition of the resurrection involves some sort of realignment of the interaction of God with his created humankind as well as his divine rule in heaven.[24]

---

[23] Henry, 1819.
[24] Dunn, 262.

196

Chapter 10

# RESURRECTION: CHRISTOLOGICAL SIGNIFICANCE

My main focal point in this chapter is to examine the Christological importance of the resurrection. Before I proceed to do my evaluation on the subject matter, it may be helpful to explain in this prelude the word *Christology*.

During the lifetime of Jesus, many groups as well as individual people – including the Sanhedrin (the Jewish Council) and Pontus Pilate – wanted to know who he was. For instance, the high priest said to Jesus, "I charge you under oath by the living God: Tell us if you are the Christ, the Son of God" (Matt. 26:63b). Matthew also stated: "Meanwhile Jesus stood before the governor, and the governor asked him 'Are you the King of the Jews?'" (Matt. 27:11a). From the citation above, it is necessary to understand the different mindsets of the Sanhedrin and Pilate about Jesus. The Jewish religious leaders thought that Jesus was claiming to be the most important expected religious leader: "Christ" the "Messiah" in the Jewish prophecy. On the other hand, Pilate was thinking that Jesus was a Jewish political figure who was "the King of the Jews" and would lead the Israelites against the Romans, helping them to defeat and usher out the Romans and liberate Palestine from the iron rule of Rome.

All people from every strata of life in Israel wanted to know Jesus' relationship to Yahweh of Israel. They wanted to know what he thought of himself and the purpose of his mission to Israel. This inquisitive attitude was compounded and intensified by his crucifixion, death, and resurrection. More than two millennia later, these issues are still being debated and discussed in a new dimension and on an ever-increasing scale.

I think this trend will probably continue for the next millennium if the world does not see the second advent of Christ Jesus himself. The vocabulary for the discussion of Christ Jesus which started in the first century in Israel and later spread to the Gentile nations which are still and will likely continue is known as *Christology*, which in Greek means "talk about Christ" (*Christ*, from the Greek *Christos*, is same word as the Hebrew *Messiah*, which means "anointed one"), just as *theology* means "talk about God". Discussion about Christ's identity is closely related to discussion of how he brings salvation to those who believe in him. Hence Christology has always been indissolubly connected with *soteriology*, or "talk about salvation".

## PAUL'S ADAM CHRISTOLOGY

I start my analysis of the Christological significance of the resurrection of Christ Jesus with Paul's Adam Christology. My main focus on the Adam Christology lies clearly in the death and resurrection of Christ Jesus. In this evaluation, I will cite two main important corpora of Paul in which he deliberately set Jesus alongside Adam as the one who answers to the clamant and long-standing emergence brought about for humankind by Adam's first disobedience. The two main scripture passages to be examined are Romans 5:12–21 and 1 Corinthians 15:20–22. But before I analyse these scriptures, I will spend a little time looking at Adam from the Old Testament perspective.

### Adam in the Old Testament

I begin with a summary account of Adam here which will help you to understand the rest of my explanation of Paul's Adam Christology. The book of Genesis gives an account of Adam as the first human, created by the Creator God in his own image on the sixth creative day (Gen. 1:27). Man was the climax of Yahweh's creative activity, and Yahweh "crowned him with glory and honour" and "made him rule" over the rest of creation (Ps. 8:5–8). Yahweh formed Adam (as a potter forms clay) out of dust from the ground (*dama*) and uniquely breathed into his nostrils the breath of life. The divine result of this was that the man became a living being.

Adam is the first human name ever recorded in the beginning of the beginning of the world, yet we notice that there are very few Scripture passages in the Old and New Testaments which record the proper name "Adam": Genesis 1:26, 2:4, 9–11, 3:17, 4:1–5, 5:1–5; Joshua 3:16; Hosea 6:7; Matthew 4:1; Luke 3:38; and 1 Timothy 2:13–14. That being said, the connotation of Adam is "mankind", a sense in which it occurs in the Old Testament about five hundred times.

Many attempts have been made to determine the etymology of the name "Adam", but so far there is no general consensus of the precise meaning. The understanding is that "mankind" does not come from the original Hebrew language, which makes it even more difficult to clarify the meaning. However, it is clear that the use of the word *dama* (ground) is juxtaposed with the name Adam in Genesis 2:7: "The Lord God formed the man from the dust of the ground and breathed into his nostrils the breath of life, and the man became a living being." Genesis 3:19 also gives a clue to the meaning of Adam when God said: "By the sweat of your brow you will eat your food until you return to the ground, since from it you were taken: for dust you are and to dust you will return." From the two citations, it is reasonable to infer, deduce, and conclude that the meaning of Adam is probably "ground". Legend has it that the ground or dust of the Garden of Eden in Mesopotamia was red, suggesting that Adam was of a red colour.

## Adam In The New Testament

Outside the Pauline corpora, Adam is referred to occasionally in the Gospels. Luke recorded the genealogy of Jesus and traced the family tree of Jesus to the first human being, Adam, and mentioned, among others, "the son of Enosh, the son of Seth, the son of Adam, the son of God" (Luke 3:38). Luke sets Adam at the head of Jesus' ancestors (although as the last name and in reverse order of Matthew 1:1), showing Jesus' relationship to the whole human race which he came to save. It is necessary to notice that by tracing the genealogy of Jesus down to Adam, who was a Gentile (the state of Israel was far off and yet to be established), perhaps Luke, also a Gentile, was making a point that both sin and salvation come to humankind from the same and one person in Adam. Although this came to fulfilment on a different timeline, in a different location, and in a different personality – and in a contrast of characters between Adam and Christ Jesus – Christ Jesus' kingship and kingdom is not confined to the catchment area in Israel (through Abraham) but extends to Eden, where the human race began through Adam, the beginner and the father of the human race.

The principal use of the figure of Adam in the Pauline literature is in contrast of Adam and Christ Jesus as stated above. This may also be alluded to in the Synoptic Gospels. For instance, Matthew recorded: "Then Jesus was led by the Spirit into the desert to be tempted by the devil" (Matt. 4:1). For a full record of the temptation of Christ Jesus, also see Matthew 4:1–11, Mark 1:12, and Luke 4:1–13. This testing of Christ Jesus is recorded to show that whereas Adam failed the great test and plunged the whole human race into sin (Gen. 3), Christ Jesus passed the same great test from the same Devil or Satan (in fact, Christ Jesus was in an even worse situation and environment than Adam).

Christ Jesus showed and demonstrated that he is faithful and divinely qualified to become the saviour for all those who accept and believe in his name in every nook and corner of the world. The temptation reflects the idea that Christ Jesus restored the state of mankind in Paradise which was lost through Adam in the Garden of Eden. Luke 3:38 referred to Adam as "the son of God", a phrase that Luke had already used for Jesus (Luke 1:35). As stated earlier, this would be a positive use of the story of Adam, because Christ Jesus is likened to Adam before his fall.

It is important to note that for Paul, there is more emphasis on the unlikeness in the midst of the likeness of Adam to Christ. This is true of both major Pauline literature in which he developed this idea: Romans 5:12–21 and 1 Corinthians 15, which will be my main textual analysis for the Paul's Adam Christology below.

## Adam's Death and Christ's Life Analogy

In Romans 5:12–21, Paul stated his Adam Christology analogy, drawing a contrast between Adam and Christ. Paul's aphorism for Christians is that Adam introduced sin and death into the world and Christ brought righteousness and life into the world. In Romans 5:12, Paul made a contrast between Adam and Christ Jesus. Adam, by sinning, set in motion a chain reaction of sin and its consequence by God's decree, which led to ultimate physical and spiritual death. Adam's disobedience brought an immediate and permanent detrimental relationship between the Creator God and the creature mankind through all ages of the world. But note, beloved child of God, that Christ Jesus, by his obedience, inaugurates a divine saving process in which those who believe in him receive God's gracious gift of righteousness and reign with him and obtain the eternal life of salvation. The Adam and Christ comparison begins in 5:12 and ends in 5:18, and these two verses sum up the whole passage. The characters of these two men also sum up the message of the book of Romans to this point. Another aphorism to understand is that Adam stands for man's condemnation (Rom. 1:18–3:20) while Christ Jesus stands for the believer's justification (Rom. 3:21–5:11).

Paul stated that "Death came to all men, because all sinned" (Rom. 5:12). Physical death is the penalty for the original sin from the original human, Adam. Physical death is also the symbol of spiritual death that can perpetually separate mankind from God. This is due to the fact that Adam's sin spiritually involved and contaminated the rest of the human race in condemnation because Adam was the father of all humankind. All the descendants from Cain onwards have inherited the vice of Adam's lasting sinful nature, which brings both physical and spiritual death. Adam by his sinful act of disobedience brought universal ruin to the whole of the human race on the earth.

The above analysis crystallises the Christological significance as I observe that Adam is the prototype of Christ, who through his righteous act of obedience brings universal blessing and salvation, but only to those who believe and have faith in him. Christ's righteous act brings justification that leads to eternal life through his resurrection, which gives salvation to all who acknowledge him as their Lord and saviour.[1] Paul alluded to the story in Genesis 2–3 to explain that the original sin of Adam and Eve was the cause of the universal misery of humankind. I thank God for the theology of Paul the Apostle in his Adam Christology analogy in Romans 5:12–21, which is the first and clearest enunciation of the universal baneful effect of Adam's sin on the human race as a whole.[2]

Please observe that in Romans 5:12–21, Paul turned to Adam as precedent (that is by way of counterexample) for the universality of Christ's atonement, without which there is no remittance of sin. Paul stated: "For just as through the disobedience of one man the many were made sinners, so also through the obedience of the one man the many will be made righteous" (5:19). Paul's divine logical statement is that if all humanity shared in Adam's disobedience, how much more might all humanity share in the obedience of Christ Jesus, the very and only Son of God. Paul's logical statement is based on the third chapter of Genesis, which recorded how "sin came into the world through one man". The proof of the ubiquity of sin is the universality of its consequence, which is both physical and spiritual death (Rom. 5:12, Gen. 3:3).

The significance of the resurrection of Christ Jesus is its ability to overturn or undo the death which was introduced by the disobedient act of Adam (which I shall develop and analyse in my consideration of 1 Corinthians 15:20–22 below). The Christological significance is that the proper order of creation which was lost in the fall of Adam is being fully restored.[3]

## SIGNIFICANCE OF THE RESURRECTION (1 COR. 15:20–22)

In previous parts of this book, I cited 1 Corinthians 15:20 when discussing the evidence of the resurrection of Christ Jesus. I stated that Paul categorically concluded and confirmed the resurrection based on

[1] NIV Study Bible, 1678.
[2] Joseph A. Fitzmyer, "Letter to the Romans", *The New Jerome Bible Commentary*, ed. with Raymond E. Brown and Roland E. Murphy (London, 2013), 845.
[3] Craig C. Hill, "Romans", *The Oxford Bible Commentary*, ed. John Barton and John Muddiman (Oxford, 2011), 1094.

the systematic and analytical presentation put forward in 1 Corinthians 15:3–8. My main focus here is to explain the significance of the Christological connection to the original sin of Adam and Eve. Paul wrote to the Corinthians and emphasised the physical resurrection and assured them that the resurrection of Christ Jesus had already taken place. He juxtaposed the disobedience of Adam, which brought both physical and spiritual death to the whole human race, with the righteous obedience of Christ Jesus, which brings both physical and spiritual resurrection. Paul stated that as death came to all humankind through a man, Adam (Gen. 3:17–19), so also the resurrection of the dead comes to all humankind through a man, Christ Jesus, who is the second Adam – "the last Adam" (1 Cor. 15:45, Rom. 5:12–21). As in Adam all human beings died (all who are his descendants suffer both physical and spiritual death), so in Christ Jesus all humankind is made alive and will eventually be made alive (resurrected). All who are "in Christ" – that is, who are connected to him by faith – will be made alive at the resurrection.[4] In Romans 5:12–21, Paul stated the Christological significance of the resurrection by juxtaposing Adam's sinfulness, which brought death and condemnation, and Christ's righteousness, which brings salvation and eternal life through his resurrection power.

The exegesis of the text under discussion, 1 Corinthians 15:20–22, is that prior to Paul's epistle, some in the church in Corinth said that there was no physical resurrection of the body. Paul wrote to the Corinthian Church in order to correct this false belief, because their doubts in the resurrection had challenged the basic element of his theology. Paul demonstrated the pivotal significance of the resurrection of Christ Jesus within the scheme of salvation by drawing a number of conclusions. This scheme of salvation is founded on an apocalyptic notion of the age of death being succeeded and overcome by an age of life, the latter being ushered in by a cosmic act of resurrection.[5] For Paul, the resurrection of Christ Jesus constitutes the first fruits of that cosmic act (1 Cor. 15:20, 23), which is the beginning of the harvest which heralds the proximity of the rest. Pairing Christ with Adam (Rom. 5:12–20), Paul found in Christ Jesus the start of a new

---

[4] John 5:25, 1 Thess. 4:16–17, Rev. 20:6.
[5] John Barclay, "Corinthians", *The Oxford Bible Commentary*, 1131.

humanity, in which the failures of the present (encapsulated in death) are replaced by the possibilities of the future (resurrection and life).

Please note that in 1 Corinthians 15:20–22, human logic gives way to the passion of the Apostle proclaiming a conviction that transcends reason and experience. What was done for Christ Jesus by God the Father can be done for others who believe in his resurrection power and saving grace; God's goodness indicates that it is possible and has already been done for others. Observe that the parallel between Adam and Christ is based on the idea of belonging (to Adam by nature; to Christ by decision) and causality (through Adam, who infected society with sin and death; and through Christ, who gives righteousness and life).[6]

I bring Paul's Adam Christology to an end by citing 1 Corinthians 15:45, where Paul stated, "So it is written: 'The first man Adam became a living being'; the last Adam, a life-giving spirit." Pay special attention to the two phrases "living being" and "life-giving spirit". Observe that the first was Adam, who had a natural body made of the dust of the ground (Gen. 2:7) and through whom a natural body is given to all his descendants through the ages. The other is the last Adam, Christ, the life-giving spirit (John 5:26) who, through his death and resurrection and at his second advent, will give to all his redeemed people a spiritual body which will be physical yet imperishable, without corruption, undefiled with purity in holiness that will be adaptable to live with the Holy God forever. That body will be similar to Christ's resurrected and glorified physical body (Phil. 3:21; Luke 24:36–43), which his disciples saw for a period of forty days before his ascension to the heavenly realm.

Paul vehemently and unequivocally stated that the last Adam (Christ) became a life-giving spirit, which is a strong affirmation of faith that the end would correspond to the beginning. It is necessary for you to understand that Jewish theology granted Adam a role in the eschaton (1 Enoch 85–90). This permitted Paul to present Christ as the last Adam. Through his resurrection, Christ Jesus became Lord (Rom. 1:3–4), and so in contrast to the first Adam, he is presented as a giver, not a recipient, of life.[7]

---

[6] Jerome Murphy-O'Connor, "The First Letter to the Corinthians", *The New Jerome Bible Commentary*, 812.

[7] Murphy-O'Connor, 813–814.

Please note that 1 Enoch is one of the books of Apocrypha which is not included in the majority of the various versions of the Bible. Hence, it is not possible to make an analysis of it, and it is of course beyond the scope and main motif of this book.

Finally, I conclude this discussion by stating that in 1 Corinthians 15:45, Paul presented the contrast between the natural body and the spiritual body by reference to their two prototypes: Adam, the first man, made from the dust, who became a living (but mortal) being (Gen. 2:7) and Christ, the final Adam, whose origin is not known even in heaven, and who is a life-giving (and immortal) sprit. Please understand that the present bodies of all believers in Christ Jesus are perishable as Adam (they bear the image of the man of dust), but the future resurrection bodies of all believers in Christ Jesus will bear the immortal and glorious body of the resurrected saviour and Lord. (1 Cor. 15:49).

Paul finished in this chapter with a triumphant declaration of the hope on which the whole Christian faith depends, and that is a "mystery" – not just the resurrected body of Christ Jesus, but a conundrum of the mission of Christ Jesus in toto, which is the motif of this book – which makes sense of the present in the light of the future (1 Cor. 15:51–58; 2:9–10).[8]

---

[8] Barclay, 1132.

Chapter 11

# FAITH IN THE RESURRECTION

In Chapter 10, I critically evaluated the Christological significance of the resurrection of Christ Jesus, which is based on Paul's Adam Christology. My main task in this chapter is to meticulously examine the importance of faith of the believer in the resurrection of Christ Jesus. I start my prelude with an explanation of the word *faith*. In order to do this and gain a good spiritual understanding of faith, I make citations from both the Old and New Testaments of the Bible, my main and divine authoritative source.

## FAITH: OLD TESTAMENT PERSPECTIVE

In the Old Testament, the word *faith* is found in only a few scripture passages.[1] Sadly, in most of these citations, the word is used in a negative form of "breaking faith" with the eternal God (El Olam) of Israel.[2] However, the rarity of the term in the Old Testament does not in any way indicate that it is not an important verb. I can say that faith in the Old Testament is indirectly and usually expressed by other verbs, such as *believe, trust,* or even *hope,* all of which are commonly found and used by Old Testament writers. *Faith, believe, hope, trust,* and *truth* in connection to salvation are stated and expressed in various ways in the Old Testament.[3]

---

[1] Exod. 21:8; Deut. 32:51; Josh. 22:16; Judg. 9:16; Hab. 2:4; Mal. 2:10.
[2] Deut. 32:51; Josh. 22:16; Isa. 14:33; Mal. 2:10, 11,14.
[3] J. D. Douglas, *New Bible Dictionary: Second Edition* (Leicester, 1994), 336.

I emphasise here that whatever other verbs are used in place of faith, the basic and fundamental expectation of the Christian is to have the right attitude towards God, which means having a firm and unshakable faith and trust in God Almighty (El Shaddai) that leads to eternal salvation in Christ Jesus. I find this absolute credence in King David, who stated:

> Trust in the Lord and do good, dwell in the land and enjoy safe pasture. Delight yourself in the Lord and he will give you the desires of your heart. Commit your way to the Lord; trust in him and he will do this: He will make your righteousness shine like the dawn, the justice of your cause like the noonday sun. (Ps. 37:3–6)

Dear beloved child of Christ Jesus, understand in the above citation that King David was wholly and utterly encouraging God's people of Israel to have an undivided, upright, and wholehearted trust in Yahweh. David inspired the people of Yahweh to put their trust in him – which was, in a way, telling them to live by faith alone. God's people are urged to trust the word of God as the Psalmist puts it: "Then I will answer the one who taunts me, for I trust in your word" (Ps. 119:42). In this passage, the "trust" may seem literary in the word of God, but a divine biblical interpretation reveals that this is faith in Yahweh himself. The writer of Proverbs put it in stronger and more unequivocal terms: "Trust in the Lord with all your heart and lean not on your own understanding" (Prov. 3:5). Here the writer instructed and encouraged his fellow people of Israel to trust God like their forefathers who trusted in God and were rescued, such as Caleb (Num.14:24, Deut. 1:36), David (1 Sam. 17:45–47), or King Hezekiah (Isa. 38:3). King David charged Solomon to serve God with wholehearted devotion as King of Israel (1 Chr. 28:9):

> And you my son Solomon, acknowledge the God of your father, and serve him with wholehearted devotion and with a willing mind, for the LORD searches every heart and understands every motive behind the thoughts. If you seek him, he will be found by you, but if you forsake him, he will reject you for ever. (1 Chr. 28:9)

Dear Child of God, please take note the consequences of not trusting and of forsaking the Lord. Yahweh frowns upon trust in one's own understanding and power. This thought is frequently and forcefully reiterated throughout the Old Testament. There are other Old Testament scriptures which support my discussion of how faith is being expressed.[4]

It is crystal clear that the people of the Old Testament thought of the Lord as the only one worthy of being trusted. They put not their trust in anything they did, or that other men did, or the good they did. Their trust indeed was solely and mainly in the God of Israel, who delivered and brought them out from slavery in Egypt. Sometimes this is picturesquely expressed. For instance, David stated: "The Lord is my rock, my fortress and my deliverer, my God is my rock, in whom I take refuge. He is my shield and the horn of my salvation, my stronghold" (Ps. 18:2).

In the discussion of faith, it is imperative to mention Abraham, who was the "father of faith" for both the Jews and the Gentiles. His whole life from the very beginning as recorded in Genesis gives evidence of a spirit of trustfulness of a deep faith in the God Most High (El Elyon).[5] The writer of Genesis stated that "Abraham believed the Lord, and he credited it to him as righteousness" (Gen. 15:6). This scripture passage is the first specific reference to faith in God's promises. It also teaches Christians that God graciously responds to people's faith by crediting righteousness to them (Heb. 11:17). Paul spoke of Abraham as "the father of all who believe" (Rom. 4:11).

## SPURGEON ON ABRAHAM'S FAITH

Here I present Charles Haddon Spurgeon's comments on Abraham's faith as follows:

Abraham justified by faith
'And he believed in the LORD; and he counted it to him for righteousness' Genesis 15: 6.
**The fact**
'He believed in the LORD'.

---

[4] Prov. 28:26, Isa. 42:17, Ezek. 33:13, Hos. 10:13, Hab. 2:18.
[5] Douglas, 366.

Leaving his country. Life in Canaan. Sodom.
Isaac's birth. Promises to him. Isaac's sacrifice.
Two sorts of faith:
(a) Historical or dead faith
(b) Living faith, producing deeds
**The result**
'He counted it to him for righteousness'.
(a) Sins forgiven
(b) Righteousness imputed – by faith
By it, gained God's favour and love, heaven, and eternal life.
These bring:
Peace How easy lies the head that does not ill!
Love When we are pure, we love God
Joy The justified person has true joy
Comfort All things work together for good
Security None can condemn, nor destroy
**As Abraham was saved, so must we be**
(a) Not by works, or Abraham would have been
(b) Not by ceremonies. Abraham believed before circumcision
(c) Reasons why sinners and Christians should believe God; exhortations to faith.[6]

# FAITH: NEW TESTAMENT PERSPECTIVE

Unlike the Old Testament, the New Testament features the term *faith* prominently; it is found more than 240 times. This abundant use of the word is to be understood against the background of the saving work of God in Christ Jesus. The central theme and thought in the New Testament is that God the Father sent his one and only son (Christ Jesus) to the world to be the saviour of the world. Christ Jesus accomplished mankind's salvation by dying an atoning death on Calvary's cross. Faith is the attitude whereby human

---

[6] Charles Haddon Spurgeon, *Spurgeon's Commentary on the Bible*, ed. by Robert Backhouse (London, 1997), 3.

beings abandon all reliance in their own efforts – whether deeds of piety, of ethical goodness, or of anything else – in order to obtain salvation in Christ Jesus. Faith is the attitude of complete and absolute trust in Christ Jesus and of wholly and holy dependence on him alone for all that salvation means.

When the Philippian jailer, who was in a state of panic and awesome fear, asked Paul and Silas the most important life-embracing question – "Sirs what must I do to be saved?" – Paul and Silas threw a lifeline answer to the spiritually drowning jailer and, without hesitation, said to him, "Believe in the Lord Jesus, and you will be saved – you and your household" (Acts 15:30–31). The evangelist John recorded the statement of Christ Jesus himself in this matter, that "whoever believes in him shall not perish but have eternal life" (John 3:16).

The word *faith* and its significance in the dogma of Christianity as recorded in the NT cannot be overemphasised. Please note that faith is clearly one of the most important concepts in the whole of the New Testament. Dear child of God, take the word of faith with you wherever you go at all times, and depend upon it in all situations and circumstances. Faith means abandoning all trust in one's own resources. It means casting oneself unreservedly on the mercy of God. Faith means laying hold of the promises of God (which are unseen and unsure in the eye of the world) in Christ Jesus; relying entirely on the finished work of the saviour for salvation; and depending on the power of the indwelling Holy Spirit of God for daily strength and sustenance. Faith implies complete reliance on God and full obedience to him.[7]

Perhaps the most famous definition of faith in the whole of Christian literature recorded in the New Testament is from the letter to the Hebrews where the writer said: "Now faith is being sure of what we hope for and certain of what we do not see!" (Heb. 11:1). This passage then turns to the very beginning of things: "By faith we understand that the universe was formed at God's command, so that what is seen was not made out of what was visible" (11:3). This is followed by an enumeration of a long history of acts of faith of noble characters in the Old Testament, from Abel and Noah through Abraham and Moses and Samuel and the prophets, ending with a list of the sufferings for their faith which men and women underwent. [8]

---

[7]  Douglas, 368.
[8]  *Christianity: The Complete Guide*, ed. John Bowden (London, 2005), 452.

# THE THEOLOGY OF MARTIN LUTHER ON FAITH (FIDE)

Before I bring my discussion of the New Testament perspective on faith to a close, it may be useful to make reference to Martin Luther, the legendary theologian of his time and founder of the Protestantism whose theology was based on *Sola fide* (justification through faith alone). Martin Luther (1483–1546) was a German monk, professor, and theologian whose quest for salvation ultimately led to the rise of the European Reformation and the division of Western Christianity. In Luther's lifetime, Pope Julius II had established a jubilee indulgence to raise funds for St Peter's in Rome.[9] While still a monk in the Augustinian order in Erfurt in Germany, Luther grew increasingly convinced of his inadequacy before God. Although he was true to his rule and observed what was expected of him, he felt that he could not meet the conditions set by God on his own works of deeds and righteousness.

Eventually, he began to doubt that sinful human beings could ever meet the divine expectations based on their own merits and credulous acts, and he became concerned with this question: "What if sinful man is unable to meet God's preconditions?" This perplexing question led him to his most significant theological insight. In his desperation to find an answer for his thirsty, hungry, and searching soul, he found one in the corpora of Paul: "For in the gospel a righteousness from God is revealed, a righteousness that is by faith from first to last; Just as it is written: 'The righteous will live by faith'" (Rom. 1:17). To be justified, to stand in a right relationship with God, a sinful human being could do nothing except live by faith and rejoice in God's grace, his undeserved and unmerited divine favour to all humanity. This was the founding principle of Luther's theology: *sola fide* (justification through faith alone). This represented a fundamental challenge to the theology and the praxis of the Medieval Roman Catholic Church, for it undermined the notion of good works, which meant that the religious culture associated with the practice (from the buying of indulgences and the giving of alms to the duties of penance and the struggles of confession) no longer had a role to play in the quest of salvation.[10]

---

[9] *Christianity*, 716.
[10] *Christianity*, 718.

I join Luther to state here that faith in the resurrection of Christ Jesus is all in all to the Christian. It is only faith and faith alone that can help the believer to trust the Lord and saviour Christ Jesus who, through his resurrection, brings salvation. As soon as the unbeliever or sinner has been prompted by the Holy Spirit of God, the soul of the unbeliever immediately and spontaneously turns to be believer and totally depends on faith in Christ Jesus for every and all aspect of life for life. For Luther and all believers in all ages, righteousness is a free gift from God which the believer receives individually by faith alone and not a demand of God in the law.

This message is the true spiritual treasure of the Church which was obscured in Luther's lifetime either by misunderstanding or a lack of hermeneutic knowledge of grace. Grace is not infused into the soul as a supernatural quality with an admixture of works and merit. It is a pure and divine spiritual unseen miracle which becomes possible by the faith of the believer in his or her first time accepting Christ Jesus as personal saviour, and continues in daily communion with God for the rest of the lifetime of the believer. This is holy and heavenly good news for all believers through the ages.

## FAITH IN THE RESURRECTION: AN EXPOSITION

I have examined the word *faith* from both an Old Testament and New Testament perspective. The main purpose of this section is to make a further analysis of the significance of faith in Christian dogma with regards to the resurrection. Faith of the believer in Christ Jesus in regards to the resurrection is paramount, because it is by faith (not by works) that the Christian believes and is assured that physical death in this earthly city will not be in vain (eternal darkness in hell) because the death of the Lord and saviour Christ Jesus – who is the author and the finisher of our faith – is not fruitless. This faith is built on Holy and solid ground which is Christ Jesus the Rock, where all the past, present, and future believers stand. Faith of the Christian in the resurrection of Christ Jesus is even most significant, as it raises an eschatological hope in the sense that all believers in Christ Jesus will be raised (resurrected) and have eternal life of salvation that emanates from him.

Paul analysed the faith of Abraham (father of faith of both the Jews and the Gentiles) in Romans 4:9–24 and drew an analogy between the faith of Abraham and that of the Gentile Christians of his generation. Paul stated: "Faith was reckoned to Abraham as righteousness". Paul explained further and stated: "Now the word, 'it was reckoned to him' were written not for [Abraham's] sake alone, but for ours also, it will be reckoned to all who believe in God the Father who raised Christ Jesus, God the Son from the dead" (Rom. 4:22–24). Paul's main point here is that it was faith, not the law that made Abraham believe in Yahweh the Father. What was credited to him as righteousness is the same faith which makes the Gentile Christians believe in the resurrected Christ Jesus who gives them salvation. In other words, both the Jews and the Gentiles are now descendants of Abraham because they share the same faith as their common ancestor in faith, Abraham, and both are now justified and have obtained salvation because of the death and resurrection of Christ Jesus.

Paul drew together the faith of Abraham and the faith of the Gentile Christians and concluded that the ultimate purpose is salvation in the resurrected Christ Jesus. The story of Abraham shows that for both Jews and Gentiles, there is only one way of justification, which is the way of faith that leads to salvation. As Abraham was justified because he believed in a God who brought life from the dead, so also the Gentiles are being justified by believing "in him who raised Jesus our Lord from the dead" (Rom. 4:24).

It is imperative to understand that Abraham was justified by faith before his circumcision, therefore independently of it. Paul argued from the sequence as presented in Genesis itself. As recorded in Genesis 15, Abraham's faith was counted as uprightness; but only in Genesis 17 was he circumcised. Therefore, circumcision has nothing to do with justification. Circumcision is called the "sign of the covenant" between Yahweh and Abraham's family (Acts 7:8). Observe that later, rabbis regarded circumcision as the sign of the Mosaic covenant, for it served to distinguish Israel from the rest of the nations (Judg. 14:3, 1 Sam. 14:6).

Significantly, Paul avoided mention of the covenant and the "sign of the covenant", because for him, that is no longer relevant. The main thing is the "seal of uprightness". Paul seemed to have identified the covenant too much with the law. Here he insinuated that God's true covenant was made with people of faith. When Abraham put his faith in Yahweh and was justified, he was as uncircumcised as any Gentile of his generation. His spiritual paternity is thus established vis-à-vis all believing Gentiles (Gal. 3:7). The Jews too must follow the footsteps of their forefather Abraham, imitating his faith, if they are to be regarded as his children.[11]

I stress here that Abraham's spiritual paternity is an important aspect of God's salvific plan for all humanity. Paul talked about the law without explicitly condemning it, but implicitly concluded that the world needs a dispensation independent of the law of Moses. The divine fact is that Mosaic Law and the promise for "all the families of the earth" to be blessed through Abraham in Genesis 12:3 cannot exist side by side; the law must yield to faith which had been accepted and pleased God before the enactment of the law. For Paul, faith is the all-important element which involves and embraces God's gracious and unconditional promise. Accordingly, the one who lives by faith lives also by grace, and the promise holds good not only for the Jews but more importantly for all humanity who share the faith of Abraham, who stands as the faithful father for both the Jews and the Gentiles who now share the same salvation from Christ Jesus.

Abraham's faith is the type of Christian faith and the pattern for Christian faith. Its objective is the same: belief in God who makes the dead live. Dear child of God, be glad and rejoice as you read about the faith of Abraham that the same accreditation is given to you. Your faith may not be recorded for people to read like Abraham's, but believe and be assured that your uprightness is already recorded to your credit which sets you free now and at the eschatological judgement. Abraham's faith in God who makes the dead live (Rom. 4:17) foreshadowed the Christian's faith in God who, in a unique sense, raised Christ Jesus from the dead.

According to the dogma of Judaism, all nations on earth except the one and only Yahweh's nation of Israel are Gentile sinners without God and without eternal hope of salvation. Here I postulate that before Abraham was called to become "God's friend", he was just like any other person of his generation who had no hope and was without God. Abraham was

---

[11] Joseph A. Fitzmyer, "The Letter to the Romans", in *The New Jerome Bible Commentary*, ed. with Raymond E. Brown and Roland E. Murphy (London, 2013), 842.

called by God to leave his family and country not because of his good deeds or services he had rendered to God – which would have made him more righteous than his contemporaries in Haran. It was God's absolute and divine prerogative to call Abraham and his descendants to become a special people of the God of Abraham, Isaac, and Jacob.

To reiterate my main point, which is faith, I cite another statement in Genesis that says: "Abraham believed the Lord, and he credited it to him as righteousness" (Gen. 15:6). The author's statement that Yahweh "credited it to him as righteousness" – which forms the climax of the episode – has rightly been seen as one of the most significant in both the Old and New Testaments scriptures. This has been taken – together with other instances of Abraham's faith, particularly his readiness to leave Haran and his willingness to sacrifice his only son, Isaac – as the foundation of the doctrine of justification by faith. Abraham's readiness to trust God's promise cannot be doubted.[12]

Abraham's faith is an interface between the Old and the New Testaments, and it is a divine source and fountain from which both the Jews and the Gentiles draw their faith and ultimate salvation in Christ Jesus. Because of the central ground on Abraham's faith, I go back once again to Romans and cite what the author said about that faith: "What then shall we say that Abraham, our forefather, discovered in this matter? If in fact, Abraham was justified by works, he had something to boast about– but not before God. What does the scripture say? 'Abraham believed God, and it was credited to him as righteousness'" (Rom. 4:1–3). Abraham was the greatest patriarch of the Jewish nation and was the true example of a justified person (Jas. 2:21–23). The Jews of Jesus' time used Abraham as an example of justification by works, but Paul holds him up as a shining example of righteousness by faith (Gal. 3:6–9).

Observe here that Paul made his first and strongest argument by appealing to the founding figure of Judaism, Abraham. What goes to Abraham and his descendants of God's people of Israel is also applicable to the rest of the Gentile nations through Christ Jesus, Paul could assume.

A careful and prayerful reading of Romans 4 reveals the basic argument as comparatively simple and direct. According to Gen. 15:6,

---

[12] R. N. Whybroy, "Genesis", *The Oxford Bible Commentary*, ed. John Barton and John Muddiman (Oxford, 2011), 50–51.

Abraham "believed God, and it was credited to him as righteousness". What Abraham actually believed was God's promise that he would have an offspring who was at that time not in view. This is an unshakable faith in God who commanded him to leave Haran for good. Yahweh considered it to be credited to him as righteousness.

Abraham, as stated earlier, was not himself upright; instead, because of his faith, he was treated ("was credited", a positive entry in "book-keeping term which figuratively applied to human conduct", as in Ps. 106:31) as though he was righteous. His standing before God as a righteous man was a gift, not an attainment from Yahweh who is righteous, merciful, and gracious to his people irrespective of their sins (Rom. 3:24). This righteousness was imputed to Abraham prior to the giving of the Mosaic Law, prior even to the requirement of physical circumcision.

The fact that Abraham had not yet been circumcised (that comes two chapters later in Genesis 17) allowed Paul to claim that Abraham is an exemplar and ancestor of all the faithful ones, both Jews and Gentiles (Rom. 3:9–12). As proof, Paul cited Genesis 17:5 ("I have made you a father of many nations", Rom. 4:17–18). Gentile Christians were for Paul (and probably for most other Jewish Christians) "children of Abraham". In Romans 4:19–21, Paul vividly described the quality of Abraham's faith. Abraham believed God against all opposing considerations, circumstances, conditions, and contrary appearances. The final reality to Abraham was God's fidelity. Yahweh does what he has promised. The character of faith as trust is nowhere more clearly depicted in Paul's writings.

Please note that in Romans 4:23–24, the content of justification by faith is spelled out more fully; that is, belief in God who "raised Jesus our Lord from the dead. He was delivered over to death for our sins and was raised to life for our justification". This formulaic of Jesus is traditional and ultimately depends upon Isaiah 52:13–53, which tells of the suffering servant on whom "the Lord laid our sins" (Isa. 53:6), who "bore their sins" (Isa. 53:12), and who will "justify many" (Isa. 53:11).

God's righteousness that called Abraham and his descendants to become the people of God has been gracefully and divinely extended to the Gentiles, who are now "a chosen people, a royal priesthood, a holy nation, a people belong to God" (1 Pet. 2:9). The righteousness of the Gentiles does not, however, come directly from Abraham or through Mosaic Law, but rather through Christ Jesus who is the end of the work and the law. Paul repeatedly said that it was not through the law that Abraham and his offspring received the promise that he would be heir of the world, but through the righteousness that comes by faith (Rom. 4:13). Here I share the same opinion with Paul and state that the righteousness of Abraham came through faith vis-à-vis the righteousness of the Gentiles; for this righteousness from God comes through faith in Christ Jesus to all who believe in him. There is no difference, for all have sinned and fallen short of the glory of God (Rom. 3:22–23).

The main point is the truth that all (both Jews and Gentiles) have sinned, and there is no difference between the two, as sin has no confinement. The righteousness of God which inspired faith in Abraham in the Old Testament is now the righteousness of God through faith in the resurrected Christ Jesus to all believers in the New Testamant. It is not the righteousness of the Jews or the Gentiles that has made them upright before God. On the contrary, it is the divine act of righteousness of Christ Jesus that has brought salvation to both Jews and Gentiles. Paul stated that "For in Christ Jesus neither circumcision nor uncircumcision has any value. The only thing that counts is faith which expresses itself through love" (Gal. 5:6).

Faith is not a mere intellectual assent (Jas 2:18–19), but a living trust in God's grace that expresses itself in acts of love (1 Thess. 1:3). God lavishes his whole, total, and complete love upon humankind through Christ Jesus, his one and only son. Christ Jesus himself expressed this divine love of God and said: "For God so loved the world that he gave his one and only Son, that whoever believes in him shall not perish, but have eternal life" (John 3:16). This is the most frequently cited scripture in the New Testament, and it is the divine interface between the Old and the New Testaments. The grand truth is that it is the divine love of God the Father that brings salvation through Christ Jesus. This salvation is grounded and anchored in the love of the Lord and saviour Christ Jesus thought faith that cannot be shaken or removed.

The focal point of faith for both Jews and Gentiles is now Christ Jesus, the central and unifying ground and the gravitational pull. As Paul stated: "Here there is no Greek or Jew, circumcised or uncircumcised, barbarian, Scythian, salve or free, but Christ is all, and is in all" (Col. 3:11). As stated

217

earlier, Christ Jesus transcends all barriers and unifies people from every culture and race, and breaks the social and economic stratum of the whole wide world. By faith in Christ Jesus, such distinction and dichotomy are no longer necessary and significant. Christ Jesus alone is the one and only God who matters to the believer.

Theretofore, God is the God for both the Jews as well as the Gentiles, and justifies both the circumcised and the uncircumcised by *sola fide* because of his righteousness, which he has shown in Christ Jesus. That means there is only one true source of righteousness (Christ Jesus) for both the people of God of Israel and the Gentile nations of believers. Here I stand on holy ground and stress again that God's righteousness is the gravitational pull for both Jews and Gentiles which first came to the Jews of Abraham and secondly to the Gentiles of Christ Jesus. The righteousness of God to the Jews of Abraham, which laid the foundation of Judaism, is the same righteousness of God to the Gentiles of Christ Jesus that established Christianity.

The holy truth is that Christ Jesus has amalgamated both the Jews and the Gentiles in the sense that all those who believe in him (both Jews and Gentiles) now have "the right to become children of God". It is vital to note that the Jews of the children of Abraham cannot be righteous and therefore cannot obtain salvation because they are descendants of Abraham. Now their righteousness and salvation come from Christ Jesus, and it is only those (both Jews and Gentiles) who have faith and belief in him that are being saved. These children are "not born of natural descent nor human decision or a husband's will, but born of God" (John 1:12–13).

"The right to become children of God" may have originally referred to wisdom finding a dwelling in the souls of the righteous. It has been recast to reflect the soteriology of the Gospel.[13] Note that all that was said before John 1:12–13 and all that follows after has its centre in those who "become children of God". The grand truth is that it is only by belief and faith that the Gentiles have life in Christ Jesus and become "children of God".[14]

The dominant and focal motif in the above analysis is God Almighty, who through his righteous act makes it possible for both Jews and Gentiles

---

[13] Pheme Perkins, "The Gospel According to John", in *The New Jerome Bible Commentary*, 951.

[14] John Kieffer, *The Oxford Bible Commentary*, 962–963.

to be in the same holy universal family of God the Creator through the final and ultimate work of salvation in Christ Jesus. In summation of the above discussion, I state that one righteousness of God leads to one salvation through one work of Christ Jesus for all people in all nations who now form an extraordinary big and universal holy family of the one holy God of the one universe.

Finally, I draw my conclusion in this chapter on faith in the resurrection in the Christian belief by bringing the two pivotal terms "resurrection" and "faith" together. The resurrection of the dead is the very centre of the eschatological transformation, the dividing line between time and eternality. The expectation of the resurrection of all believers is the distinctive faith of all Christians through the ages, and it is the one and only hope that marks off the Christians' doctrine from the pagan wisdom of the ancient and modern world. The resurrection is the one and only vision of lasting happiness promised to all Christians, and if the theme of the resurrection of the dead is taken away from the doctrine and teaching in Christianity, all the Christian ideologies and dogmas will automatically and instantaneously fall apart, crumble, and perish. The main ground for the Christian divine present and eschatological hope is based on the resurrection of Christ Jesus as the culmination of his work of salvation.[15]

---

[15] Allen D. Fitzerald, *Augustine through the Ages: an Encyclopaedia* (Cambridge, 1999), 722.

# Chapter 12

# THE RESURRECTION: A DIVINE TRUE EVENT

The main thrust in this chapter is to probe the validity of the resurrection of Christ Jesus and ascertain that he indeed rose from the dead. I will do this by citing some of the prominent theologians who have contributed in this area and compare their viewpoints and comments with the biblical (especially the New Testament) accounts of the resurrection of Christ Jesus.

The starting point is probably the statement that came from the holy lips of Christ Jesus himself who is the resurrection. Immediately after Peter confessed that Jesus is the Christ, "Jesus then began to teach them that 'the Son of Man must suffer many things and be rejected by the elders, chief priests and teachers of the law, and that he must be killed and after three days rise again" (Mark 8: 31). This is the first of Jesus' passion predictions which will be addressed in subsequent paragraphs below; meanwhile, my interest here is the key phrase "after three days rise again". The synoptic writers who recorded the passion prediction wrote that Christ Jesus said this regarding the resurrection that would happen within three days of his death and burial.

# SIGNIFICANCE OF THE "THREE DAYS" IN THE OLD TESTAMENT

What is the meaning and significance of three days? Is there any Old Testament scripture which can help to explain its meaning and make it easy to understand the phrase? The appropriate place to start in the Old Testament is the dialogue reported by the writer of the book of Esther:

> Then Esther sent this reply to Mordecai "Go, gather together all the Jews who are in Susa, and fast for me. Do not eat or drink for three days, night or day. I and my maids will fast as you do. When this is done, I will go to the King, even though it is against the law. And if I perish, I perish". On the third day Esther put on her royal robes and stood in the inner court of the palace, in front of the King's hall. (Esther 4:15, 5:1)

In this account, Esther fasted for three days and ended her fast on the third day. She disobeyed royal law and custom of Persia (Esther 4:9–11) and took the risk, even taking her life in her hands, and appeared before King Xerxes. At the end of the three-day fast, she rose up and put on her royal robes (kept aside her sackcloth and ashes for the three-day fast) and presented herself to the king in order to save the lives of the Jews in Susa.

Note that in this account, Esther prefigured Christ Jesus. As Esther fasted for three days and presented herself to the king in order to save the Jews in defiance of the law, in the same way Christ Jesus stayed in the grave for a three-day period, disobeyed the natural order of death, and rose on the third day (leaving behind in the grave the strips of linen as well as the burial cloth) and put on his royal robe and diadem to bring salvation not only to the Jews but to the whole Gentile world.

The salvation Esther brought to the Jews – but reluctantly and after forceful persuasion and pressure by Mordecai – was only for the Jews in Susa and was on temporary basis; but Christ Jesus brings salvation for all, which is permanent for the whole wide world. More significantly, he voluntarily laid down his life according to his will and in agreement with God the Father. He laid down his life of his divine volition according to his statement: "The reason my father loves me is that I lay down my life – only to take it up again. No-one takes it from me, but I lay it down of my own accord. I have authority to lay it down and authority to take it up again" (John 10:17–18). The fact that Christ Jesus would die (and eventually died) for his people runs through all four Gospels. In his death, both the love and the plan of God the Father are involved, as well as the authority God the Father gave to God the Son. Christ Jesus obediently chose to die; otherwise, no one would have had the power to put him on the cross to kill him.[1]

Another Old Testament scripture which helps us to understand the phrase "three days" is Hosea 6:1–2. Here the prophet pleaded with the unrepentant people of Israel and said to them: "Come, let us return to the Lord. He has torn us to pieces, but he will heal us; he has injured us, but he will bind up our wounds. After two days he will revive us; on the third day he will restore us that we may live in his presence." Israel's hope for restoration is depicted in this citation. Here Hosea spoke of both physical and spiritual restoration of Israel by Yahweh if only they would wholeheartedly repent and return to Israel's God of Abraham, Isaac, and Jacob.

With regards to our main focus in this section, which is resurrection, there is no doubt that Hosea spoke about it by using the verbs *revive* and *restore* as they appear together in the same sentence. There are other Old Testament prophets who used similar expressions to denote resurrection (Isa. 26:19). There are impressive parallels between Hosea 5–6 and 13–14 (lion image, 5:14, 13:7–8; exhortation to return, 6:1, 14:1; dew or rain imagery, 6:3, 14:4), and since in 13 it is clearly a case of death (see 13:1, 9, 14), this should also be the case in 5–6 (mainly Ezek. 47 for death and resurrection as symbolic of exile and restoration).[2]

The phrases "two days" or "third day" mean after a short while, a brief time, and anything which lasts for a moment – a temporary situation or event. It is probable that this particular scripture is an allusion to the resurrection of Christ Jesus (which is my focal point here); and the time expressed by the "third day" is to be a type and figure of Christ's rising on the third day, which was fulfilled eight hundred years later. I will address

[1] NIV Study Bible, 1584.
[2] John Day, "Hosea", in *The Oxford Bible Commentary*, ed. John Barton and John Muddiman (Oxford, 2011), 574–575.

the resurrection of Christ Jesus on the third day on the first Easter Sunday morning later in my conclusion, but in the meantime, I will put forward the theories and opinions of some of the theologians in the Enlightenment era who cast doubt on the resurrection.

## THE ENLIGHTENMENT PERIOD: THE RESURRECTION – NON-EVENT?

The movement which is now generally known as the Enlightenment in the eighteenth century ushered in a period of considerable uncertainty for Christianity in Western Europe and North America (see background in Chapter 8). The Enlightenment period saw the intellectual credentials of Christianity itself (rather than any one of its specific forms) facing major threats on a number of fronts.[3] Over the centuries, the question of the relation between faith and history often comes to focus on the question of the resurrection of Christ Jesus. The main question here is more specific: whether Christ Jesus was indeed raised from the death – and if it happened, what that event might mean. Before I proceed, I want to state here unequivocally that I do wholeheartedly belief and certain that Christ Jesus physically rose from the dead.

The Enlightenment emphasis on the omni-competence of reason and the importance of contemporary analogues to past events led to the development of an intensely sceptical attitude toward the resurrection in the eighteen century.[4] In this chapter, I will summarise the opinions of some of the theologians who were very critical with negative viewpoints of the resurrection, and also cite Holy Scripture to help us to decide whether their opinions and teachings are false or true.

I start with Gotthold Ephraim Lessing, a prominent theologian in the Enlightenment period. Lessing expressed a negative opinion on the resurrection contrary to the biblical account of the Gospel writers, Pauline corpora, and other scriptures in the New Testament. Lessing was very sceptical of the resurrection of Christ Jesus because he did not have a personal, first-hand experience of the resurrection like the biblical

---

[3] Alister E. McGrath, *Christian Theology: An Introduction* (4th edn, Oxford, 2007), 66.
[4] McGrath, 320.

Apostles, who saw the post-resurrected physical body of Christ Jesus. Lessing put forward his sceptical viewpoint forcefully and questioned the validity of the resurrection, saying, "So why should he be asked to believe in something which he has not seen?" The problem of chronological distance, according to Lessing, was made all the more acute on account of his doubts (which he evidently assumed others would share) concerning the reliability of the eyewitness reports: "Our faith eventually rests upon the authority of others, rather than the authority of our own experience and rational reflection upon it."

Lessing made further comments on the resurrection, including the following statement:

> That, then, is the ugly great ditch which I cannot cross, however often and however earnestly I have tried to make this leap. If anyone can help me to cross it. I implore them to do so. And so I repeat what I said earlier. I do not for one moment deny that Christ performed miracles. But since the truths of these miracles has completely ceased to be demonstrable by miracles happening in the present, they are no more than reports of miracles. I deny that they could and should bind me to have the smallest faith in the other teachings of Jesus.

In other words, according to Lessing, as men and women are not raised from the dead in his lifetime now, why should we believe that such a thing happened in the past?[5] Lessing argued that being forced and obliged to accept the testimony of others on the resurrection is tantamount to compromising on human intellectual autonomy. He stated that there is no contemporary parallel for classic resurrection. That is to say, the resurrection cannot be experienced by modern persons of the Enlightenment era and beyond in the Western modernism. For these and other reasons, Lessing put the New Testament account on the resurrection into doubt and concluded that the resurrection was little more than a misunderstanding and "non-event".

---

[5] McGrath, 320.

You may have noticed that the main point raised by Lessing was his confession that he did not experience the resurrection phenomenon and did not personally see the post-resurrected physical body of Christ Jesus the way the first-century Jewish Apostles like Peter, John, Mary, or even Paul, and more than five hundred disciples over a period of forty days. If that was the main reason (which was the case) for Lessing to conclude that the resurrection is a "non-event", the whole of his Christian faith and belief "stood on a shaky and sinking ground" and his Christian credo was seriously questionable and doubtful. Why? The reason is of fundamental importance because the entire Bible (both Old and New Testaments) stands on faith alone and not by sight. In other words, the Bible's main principle is "believing is seeing" and not "seeing is believing".

Lessing based his argument on the resurrection of Christ Jesus on the latter instead of the former. Just to emphasize the principle of faith in the Bible, I cite two main patristics in the very beginning of the Old Testament. It is faith and belief which led Noah to galvanise himself into action and build the ark, as "[Noah] did everything just as God commanded him" in order to preserve Yahweh's creation. Noah had not experienced a flood or had knowledge of a previous flood, but by faith he believed that what God said to him and commanded him to do would surely and truly be fulfilled (Gen. 6:22). The father of faith, Abraham, "believed the Lord, and he credited it to him as righteousness" (Gen. 15:6). Abraham is the "father of all who believed" (Rom. 4:11), and this is the first specific reference to faith in God's promises. It also teaches that God graciously responds to a man's faith by crediting righteousness to him (Heb. 11:7).

I confront Lessing and those who share a similar viewpoint on the resurrection with the following questions:

- Did Lessing personally see and observe God when he created the universe by his own unequivocal and explicit authoritative command and personally cast man and moulded Adam in his own image, and blessed both Adam and Eve to increase in number and multiply? (Gen. 1–2)
- Was Lessing present in the Garden of Eden when Adam and Eve committed the sin of disobedience which brought God's anger upon them and their descendants? (Gen. 3)

- Did he see and hear from God when Noah was instructed by God to build the ark, or did Lessing himself experience the flood with Noah? (Gen. 6–8)
- Was Lessing a contemporary of Abraham in Haran and heard God when the Lord said, "Leave your country, your people and your father's household and go to the land I will show you"? (Gen. 12:1)
- Did Lessing observe the Exodus of the Hebrews from Egypt, and was he one of them who crossed both the Red Sea and the Jordan River via usual and unnatural phenomenon wrought by the divine power of Yahweh of Israel (Exod. 14:15–31, Jos. 3–4)?
- Did Lessing participate or help Joshua to establish the Jewish nation in the land of Palestine? (Jos. 5:13–12:24).
- Did he help Moses to write the Pentateuch of the Old Testament?
- Did Lessing see and observe the virgin birth of Christ Jesus? (Matt. 1:18–25; Luke 1:26–2:20).
- Was he one of the disciples of Christ Jesus who were with him from the beginning to the end of his ministry in Palestine?
- Did Lessing see all the mighty and wonderful miracles Christ Jesus performed and all the good works he did?
- Did Lessing know the four gospel writers and the authors of the epistles and agree with them in all their accounts and recordings in the New Testament except the doctrine of the resurrection?
- Did Lessing join John the Apostle to receive the "revelation of Jesus Christ, which God gave him to show his servants what must soon take place"? (Rev. 1:1)

These probing questions together with Hebrews 11 refer to some of the major events in both the Old and the New Testaments that culminated in the resurrection of Christ Jesus with the ultimate work of salvation for the seeds of Adam and Eve. These questions also give a clear and divine message that the people of God (both in the Old and New Testaments) carried out extraordinary tasks and did great exploits for their God in varied and difficult situations and circumstances through the ages because of their faith in their God. That is to say that Holy Scripture from Genesis to Revelation must be accepted wholeheartedly by faith alone and nothing else.

Faith is the flagship and bulwark in the entire Bible, and it is because of this that the author of Hebrews 11 defined faith as "being sure of what we hope for and certain of what we do not see". The writer listed the names of those who were commended for their faith and enumerated their acts for recognition for their faithfulness, which started with the faithful Abel. Among the acts these faithful ones were commended for, the author included those who "were tortured and refused to be released, so that they might gain a better resurrection" (Heb. 11:35).

With regards to the subject matter which is resurrection, Christ Jesus who is the resurrection said to Thomas, "Because you have seen me, you believed, blessed are those who have not seen yet have believed" (John 20:29). This is the concluding blessing which drooped from the holy lips of Christ Jesus that guarantees that all those Christians who have believed without seeing the resurrection but believe in faith are not different from the first disciples and those named in Hebrews 11, including all those names outside the New Testament. They all share and obtain the same salvation in Christ Jesus. Their faith is grounded in the presence of the Lord Christ Jesus through the Holy Spirit.[6]

In John's Gospel, besides 13:17, this is the only formula using *blessed*. This blessedness concerns the future believers who Christ Jesus had already prayed for in John 17:20–24. Here Christ Jesus said: "My prayer is not for them alone. I pray also for those who will believe in me through their message" (17:20). Christ Jesus had just spoken of the mission and the sanctification of his followers (17:18–19). He was confident his disciples would spread the gospel, and he prayed for those who would believe as a result.

Be encouraged that Christ Jesus has already prayed for you and he is still interceding for you as a believer. Though you did not see his resurrected physical body, you believe he rose from the dead. Surely you will also be raised up on the last day of his second advent. Thomas should have believed without seeing the marks of the cruel nails and fierce spear. However, his negative doubt turned out with a positive outcome as he exclaimed "My Lord and my God!" (John 20:28). Thomas clearly made

---

[6] Pheme Perkins, "The Gospel According to John", in *The New Jerome Bible Commentary*, ed. Raymond E. Brown, Joseph A. Fitzmyer, and Roland E. Murphy (London, 2013), 984.

his confession wholeheartedly which is an act of solid and steadfast faith in Christ Jesus. This confession is the highest point of faith, and for the first time in the New Testament, Jesus is confessed not just as "you are the Christ" but most significantly, "My Lord and my God".

There is no doubt that Jesus is elevated and exalted to the highest divine level of Yahweh of Israel. The Jews worship only one God of Abraham, Isaac and Jacob, but for a Jew (Thomas) to proclaim Jesus (man) as "God" is not dogmatism and contrary to monotheism in Judaism. The Holy Spirit of the Father who prompted Peter to confess Jesus as "the Christ" is the same spirit which revealed to Thomas that Jesus is both Lord and God. Christ Jesus is not John the Baptist, Elijah, Jeremiah, or one of the prophets, but "Lord and God". No other title or description is good or adequate enough for him in his divinity except "Lord and God". Be sure that he is your Lord and God in all and every aspect and moment in your life. That is all you need now here in this earthly city, and it will lead you ultimately to your desired city of God.

Finally, I conclude my remarks on Lessing by citing one of Paul's corpora in Romans 1:17: "For in the gospel a righteousness from God is revealed, a righteousness that by faith from first to last, just as it is written, 'the righteous will live by faith.'" The key phrase here is "faith from first to last", which is taken to refer to the requirement of faith alone (sola fide). Faith is the all-inclusive word for everything in the scripture from the Old Testament to the New Testament; "from the first to last" and from the "beginning to the end".

I totally and utterly disagree and reject the opinion of "non-event" which Lessing expressed on the resurrection. I think Lessing put too much emphasis on sight and experience. The pivotal point from Genesis to Revelation in the Bible is faith, and Christians live by faith, not by sight. All the righteous people of God through the ages live by faith, and it is paramount that both the Jews and the Gentiles who have faith in the Lord Christ Jesus should be prompted by the Holy Spirit to accept the whole and not part of the Bible in faithfulness and in divine obedience.

Another author who was very critical of the resurrection was the modern theologian David Friedrich Strauss, who regarded the resurrection as a "myth". Strauss devised a radical approach to the event of the resurrection of Christ Jesus. He noticed that the resurrection is of central importance to the Christian faith. He therefore placed the original classic belief of the resurrection at the purely subjective level and stated that the belief in the resurrection is not to be explained as a response to a life objectively restored but is a subjective concept in the mind of the first disciples and subsequent followers of Christ Jesus.

According to him, faith in the resurrection of Christ Jesus is an outcome of an exaggerated recollection of the personality of Jesus himself by which a memory has been projected into the idea of a living presence. For that reason, Strauss stated that a dead Christ Jesus is thus transfigured into an imaginary risen Christ Jesus who is a "mythical" risen Christ Jesus. Strauss's opinion was that the resurrection of Christ Jesus is a myth and a reflection of the gospel writers' social condition and cultural outlook in Israel in the first century.[7]

I totally and utterly disagree with Strauss for dismissing the resurrection as a myth. His effort and reason to conclude that the resurrection is a myth is tantamount to trying to square the circle. The whole of his Christian faith, belief, and theology was seriously topsy-turvy. For him to sweep aside the resurrection event and regard it as myth means that the whole of the divine Bible story from Genesis to Revelation is mythological. What did Strauss mean by the word *myth*? Generally, a myth is a traditional or legendary story, usually concerning some being or hero or event, with or without a determinable basis of fact or a natural explanation, especially one that is concerned with deities or demigods and explains some practice, rite, or phenomenon of nature. Myth can also be explained as a traditional story, especially one concerning the early history of a people or explaining a natural or social phenomenon.

I have earlier shown that the Bible is full of legendary stories, heroes, and events which the children of God in both the Old and New Testaments believe to be true and dependable with determinable basis of fact, the only and one source of which is from the Almighty God, Israel's Yahweh, who is worthy to be trusted in all generations and at all times. There are more than seventy important events in the Bible which are not mythology, but rather apparent, clear, and intelligible milestones divinely planned and excellently executed by the omniscient God himself. Among these events are the birth, mission, crucifixion, and resurrection of Christ Jesus; his ten

---

[7] McGrath, 321.

glorious appearances; his great commission; and his ascension. All these events (not in part but the whole) pertaining to Christ Jesus as recorded in the four Gospels are divinely interwoven and culminate in the glorious and ultimate result of his victorious resurrection which wrought salvation.

The Bible, not in part but as a whole, is the handiwork of God the Father, as Paul stated: "All scripture is God breathed and is useful for teaching, rebuking, correcting, and training in righteousness" (2 Tim. 3:16). Paul asserted here that all the events, including the resurrection phenomenon recorded in both the Old and the New Testaments, are considered equal in authority and value. Peter affirmed that God's active involvement in the writing of scripture is so powerful and awesome that what is written is the infallible and authoritative word of God (2 Pet. 1:20–21). I have more to discuss under the subheading "Evidence of the Resurrection", which will show support for my viewpoint of the truth of the resurrection.

McGrath in his book enumerated the work of other theologians who postulated and expressed similar views to Lessing and Strauss in the Enlightenment era. They all made a common conclusion and stated that belief in an objective resurrection of Christ Jesus might have been properly legitimate and intelligible in the first century but cannot be taken seriously in the modern age. They solidified their points by stating that it is impossible to use electric light and radio equipment and, when ill, to claim the assistance of modern medical and clinical discoveries, and at the same time believe in the New Testament world of spirits and miracles. They forcefully and emphatically stated that a modern scientific and existential world view means that the New Testament is now discarded and unintelligible. All in all, they concluded that the resurrection is to be regarded as non-event, a myth, a mythical event, an historical event, and an event of dubious historicity, pure and simple.[8]

Please note that I do not concur with the opinions and theories which have been postulated by those theologians, and I believe that the effort and evidence they provided to dismiss the resurrection event is too flimsy and without substance. I will support this last statement below.

---

[8] McGrath, 322.

## Evidence of the Resurrection

The evidence of the resurrection which has been recorded and presented by the four gospel writers, as well as the author of the Acts of the Apostles, Paul's corpora, and writers of other epistles, and what has been unfolded in the book of Revelation, are far too numerous and unequivocally more convincing than the scanty, unsatisfactory opinions and viewpoints presented by those theologians of the Enlightenment era. In any case, it will be unfair and academically empty and unsound to dismiss their opinion just with the last statement without presenting better and more substantiated evidence that will surpass the viewpoints of the sceptical theologians of the resurrection. In order to do this, I will present evidence based in the account recorded in the New Testament – the only divine authoritative and reliable source of information on the subject matter of the resurrection of Christ Jesus and his free gift of salvation which form the Christian theology of Christology and Soteriology.

I think it is appropriate to start the evidence of the resurrection with the dialogue between Christ Jesus the Lord and Martha, the sister of Lazarus, in the initially sad event but eventually happy occasion of the resurrection of Lazarus:

> "Lord", Martha said to Jesus, "if you had been here, my brother would not have died. But I know that even now God will give you whatever you ask." Jesus said to her, "your brother will rise again". Martha answered, "I know he will rise again in the resurrection at the last day". Jesus said to her, "I am the resurrection and the life. He who believes in me will live, even though he dies; and whoever lives and believes in me will never die. Do you believe this?" "Yes, Lord", she told him, "I believe that you are the Christ, the Son of God, who was to come into the world." (John 11:21–27)

It is imperative to understand the above statements of Christ Jesus. He did not just say that he *gives* resurrection and life, but that he *is* the resurrection and life. In some way, these are identified with him, and his nature is that final death is impossible for him.

Christ Jesus said that he himself is life (John 14:6; Acts 3:15; Heb. 7:16); not only that, but he conveys life to all believers in him so that final death will never triumph over them (1 Cor. 15:54–57). In this dialogue, Christ Jesus authoritatively and unequivocally declared that he is the resurrection and the life. Both the resurrection and the life are rooted in him and directly come from him (Rom. 6:8–9; Col. 1:18; 1 Thess. 4:16).

Dear believer in the resurrection of Christ Jesus, please take note of the sequence of the words which came from the divine lips of the Lord. First the resurrection, and then the life, because resurrection opens the pearly gates to immortality in heaven. Christ Jesus is the resurrection and the life in person (John 1:3–4). Christ Jesus is the full and blessed life of God in all his glorious attributes: omniscience, omnipresence, omnipotence, loving kindness, mercy, holiness, and more. As such, he is also the cause, source, or fountain of the believers' glorious resurrection and of their everlasting life. Praise be to God the Father, because Christ Jesus who is God the Son lives forever, and all believers in him shall live eternally and reign with him in his kingdom which shall never end. Christ Jesus is the prince and originator of life, and he is forever the conqueror of both physical and spiritual death.[9]

I have stated in the previous section that Christ Jesus himself predicted that he would die and after three days come back to life. The authors of the four Gospels gave detailed accounts of the escalation of events which culminated in the ultimate and eventual crucifixion of Christ Jesus. They also presented literal and graphic records of how Christ Jesus died and showed that he was indeed and really dead; and they gave a full and comprehensive account of how his burial took place. In fact, they recorded how the tomb of Christ Jesus was secured because of the effort and request made by the chief priest and the Pharisees – as ironically they wanted to make sure that the resurrection of Christ Jesus, which he had predicted, did not come through by any means of deception by his disciples.

The gospel writers stated that the women went to the tomb which had been sealed with a heavy stone and was guarded by well-armed Roman soldiers. The women approached the grave of Christ Jesus and contemplated how to get help for the removal of the heavy stone on top of the tomb. The four gospel storytellers recorded the scene of the heavenly

[9] William Hendriksen, *New Testament on John*, 150.

person who the women thought to be a gardener who eventually turned out to be an angel of God Almighty who gave them the unexpected and surprising good news: "Do not be afraid, for I know that you are looking for Jesus, who was crucified. He is not here; he has risen, just as he said. Come and see the place where he lay. Then go quickly and tell his disciples: He has risen from the dead and is going ahead of you into Galilee. There you will see him. Now I have told you" (Matt. 28:5–7).

The heavenly messenger of God did not stop at telling the women that Christ Jesus has risen; reassuringly, he added, "Come and see the place where he lay". According to Mark 16:5, by this time the women were already inside the tomb. However, the angel bid them to come even closer, so that they might see whatever was there to be seen – not only the empty tomb which showed that "He is not here" but also "the linen bandages lying there, and the sweatband not lying with the linen bandages but folded up in a place by itself" (John 20:7). The angel showed the scene to the women who must convince themselves that everything is orderly in this tomb. The women must gain the confidence of the fact that no disciples have been there to physically remove the body, nor have enemies pillaged the tomb. In either case the bandages would no longer have been present.

The women, just like Peter and John that same morning, had to see that the Lord Christ Jesus was indeed and truly restored from temporary death to glorious and eternal life. Christ Jesus himself graciously, of his own divine accord, removed the bandages and the sweatband. He left them behind because these are for the dead, and he had provided for himself a garment such as was worn by the living, as he was no longer dead but alive. Christ Jesus calmly and majestically put everything in its place for the dead in the tomb, and departed from the tomb gloriously and ascended to heaven, where he is now preparing a place for you. After completion he will descend (second advent) and take you home, where you will spend eternity with him in his kingdom.

Dear begotten and beloved child of the risen living Christ Jesus, I implore you to reject the poisonous ideas and ill-conceived opinions of the theologians of the Enlightenment era who were sceptical of the resurrection of Christ Jesus. In addition to what has been presented above, you might have read or heard similar negative and antichrist viewpoints about the resurrection. I sincerely and earnestly implore you in the name of the resurrected Christ Jesus to dismiss and dispel all contrary opinions on the resurrection. They are from the Devil, who is the deceiver and father of liars. For you to believe that Christ Jesus rose from the dead is the first and most blissful step; it is perfect, marvellous, and wonderful in the sight of God. However, that on its own is not good enough.

As you read this book, my earnest and fervent prayer is that it should feed and nourish you spiritually and help you also to learn and know more for yourself the kind of saviour who actually rose from the dead. Christ Jesus who was resurrected is the same God who voluntarily went to the cross and died. He is a compassionate, kind, merciful, and loving redeemer who healed the sick, cleansed the lepers, physically and spiritually fed the hungry, comforted the mourners, raised the dead, and pardoned sinners even as he hung on the cross. Careful biblical study of the resurrection account overwhelms and surpasses the few unsubstantiated reasons of the sceptics of the resurrection.[10]

The literal and graphic presentation by the gospel narrators in the New Testament about the resurrection of Christ Jesus is too compelling and convincing. It cannot be simply brushed aside, dismissed, or cancelled with a stroke of a pen by a handful of theologians of doubtful belief and corrupt faith. Furthermore, on the proof of the resurrection, Luke also stated: "After [Jesus] suffering, he showed himself to those men [Apostles] and gave many convincing proofs that he was alive. He appeared to them over a period of forty days and spoke about the Kingdom of God" (Acts 1:3). Dear believer in the resurrection of Christ Jesus, it will be a spiritually profitable exercise if you can devote quiet time with the risen Lord and saviour Christ Jesus to study the resurrection appearances.[11] An analysis of these passages shows that Christ Jesus made ten post-resurrection bodily appearances altogether in different places and at various times.

I have meticulously and extensively examined the resurrection event of Christ Jesus and commented on several important points, but in this paragraph it may be useful to explain the phrase "over a period of forty days". I think the number forty is symbolic as recorded in Acts 1:3 and divinely presented. I do not know whether Luke derived it from an existing tradition concerning the duration of the resurrection appearances or

[10] William Hendriksen, *New Testament on Matthew*, 991.
[11] Matt. 28:1–20; Luke 24:1–53; John 20:1–29; 1 Cor. 15:3–8.

invented it himself, but that is a different matter. I believe that Luke presented an accurate record of a period of forty days as he himself had "carefully investigated everything from the beginning" (Luke1:3). In fact, Luke was an eyewitness of the activities of the Holy Spirit which galvanised the Apostles into action, and he also participated in the missionary journeys of Apostle Paul (Acts 16:16). I think the period of forty days is understood as the sufficient space of time for the preparation of the Apostles to be witnesses of the resurrected Christ Jesus (Acts 13:31). There are other furnished precedents for such a rounded forty-day period of preparation, such as Genesis 8:6 (Noah). Exodus 24:18, 34: 28 (Moses); Numbers 13:25 (Israelite explorers of the land of Canaan), Numbers 14:33–34 (Israelites in desert); and 1 Kings 19:8 (Elijah).

I make further analysis of the forty-day period in the New Testament and understand that it was the period of Jesus' fasting and temptation, which preceded his first preaching (Luke 4:2, 14–15), although the Gospel did not stress its preparation aspect. There is also a heavenly relationship between the forty days appearances and the fiftieth day of Pentecost just "in a few days" (Acts 1:5). The day of the Pentecost came ten days later than the forty days period of the appearances after the resurrection of Christ Jesus. In order words, the ascension of Christ Jesus occurred forty days after the resurrection, and the Holy Spirit came at Pentecost ten days after the ascension.[12]

Paul, in his first epistle to the Corinthians, stated:

> For what I received I passed on to you as of first importance, that Christ died for our sins according to the Scriptures, that he was buried, that he was raised on the third day according to the scriptures, and that he appeared to Peter, and then to the Twelve. After that, he appeared to more than five hundred of the brothers at the same time, most of whom are still living, though some have fallen asleep. Then he appeared to James, then to all the apostles, and last of all he appeared to me also, as to one abnormally born. (1 Cor. 15:3–7)

---

[12] Richard J. Dillon, "Acts of the Apostles", *The New Jerome Bible Commentary*, 727.

In this citation, Paul recorded six resurrection appearances. It is vital to note here that Paul summarises the central and main heart of the gospel of Christ Jesus as follows:

- Christ died for our sins, not his own (Heb. 7:27).
- He was buried (confirmation that he really physically died).
- He was raised from the dead on the third day. The appearance to Peter is the one mentioned in Luke 24:34, which occurred on the first Easter Sunday morning. The appearance to the Twelve probably took place on the same Sunday but in the evening (Luke 24:36–43; John 20:19–23). "The Twelve" seems to have been used to refer to the group of the original Apostles, although Judas was no longer with them (notice, however, that the eleven disciples, the eleven Apostles, or "the Eleven" are referred to in Matt. 28:16; Mark 16:14; Luke 24:9, 33: Acts 1:26). Paul included the appearance of "more than five hundred", which is a large crowd, mainly to help bolster the faith of those Corinthians who evidently had some doubts about the resurrection of Christ Jesus (1 Cor. 5:12). Paul also added to the list of the Apostles the name of James, who was the half-brother of Christ Jesus (Matt. 13:55), who did not believe in Christ Jesus before the crucifixion and resurrection (John 7:5) but afterwards joined the apostolic band (Acts 1:14) and later became prominent in the Jerusalem Church (Acts 15:13). However, it is not clear in the New Testament when, how, and where this appearance to James took place.
- Last of all, but of most significance, Christ Jesus appeared to Paul himself in his post-resurrection body. This appearance to Paul came several years after the resurrection.[13]

The purpose of the above analysis of the resurrection appearances of Christ Jesus is to support the event of the resurrection and utterly and totally condemn and dismiss unequivocally the ungodly and antichrist opinions of theologians of the Enlightenment era. Even today, some ministers of God still cast doubt on the resurrection phenomenon.

For the sake of argument, let's say that all the disciples who saw the post-resurrection body of Christ Jesus were deceived. It was all a figment

---

[13] NIV Study Bible, 1721.

of their imagination, perhaps due to lack of or inadequate education, understanding, and knowledge. The probing question here is what happened to Paul the persecutor of the disciples of Christ Jesus? According to Paul, Christ Jesus also appeared to him "as to one abnormally born".

Luke recorded Saul's (Paul) extraordinary conversion from Judaism as a persecutor of "the way" who was later persecuted because of "the way" (Acts 9). Later in Acts 21:37–22:5, Luke recorded Paul's address to the crowd. In his defence, Paul began with his credentials as a prominent Jew and a persecutor of the disciples of Christ Jesus. Paul explained that he was not just an ordinary Jew, but rather he was born a Jew and had a strict Jewish upbringing. He studied under the tutelage of legendary Gamaliel (Acts 5:4) and had completed his training in the Jewish law. There is no doubt that Paul was extraordinary and extremely zealous in his Jewish faith. He was not just a passive observer of the Mosaic Law; he actually put his Jewish religious faith into action against the followers of Christ Jesus.

Luke stated: "Meanwhile, Saul was still breathing out murderous threats against the Lord's disciples. He went to the high priest and asked him for letters to the synagogues in Damascus, so that if he found any there who belonged to the Way, whether men or women, he might take them as prisoners to Jerusalem" (Acts 9:1–2). In his address to the crowd in Jerusalem, Paul directly appealed to the high priest as someone who could testify to the truth of what he was saying. As cited above, Paul had even pursued the Christians beyond Jerusalem by obtaining special permission to hunt them down in Damascus. As you may have noticed, this is an impressive set of credentials for Paul, which show his indisputable good background as a zealous Jew and guardian of Mosaic Law.[14]

Paul was one of the most educated person in his generation, a fervently dedicated observer of Mosaic Law, and a fierce persecutor of the Jewish Christians of his own generation. He was trained and brought up in the strictest teaching of Judaism under the tutelage of "a Pharisee named Gamaliel, a teacher of the law, who was honoured by all people" and a prominent member of the Sanhedrin, which was the Jewish Supreme Court (Acts 5:34). Paul was probably the most educated, knowledgeable, and intelligible Apostle of Christ Jesus, and he was well acquainted with the

---

[14] Stephen Gaukroger, "Acts Free to Live", *Crossway Bible Guides* (Nottingham,1993) 183–184.

237

Jewish laws and tradition. He was very zealous about the new sect of the Way and wanted to protect Judaism by all means, which led him to bitterly hostile to the followers of Christ Jesus. He wanted to make sure that "the Way" came to an abrupt end in its embryonic stage and did not to develop to become "the way to eternity and salvation for all people on earth".

The appearance of the resurrected Christ Jesus to Paul as he travelled on the road to Damascus to take the followers of Christ Jesus as prisoner made an indelible impact in his mind, which is recounted in Acts 22:4–21. Paul was very frank and emphatic that he saw the post-resurrection physical living body of Christ Jesus. Indeed, he was so sure of this that he devoted the rest of his life to serving the risen Christ Jesus who appeared to him. Paul was probably converted (the Damascus experience) within five years of the crucifixion and, of course, the resurrection of Christ Jesus. That being the case, the evidence for the crucifixion, resurrection, and especially the appearance of Christ Jesus in bodily form to him would have been very fresh and remained so as a photographic image in his mind, which persisted and became absolutely permanent throughout his missionary journeys as the Apostle for the Gentiles.

It is worth noticing that the original Apostles, including Paul and those who followed them, were ready and willing to go to prison and even be martyrs (which happened to most of them) for the sake of Christ Jesus because of their conviction of the resurrection phenomenon that some had observed, although others believed by faith.

I now bring this chapter to a close by stating that the resurrection of Christ Jesus is not a myth, mythical event of dubious historicity, or a figment of the imagination of the disciples in a state of hallucination. Hallucination comes to those who are in some sense prepared and looking forward for it. From the detailed presentation above of the resurrection, there is no evidence in the New Testament to show that the disciples were in a state of hallucination. Hallucination is an individual experience, whereas in the case of the resurrection, there were more than five hundred people at one time who saw the bodily form of the resurrected Christ Jesus all at once. The disciples saw the risen Lord in various locations and at different periods over forty days and observed many convincing proofs from him that he was alive (Acts 1:2–3, 38–40). The key statement in Acts 1:3 is "he showed himself to these men and gave many convincing proofs that he was alive". It may be possible to deceive all people, but it is impossible to deceive all people all the time at same time.

In order to dispel speculation, myth, hallucination, uncertainty, or any related negative ideas regarding the resurrection, Christ Jesus appeared to his disciples. This is Luke's account:

> While they were still talking about this, Jesus himself stood among them and said to them, "peace be with you". They were startled and frightened, thinking they saw a ghost. He said to them, "Why are you troubled, and why do doubts rise in your minds? Look at my hands and my feet. It is I myself! Touch and see; a ghost does not have flesh and bones, as you see I have". When he had said this, he showed them his hands and feet. And while they still did not believe it because of joy and amazement, he asked them, "Do you have anything here to eat?" They gave him a piece of broiled fish, and he took it and ate it in their presence. (Luke 24: 36–43)

Christ Jesus knows the hearts and minds of his disciples and all believers in him through the ages. He appeared to his disciples, "stood among them" mysteriously, and spoke to them as their risen Lord in order to quell their doubts and also dismiss uncertainty in the hearts and minds of all subsequent believers regarding his resurrection. The words from the divine lips of the living Lord were not only for his original Jewish Apostles of the first century but are also addressed in anticipation to all those who believe in him through the ages.

Christ Jesus noticed that his disciples were filled with fear and doubt, and so he directed their attention to his hands and feet. According to John, "He showed them his hands and side" (John 20:20). What Christ Jesus wanted to show to them was undoubtedly the stigmata, the marks of his crucifixion. Dear believer in the resurrected Christ Jesus, take comfort from the fact that Christ Jesus is always sympathetic, loving, merciful, and kind; and he is the same Lord and saviour before and after his crucifixion and resurrection. With marvellous condescension and humility he stood among his "startled and frightened" disciples and showed them his hands, feet and side". This physical appearance and demonstration of Christ Jesus is in no doubt to assure and prove to them that he is not a ghost but is indeed their resurrected Lord and saviour, and because he lives and reigns for ever, all his disciples through all the ages also live and reign with him for eternity. The risen Lord and saviour ate a piece of broiled fish in their presence, not because he was hungry and needed any earthly food; but to convince and confirm to them that they were not looking at a ghost but seeing and gazing on the resurrected Christ Jesus the Crucified God who died on the cross temporarily but now lives forever and brings salvation to the whole wide world.[15]

There is absolutely no grounds to regard the resurrection as a non-event, mythical event, or event of dubious historicity or hallucination. The resurrection is real, and it is the final and grand act of God the Father and his divine intervention in his righteousness to complete the ultimate and supreme work of salvation through the death of Christ Jesus on the cross and his resurrection power.

The resurrection is no flash-in the-pan experience, a glimpse of Christ Jesus in an unexpected moment. The enduring and proven fact for more than two millennia is that Christ Jesus is alive forever. As stated earlier, the resurrection is not phantom or a figment of the imagination of a few disciples. The disciples saw the post-resurrected body of Christ Jesus, he instructed and taught them, he performed post-resurrected miracles, and he prepared breakfast and ate with them. This is not the normal behaviour of a ghost or hallucinatory act. If Christ Jesus was in fact permanently dead and did not resurrect; then God built his living Church on dilution, which is an unthinkable conclusion.

The secret of how Christ Jesus sets people free from their sins through his death and resurrection cannot be grasped and set into words. It is the experience of being grasped when words fail, and all we can do is point to the divine and true story of the resurrection phenomenon and expose ourselves to the experience.[16]

---

[15] William Hendriksen, *New Testament on Luke*, 1074.
[16] Stephen Verney, *Into the New Age* (Glasgow, 1976), 58.

## Chapter 13

# RESURRECTION: ESCHATOLOGICAL DIMENSION

In Chapter 9, I analysed the significance of the resurrection phenomenon and its importance to the Christian faith, and I critically examined the validity of it. The primary purpose of this chapter is to ascertain whether the work of salvation would have been possible without the resurrection event. My main task in this chapter is to make an in-depth exposition of the word *salvation*, juxtapose it with the word *resurrection*, and critically examine both of them together. These two nomenclatures are the two dominant watchwords in this chapter.

In previous chapters, I critically analysed and evaluated salvation and resurrection. I also examined their significance, showed the evidence, and stated that resurrection and salvation are divinely linked in Christ Jesus. Without the resurrection phenomenon, there would be no eternal salvation. Most of my discussion has focused on the past and present elements of resurrection and salvation.

The main focal point of this chapter is to examine the eschatological dimension of the resurrection and the salvation. In other words, this chapter will unveil for you the aspects of resurrection and salvation which are yet to happen and await final fulfilment. I will start with the "yet to happen" in the resurrection.

# ESCHATOLOGICAL DIMENSION OF THE RESURRECTION

Eschatology is not an easy word to explain or define. It has to do with the study of the "last things" – events that will bring history and this cosmos to a close. That being said, eschatology can also be explained in a variety of senses. For instant, the word *eschatology* can be used to describe the fate of an individual believer's soul after death, the termination of this world order and a setting up of another, and events like the last judgement and the resurrection of the dead. Eschatology is also a convenient way of referring to future hopes about the coming of God's kingdom on earth, irrespective of whether they involve an ending of the historical process. Generally, biblical study shows that many scripture passages, both Old and New Testaments, are about a future hope and its fulfilment in this world as well as in the kingdom of God in heaven.

The heart of the first century Christian message is eschatology, which is the second advent of the promised Messiah king and the pouring out of the prophetic spirit that will bring about the ultimate eternal salvation. In fact, Luke forcefully and emphatically brought to the fore the second advent of Christ Jesus in the very beginning of his second book:

> After he said this, he was taken up before their very eyes, and a cloud hid him from their sight. They were looking intently up into the sky as he was going, when suddenly two men dressed in white stood beside them. "Men of Galilee," they said, "why do you stand here looking into the sky? This same Jesus, who has been taken from you into heaven, will come back in the same way you have seen him go into heaven." (Acts 1:9–11).

I speculate that these "two men dressed in white" were angels who represented God the Father and God the Holy Spirit. They were united to divinely confirm the finished work of salvation in Christ Jesus the Son of God. They also made a grand promise of the second advent (which pointed to the eschatological resurrection and salvation) of Christ Jesus.

Here, I also see the Trinity in action, like the time when Christ Jesus was baptised before he formally and officially started his earthly mission (Luke

3:21–22). Observe God's glorious and wonderful plan of salvation in Christ Jesus. As God the Father and God the Holy Spirit confirmed the earthly mission of salvation of God the Son in the beginning, so in the same way they proclaimed the accomplished mission of salvation in Christ Jesus at the end of the earthly mission. For most New Testament writers (especially Paul, as will be discussed below), there is still an unfulfilled element of salvation currently awaiting its final and ultimate stage of completion. Believers may have tasted the heavenly gift and participated in the Holy Spirit now (Heb. 6:4), but they are eagerly and honestly looking forward to a future of bliss, and while they wait, they endure privations, merely tasting the glory to come.

The resurrection of Christ Jesus is the main message of the apostolic writers in the New Testament, and for both the first century Jewish and Gentile Christians, it was an essential component of future hope. To speak of the resurrection of the dead was to speak of the life of the age to come. The New Testament has recorded in many passages the very close link between resurrection and the eschatological events (e.g. 1 Cor. 15:20 and Phil. 3:21). The resurrection of Christ Jesus is the first fruits, an anticipation in which a key feature of the last days (Acts 2:17) becomes a reality in the old age.[1]

It is a tested and proven fact for more than two millennia that the resurrection of Christ Jesus has already brought a new heavenly quality to the fabric and life of his followers both as individuals and as the Christian community of the Church of Christ Jesus. The first-century Jewish believers, the early Gentile Christians, and all subsequent Christians believe that because of the resurrection of Christ Jesus, resurrection has already taken place in part and temporarily; but not in full and permanently in their lives in the present age in this earthly city. The full and permanent resurrection will come to reality in the future, which is the eschatological hope for all believers through the ages.

In view of the importance of the New Testament material to the shaping of Christian thinking on eschatology, I shall consider some of its main sources. The two main sources of outstanding importance are the preaching of Christ Jesus himself before and after his death on the cross and resurrection, and the corpora of the Apostle Paul. In the following paragraphs, I will examine the two main sources, starting with the one from Christ Jesus himself who is the resurrection and life both now and future.

---

[1] *Christianity: The Complete Guide*, ed. John Bowden (London, 2005), 379–380.

# ESCHATOLOGY: THE PREACHING OF CHRIST JESUS

The dominant theme in the preaching of Christ Jesus which relates to eschatology is the coming of the kingdom of heaven or God. The phrase "kingdom of heaven or God" was rare in contemporary Jewish writings and was widely regarded as one of the most distinctive aspects of the preaching of Christ Jesus. This phrase and closely related ideas occur some seventy times in the synoptic Gospels. The phrase has strong eschatological associations in the preaching of Christ Jesus. It is very noticeable that the phrase has both present and future associations. For instance, the kingdom is something which is "drawing near" (Mark 1:15), yet still belongs in its fullness to the future. The Lord's Prayer, which remains of central importance to individual and corporate Christian prayer and worship, includes reference to the future coming of the kingdom (Matt. 6:10).

At the Last Supper, Christ Jesus spoke to his disciples of a future occasion when they would drink wine in the kingdom of God (Mark 14:25). A general consensus among New Testament scholars is that there is a tension between the "now" and the "not yet" in relation to the kingdom of God, similar to that envisaged by the parable of the growing mustard seed (Mark 4:30–32). It is imperative to state that the New Testament writers did not think of Christ Jesus' resurrection as an odd isolated phenomenon but rather a resurrection which includes and embraces all believers through all ages, and for both the "now" hope as well as the "not yet" expected eschatological hope of salvation. Christ Jesus himself spoke of the "not yet" resurrection of believers and said: "The people of this age marry and are given in marriage. But those who are considered worthy of taking part in that age in the resurrection from the dead will neither marry nor be given in marriage, and they can no longer die, for they are like the angels. They are God's children, since they are children of the resurrection" (Luke 20:34–36). The resurrection order cannot be assumed to follow present earthly lines and be confined or restricted to the "now" salvation.

There are several scripture passages to support the eschatological resurrection of those who are to take part in the resurrection of the righteous.[2] The children of God who are the children of the resurrection are those who will take part in the resurrection of the righteous. Christ Jesus'

---

[2] Matt. 22:23–33; Mark 12:18–27; Acts 4:1–2, 23:6–10.

God is the living "Abba" who gives and sustains life beyond the grave. Christ Jesus demonstrated his faith and confidence in the life-giving power of the God he proclaimed.[3] Christ Jesus spoke of those who, apart from any merit of theirs but only by virtue of God's sovereign grace, are considered worthy of partaking in the glories of the coming age, the new heaven and earth, and to be sharers in the resurrection of the righteous (John 5:29).

Christ Jesus comforted his disciples before his crucifixion and told them of his second advent, and of the future and permanent salvation which he will give to them and all believers in him: "Do not let your hearts be troubled. Trust in God, trust also in me. In my Father's house are many rooms; if it were not so, I would have told you. I am going there to prepare a place for you, I will come back and take you to be with me that you also may be where I am" (John 14:1–3). The New Testament is full of stories of how Christ Jesus met with his first and subsequent disciples after his resurrection; and he is still meeting with his people in all circumstances and situations in all places. Please understand that in the passage above, Christ Jesus himself is divinely and in holy confidence telling his Galilean disciples and you of his second advent when he will finally finish and seal the work of salvation, which will make it possible for you to forever be with Christ Jesus, your saviour, Lord, and God.

## ESCHATOLOGY: PAUL'S CORPORA

Like that of his Lord and God Christ Jesus, Paul's eschatology theology shows a tension between the "now" and "not yet". This is articulated in terms of a number of key images:

- The presence of a "new age" – at several points, Paul emphasised that the coming of Christ Jesus inaugurates a new era or "age". Although this new age which Paul designated a "new creation" (2 Cor. 5:17) has yet to be fulfilled, its presence has already been experienced. For this reason, Paul could refer to the "end of the ages" in Christ (1 Cor. 10:11).

---

[3] Robert J. Karris, "The Gospel According to Luke", in *The New Jerome Bible Commentary*, ed. Raymond E. Brown, Joseph A. Fitzmyer, and Roland E. Murphy (London, 2013), 713.

- The resurrection of Christ Jesus was seen by Paul as an eschatological event, which affirms that the "new age" has really been inaugurated. Paul clearly saw Christ Jesus' resurrection as an event which enables believers to live in the knowledge that death – a dominant feature of the present age – has been overcome and will finally be overcome at the second advent of Christ Jesus.

- Paul looked forward to the future coming of Christ Jesus in judgement at the end of time, confirming the new life in believers and their triumph over sin and death. A number of images are used to refer to this, including "the day of the Lord". In fact, at one point (1 Cor. 16:22), Paul used an Aramaic term, *Maranatha* (literally, "come, our Lord") as an expression of the Christian hope. Other passages which refer to the future coming of Christ Jesus include 1 Corinthians 15:23 and 2 Thessalonians 2:1, 8–9. For Paul, there is an intimate connection between the final coming of Christ Jesus and the execution of final judgement.

- A major theme of Paul's eschatology is the coming of the Holy Spirit. This theme, which builds on a longstanding aspect of Jewish expectations, sees the gift of the spirit as a confirmation that the new age has dawned in Christ Jesus. One of the most significant aspect of Paul's thought at this point is his interpretation of the gift of the Holy Spirit to believers as a deposit (2 Cor. 1:22, 5:5). This unusual word *deposit* has the basic sense of a "guarantee" or "pledge", affirming that the believer may rest assured of ultimate salvation on account of the present possession of the Holy Spirit. Although salvation remains something which will be consummated in the future, the believer may have present assurance of this future event through the indwelling of the Holy Spirit.[4]

- Paul looked forward to the "not yet" salvation: "I have fought the good fight, I have finished the race, I have kept the faith; now there is in store for me the crown of righteousness, which the Lord, the righteous Judge, will award to me on that day –and not only to me, but also to all who have longed for his appearing" (2 Tim. 4: 7–8).

[4] Alister E. McGrath, *Christian Theology: An Introduction* (4th edn, Oxford, 2007), 465–466.

Regarding the "not yet" aspect of salvation, Paul emphasised to Timothy in his second epistle the final and ultimate salvation in Christ Jesus. Paul convinced and assured himself of the eschatological salvation he hoped for: "Now there is in store for me the crown of righteousness". The "store" Paul spoke of metaphorically is the kingdom of Christ Jesus which has not come (not open yet) but will come eventually. Paul and all the believers in the Lord who had physically departed had received the crown of righteousness in the spirit in the kingdom of our Lord and God Christ Jesus. This crown of righteousness will be awarded physically not only to Paul but to all believers, dead and living, in Christ Jesus who faithfully wait for his second advent. Paul truly and really fought a divine fight for his Lord and God Christ Jesus as an Apostle for the Gentiles and laboured to get the crown of righteousness for over thirty years (36–66 AD) from the moment he encountered the Lord Jesus in his Damascus divine experience (Acts 9:1–19).

Paul wrote to Timothy in his second epistle and forcefully and confidently concluded his theology on the motif of "not yet" salvation, stating "the Lord will rescue me from every evil attack and will bring me safely to his heavenly Kingdom" (2 Tim 4:18). Paul knew very well that he would depart from this earth very soon (2 Tim. 4:6). Yet in the text above, he stated that the Lord would rescue him from every evil attack. Are these statements of Paul – "For I am already being poured out like a drink offering, and the time has come for my departure" and "The Lord will rescue me from every evil attack and will bring me safely to his heavenly Kingdom" (2 Tim 4:6, 18) – contradictory to one another? In other words, was Paul not sure of what he was writing to Timothy?

The answer is absolutely no. Paul had a divine revelation and was quite aware that he would very soon depart (die) physically and leave behind this earthly city. He also knew by the same holy revelation that the Lord Christ Jesus who called him to serve would rescue him from every evil attack (which is to say, his physical dead body and spirit would not end in the grave and swallowed up by the evil power of death). Paul hoped in the "not yet" salvation and assured himself that after his physical death, the Lord would spiritually rescue and divinely transport him to safety to be with his Lord and God Christ Jesus who Paul had served and laboured for over thirty years in his ministry to the Gentiles.

Paul drew an analogy between the death and the resurrection of Christ Jesus and the baptism of the believers in Romans 6:1–14 and emphasised the "not yet" future hope of all believers: "We were therefore buried with him through baptism into death in order that just as Christ was raised from the dead through the glory of the Father, we too may live a new life" (Rom. 6:4). This "new life" the baptised believer is currently experiencing and enjoying "now" is but a foretaste in this earthly city, while waiting for the "not yet" hope which will be the final and eternal salvation in the city of God. The resurrection of Christ Jesus gives a guaranteed eschatological hope that one day all who believe in Christ Jesus will rise to eternity in glory with him and be like the angels in his kingdom.

It is necessary to note that among all the New Testament writers, Paul's corpora most pointedly exhibits the eschatological tension between the "now" and "not yet". With respect to individual Christians, all references to the resurrection and eternal life are future tense. For example, Paul stated: "We too may live a new life" (Rom. 6:4), "We will certainly also be untied with him in his resurrection" (Rom. 6:5), and "We believe that we will also live with him" (Rom. 6:8). Generally, the believers' "now" existence, life, and activity in this earthly city is a shadow which is not fully realised and waiting for the "not yet" to be materialised.[5]

I bring this section of my discussion to a close by citing John the Divine, who recorded what God revealed to him regarding the eschatological resurrection. According to John:

> The rest of the dead did not come to life until the thousands years were ended. This is the first resurrection. Blessed and holy are those who have part in the first resurrection. The second death has no power over them, but they will be priests of God and of Christ and will reign with him for a thousand years. (Rev. 20:5–6)

My purpose here is not to discuss the subject of the millennium, because theologians are divided down the middle of what it stands for and have different hermeneutical understandings. For instance, some

---

[5] Craig C. Hill, "Romans", *The Oxford Bible Commentary*, ed. John Barton and John Muddiman (Oxford, 2011), 1094.

theologians take the "a thousand years" literally as 1,000 actual years, while others interpret it metaphorically as a long but undetermined period of time. However, it suffices here to state that both the living and the dead who believe in Christ Jesus are eagerly and faithfully yearning for the expected eschatological first resurrection because they believe that "the second death has no power over them". This has been made possible for them because of the death and resurrection of Christ Jesus, who wrought both present and eschatological salvation.

It is important to note that this does not mean that all those who rise will rise to heavenly blessing. Christ Jesus himself spoke of "the resurrection of life", but he also spoke of "the resurrection of judgement" and stated: "Do not be amazed at this, for a time is coming when all who are in their graves will hear his voice and come out – those who have done good will rise to live, and those who have done evil will rise to be condemned" (John 5:28–29) Here I notice a reference to the future raising of the death for both the righteous and the unrighteous.

Observe that the first part of the citation deals with the first resurrection, which is the soul; while the second subdivision describes the second resurrection, which is the body. Also take note of the same sequence of events in another work by the same author (John) in the Book of Revelation, which has been cited above (Rev. 20:5–6). It will not be possible to discuss the nature of the resurrected body because of its complicated dogmas for both the "spiritual" and the "physical", which is beyond the scope of this book.

# ESCHATOLOGICAL TENSION OF SALVATION: "NOT YET"

Eschatological future hope is a common feature of Paul's religious heritage. Fundamental to Paul's conception of the process of salvation is his conviction that the believer has "not yet" arrived, is "not yet" perfect, and is always in transit. It is this which determines the experience of being saved as a process of eschatological tension. This is the tension between a work begun but not complete, between fulfilment and consummation, and between decisive "already" and a still to be worked out "not yet".[6]

---

[6] James D. G. Dunn, *The Theology of Paul the Apostle* (London, 2008), 465.

## Already – not yet

The eschatological tension implicit in Paul's schema of salvation runs through all his soteriology. Soteriological theology (the Christian doctrine of salvation) teaches believers that Christ Jesus came to the world to save them from their sins – that is, salvation already obtained by believers through the death and resurrection of Christ Jesus in this earthly city. At the same time, Christians also believe that they will be saved and spend eternal life with Christ Jesus in the age to come in the city of God. That is to say, they are presently waiting for the final salvation which has "not yet" arrived. If I link both the present and the future salvation together, I can finally put them together as "already – not yet", which is a way of summarising the recognition that something decisive has already happened in the event of coming to have faith in Christ Jesus; but the grand work of God is waiting for its final materialisation, which is not yet complete.[7] For example, Paul spoke more frequently of the kingdom of God as an inheritance still outstanding realm to be reached in future.[8]

Christians are presently saved and are in the "already" spiritual state, which is temporarily in the earthly city. All should put their faith and focus on the "not yet" expected aspect of salvation that is eternal life with Christ Jesus in the city of God. This eschatological salvation cannot be compared with any other materialistic and secular luxuries. With regards to the conflicts between eschatological salvation and earthly pleasures and affluence, Christ Jesus warned his disciples and said to them: "For whoever wants to save his life will lose it, but whoever loses his life for me will find it. What good will it be for a man if he gains the whole world, yet forfeits his soul? Or what can a man give in exchange for his soul?" (Matt. 16:25–27). Christ Jesus' logic is loud and clear, indicating that the thought of future salvation of the soul should encourage acts of discipleship in the present, for only the final state of the human soul matters.[9] Christ Jesus told his disciples to pay more attention to the eschatological salvation which is yet to come. The future salvation of the soul is far greater, and it

---

[7] Dunn, 466.
[8] 1 Cor. 6:9–10, 15:50; Gal. 5:21; Col. 3:24; Eph. 1:14, 18:55.
[9] Dale C. Allison, "Matthew", in *The Oxford Bible Commentary*, ed. John Barton and John Muddiman (Oxford, 2011), 865.

is incomparable to all the splendour and glamour of King Solomon and all his personal splendour and aggrandizement.

To buttress my view of eschatological salvation, I cite another statement of Christ Jesus who warned his disciples regarding secular pleasures and worldly treasures: "Do not store up for yourselves treasures on earth, where moth and rust destroy, and where thieves break in and steal. But store up for yourselves treasures in heaven, where moth and rust do not destroy, and where thieves do not break in and steal" (Matt. 6:19–20). What Christ Jesus said is that to "store up" for yourself perishable earthly treasures now in this earthly city will lead you to lose the imperishable heavenly riches in the future in the heavenly city of God. The eschatological "treasures in haven" are those blessings that are reserved for the believer in heaven (1 Pet. 1:4) – that are heavenly in character, but of which the believer experiences a foretaste even now.

The heavenly treasures are mothproof, rustproof, and burglar-proof (Matt. 6:20). In other words, they endure forever in all their sparkling lustre, the irremovable possession of the children of the heavenly Father. This is in agreement and confirmation of the teaching of both Old and New Testament scriptures, which tell us about the following:

- a faithfulness that will never be removed (Ps. 89:33; 138:8)
- a life that will never end (John 3:16)
- a spring of water that will never cease to bubble up within the one who drinks of it (John 4:14)
- the gift that will never be lost (John 6:37, 39)
- the strong divine hand out of which the good shepherd's sheep will never be snatched (John 10:28)
- the chain that will never be broken (Rom. 8:29, 30)
- the love from which we shall never be separated (Rom. 8:39)
- the calling that will never be revoked (Rom. 11:29)
- the foundation that will never be destroyed (2 Tim. 2:19)
- an inheritance that will never fade out (1 Pet. 1:4, 5)[10]

The ultimate and final salvation is yet to come; that is in heaven where Christ Jesus is preparing a permanent place for each and every believer in him. Christ Jesus himself comforted and promised his distressed disciples and said to them:

---

[10] William Hendriksen, *New Testament on Matthew* (Edinburgh, 1978), 343–345.

Let NOT your heart be troubled. You are trusting God, now trust in me. There are many homes up there where my father lives, and I am going to prepare them for your coming. When everything is ready, then I will come and get you, so that you can always be with me where I am. If this weren't so, I would tell you plainly. (John 14: 1–3)

This is the promise of the second advent and eschatological salvation which will be finally and permanently fulfilled in the kingdom of Christ Jesus.

Christ Jesus had already given salvation to his disciples (especially the eleven) who believed in him while he was physically with them on earth. However, the salvation he gave to them was temporary, because he himself was still on earth and with them just for a limited period of time. This cosmos is not the permanent dwelling place for Christ Jesus and all those who believe in him. As stated earlier in this book, Christ Jesus condescended and descended from his permanent place in his heavenly kingdom and came down to this earth temporarily to bring salvation to all those who believe in him.

As has been explained, after his death and resurrection, he showed himself to his disciples in a period of forty days and finally ascended into heaven where he originally came from. For the sake of the disciples and all believers through the ages, he promised to come back (second advent) and "get" the disciples and all believers with him that all his children will eventually be with him where he is forevermore. Christ Jesus will definitely make his promise absolutely good, and all believers are eagerly and sincerely expecting his second advent, which has not yet been fulfilled. Christians are focusing and waiting for the eschatological salvation which will eventually take place at the appointed and appropriate divine time of God the Father.

Note that no one knows the precise time of the second advent of Christ Jesus as he himself confessed to his disciples: "No-one knows about that day or hour, not even the angels in heaven, nor the Son, but only the Father. Be on guard! Be alert! You do not know when that time will come" (Mark 13:32–33). For Christ Jesus to draw a road map or an itinerary for the future and give it to the disciples would have been a hindrance, not a help, for their faith. Certain signs have been given (Matt. 24:36–51). These signs are not for the purpose of making detailed chronological predictions. Here God the Son (Christ Jesus) himself said that he did not know when his second advent will be fulfilled. The time and hour is entirely within the power and authority of God the Father who alone has the divine prerogative to decide as God the Father sent his son Christ Jesus in the First Advent at the fullness of time. For Paul stated: "But when the time had fully come, God sent his Son, born of a woman, born under the law" (Gal. 4:4).

I stress that while the believer is eagerly and earnestly waiting for eschatological salvation in the second advent of Christ Jesus, the child of God should not rest on his or her oars but vigorously row across every lake, stream, river, sea, and ocean and transverse from east to west and north to south and into the arid desert to carry out the task of the Great Commission of Christ Jesus of making disciples of all nations (Matt. 28:19–20).

Finally, I come back to the theology of Paul the Apostle and state that a cardinal point of his eschatological theology is his conviction that the believer in Christ Jesus has not yet arrived, is not yet perfect, and is always in transit, moving toward the end. Eschatological hope for salvation was a common teaching of Paul, who talked of the "faith we eagerly await through the spirit of righteousness for which we hope" (Gal. 5:5). In this scripture, Paul made an eschatological statement regarding the salvation the Christians expect to attain in the future. Paul had confidence in what God has already done for all believers, but he had more conviction in what God intends to do in the future in his salvific work. Paul stated: "Being confident of this, that he who began a good work in you will carry it on to completion until the day of Christ Jesus" (Phil. 1:6). Paul was confident not only of what God has already done for the audience (forgiveness of their sins) who listened to the letter he sent to them which was read to the Philippian Church, but moreover, of what God has done as they had "been filled with the fruit of righteousness that comes through Christ Jesus to the glory and praise of God" (Phil. 1:11).

God has already done a good work of salvation through Christ Jesus, but when Christ Jesus finally returns (second advent), then the salvation of all believers will be brought to perfect completion.[11] It is God the Father who initiates salvation, who alone continues the process of salvation now, and who will one day in the future bring it to its consummation.[12] The day of Christ Jesus is that final and divine time when he will return, and this will be the moment when the eschatological salvation of all the believers in Christ Jesus will be brought to a perfect materialisation. The process of the fulfilment of salvation will be arbitrarily initiated and peculiarly carried out by God the Father alone who continues the process now and who will one day (only known to the Father) bring salvation to its final and perfect completion.

## The Mysterious Sixth and the Resurrection

In Chapter 5, I analysed the term *salvation* and examined its meaning and relevance in the Old and New Testaments. Also, in Chapter 8, I critically evaluated the significance of resurrection in both testaments and stated that without the resurrection phenomenon, there would be no work of salvation. My main point here is to discuss the motif of the mysterious sixth in both the Old and New Testaments and its significance to both resurrection and salvation.

It is very mystifying and intriguing to observe that the resurrection phenomenon is recorded in the sixth verse of the last chapters in each of the three Synoptic Gospels.[13] It is awesome to notice this, which made me excited and encouraged me to further investigate in order to ascertain whether this motif of the sixth verse is just a coincidence or a biblical pattern that requires further theological study.

In order to get more divine revelation of this mystery, I tried to make further investigation of the mysterious sixth verse and traced its biblical origin and significance in Genesis 1:26–31. In this passage, God planned to make man in God's own image and executed his plan on the sixth day: "So God created man in his own image, in the image of God he created him, male and female he created them. God saw all that he made, and it was very good. And there was evening, and there was morning the sixth

[11] Phil. 1:10, 2:16; 1 Cor. 1:8, 55; 2 Cor. 1:14.
[12] NIV Study Bible, 1760.
[13] Matt. 28:6; Mark 16:6; Luke 28:6.

day." It is paramount to note that the Creator God completed his work of creation of the earth, including the head and crown of his handiwork – Adam and Eve – on the sixth day.

On the same sixth day, God also made a final self-assessment of his divine creative skill, made a holy approval, and concluded that everything he had made from the first to the sixth and final day was "very good". God the Father made this grand and absolute declaration of his finished work of creation on the final (sixth) day. Dear beloved child of the resurrection, observe that God made a daily self-assessment of his creative skill, and on each day he concluded that it "was good". Note that in order to stress the divinity and importance of his (God's) work on the sixth day, the Creator God declared that it was "very good". In other words, God the Creator of the world identified the sixth day as more noticeable and honourable, which indicates that it surpasses all the preceding creative days.

Please note that I am not in any way suggesting that the other days of creation and their created things are less significant. The point here is that the sixth day is excellent, and it excels over all the other creative days. It is noteworthy above all other days because everything that was made (man and woman) in it "was very good". Genesis 1:27 is a highly significant verse, and it is the first occurrence of poetry in the OT. "Created" is used here three times to describe the central divine act of the sixth day. The importance of the occurrence of the word "created" three times in a single verse is to be considered and examined very carefully.

On the sixth day of creation, God the Father, God the Son, and God the Holy Spirit (the three divine persons of the Holy Trinity) unanimously planned and executed the creation of Adam and Eve. Just like God the Father, God the Son who is Christ Jesus the bringer of salvation also concluded his completed work of salvation in the final moment on the cross and shouted "it is finished" (John 19:30).

Furthermore, it is interesting to discover that the exposition of the fall of man is also recorded in Genesis 3:6, which states, "When the woman saw that the fruit of the tree was good for food and pleasing to the eye, and also desirable for gaining wisdom, she took some and ate it. She also gave some to her husband, who was with her, and he ate it" (Gen. 3:6). The very moment of the fall of humankind and culmination of sin occurred in the sixth verse.

Child of the triumphant and the victorious Christ Jesus, please observe the significance of the human tragedy which occurred in the sixth verse and started the original sin that pervades the rest of human history in all generations and in all the world. Instead of recognising their creaturely dependence and rendering obedience to Yahweh the Creator God, who made Adam and Eve in his own image, they attempted to break out of their status as being the "image of God" that was without sin and perfect both physically as well as spiritually – and unfortunately succeeded in doing so. They wished to possess the power that belongs to omni-powerful God alone, who has unlimited knowledge and is immortal. The creatures Adam and Eve wanted to become the Creator God; the subordinates wished to become predominant. Their rebellion against their Creator God (like their deceiver Satan) alienated them from Yahweh, and they ended with quite the opposite of what they had planned and hoped to attain. Their disobedience and rebellion brought fear and shame to them and separated them from God.

Moses stated: "Then the man and his wife heard the sound of the Lord God as he was walking in the garden of the cool of the day, and they hid from the Lord God among the trees of the garden. But the Lord God called to the man, 'Where are you?' He answered, 'I heard you in the garden, and I was afraid because I was naked; so I hid'" (Gen 3:8–10). In response to their human craving to be like God, Yahweh in his anger cursed the ground and expelled them from the Paradise garden.[14]

It is paramount to note a very important point in the story of Paradise lost: God cursed the serpent, but God did not curse Adam and Eve. In fact, God made sure that Satan, who is the source and originator of sin and tempted Adam and Eve, had the most severe curse and punishment. So the Lord God said to the serpent, "Because you have done this, cursed are you above all the livestock and all the wild animals! You will crawl on your belly and you will eat dust all the days of your life. And I will put enmity between you and the woman, and between your offspring and hers; he will crush your head, and you will strike his heel" (Gen 3:14–15).

The antagonism between human beings and snakes from the fall of Adam and Eve has been used to symbolise the outcome of the titanic struggle between God and Satan.[15] This struggle has been very dominant

---

[14] Edward P. Blair, *The Word Illustrated Bible Hand Book* (London, 1988), 105.
[15] NIV Study Bible, 12.

in the hearts and history of human beings in the whole wide world and will continue until the second advent of the "offspring of the woman" who is Christ Jesus. God's divine original blessing which he pronounced on Adam and Eve before their fall – "Be fruitful and increase in number, fill the earth and subdue it. Rule over the fish of the sea and the birds of the air and over every living creature that moves on the ground" (Gen. 1:28) – was not withdrawn from them.

Observe, Adam and Eve "sewed fig leaves together and made coverings for themselves" (Gen. 3:7), but "The Lord God made garments of skin for Adam and his wife and clothed them" Gen. 3:21). Here you can understand the merciful and forgiving God who immediately made better and more effective clothes to cover the shame of Adam and Eve. God castigated them and removed them temporarily from the Paradise garden, but he immediately made provision for their descendants for atonement and remission of sin, restoration, and reconciliation to himself through Christ Jesus. Christ Jesus who is God the Son ("the offspring of the woman") came to this world more than two millennia ago and fulfilled the curse the Lord God pronounced upon Satan. The Lord God executed his curse upon Satan when the Lord God sent his one and only son Christ to this world. Through his birth, mission, and death on the cross on the first Good Friday and ultimate resurrection on the first Easter Sunday Morning, Christ Jesus crushed the head and power of Satan. In his resurrection power, Christ Jesus has set free from sin the offspring (human beings in the whole universe) of the woman and wrought salvation for all those who believe in him.

As stated earlier, it is wonderful to note that the glorious resurrection phenomenon is recorded in the sixth verse in the last chapters in each of the three synoptic gospels in the New Testament. I start with Matthew, who recorded the resurrection and stated what the angel said to the women: "He is not here, he is risen, just as he said. Come and see the place where he lay" (Matt. 28:6). The heavenly messenger of God did not stop by telling them that "he is risen"; but reassuringly, he added, "Come and see the place where he lay." The angel invited them and asked them to come closer to the tomb where Christ Jesus was buried. The angel did not just want them to hear from him; he wanted them to see for themselves and observe, and convince themselves that "He is risen". When they had convinced themselves, they would be able to tell others with conviction.

Are you sure, and have you convinced yourself that "He is risen"? May the risen Christ Jesus spiritually open your ears to hear the voice of the angel who is saying to you, "Come and see where he lay." Accept the invitation of the angel and make a spiritual journey to the place where he was buried. See for yourself and assure yourself that "He is risen". Christ Jesus is indeed and really restored from temporary death to glorious and eternal life. He departed from the tomb majestically and ascended to heaven, where he is preparing a place for you. After completion, he will definitely descend (second advent) and take you home where you will spend eternity with him in his kingdom.

Mark also recorded the resurrection event and cited the statement of the angel to the women: "Don't be alarmed', he said. 'You are looking for Jesus the Nazarene, who was crucified. He is risen! See the place where they laid him" (Mark 16:6) The climax of Mark's Gospel is the resurrection. Without the resurrection, Jesus' death, although it may have been noble, would have been undeniably tragic. His opponents and critics would have been proven right. On a positive note, in his resurrection, Christ Jesus is declared to be the Son of God with power (Rom. 1:4). In his resurrection power, his main enemy (Satan) has been crushed and put to shame, and Christ Jesus is exonerated in exultation and is now in his heavenly kingdom in glory and power for eternity.

Finally, we finish the motif of the sixth verse with Luke. According to Luke, "two men in clothes that gleamed like lightning" said to the women "He is not here; he has risen! Remember how he told you, while he was still with you in Galilee" (Luke 24:6). Jesus had predicted his shameful death and glorious resurrection on several occasions (9:22), but his disciples failed to comprehend or accept in human terms what he said to them.

It is puzzling to observe that Moses recorded the creation story of Adam and Eve in Genesis 1:26–31 on the sixth day, and in the same vein, he inserted the incident of how sin came into the cosmos in 3:6 through Adam and Eve, which eventually cost them and all humanity eternal life and Paradise, if only temporarily.

My main task for the remaining part of this chapter is to unravel the mystery of the resurrection phenomenon which is recorded by all three

Synoptic Gospel writers who give account of the resurrection event in the sixth verse in the last chapter in their respective books – and also to understand the reason for Moses to record the creation story of human beings on the sixth day (Gen. 1:27–31) and the spiritual demise of the same human beings in the sixth verse in Genesis 3. The time lapse between the record of Moses in the book of Genesis in the Old Testament and the account given by the three Gospel writers in their respective books in the New Testament is about 1,406 years, yet there is a motif of sixth which is a common factor.

I put together the jigsaw puzzle by stating that the motif of sixth which connects both the Old and the New Testament scriptures is not a coincidental presentation of structures in the Bible, and it is not intentionally written text recorded by human hand. I postulate that the sixth verse motif which joins the two testaments is God's own divine plan of action to restore the fallen human beings Adam and Eve and their offsprings by cleansing them from all their sins through the birth, mission, death on the cross, and eventual resurrection, which wrought salvation that is in the Lord and saviour Christ Jesus.

It is recorded in Genesis 1:26–31 that man was created on the sixth day in the image of his Creator God and was perfect without sin. Man is the crown of God's creation and was made for the presence and fellowship of God. God blessed both Adam and Eve and said to them, "Be fruitful and increase in number; fill the earth and subdue it." Adam and Eve lived in Paradise with divine benediction and flourished and exercised dominion over all earthly creatures. Adam and Eve initially actually bore the image of their Creator God and became God's servants in God's kingly rule. As God's representatives in the earthly realm, they were good stewards of God's creatures. They were godly and perfect, and they had communication with their Creator God on a daily basis. In fact, they became God's vice regents (Gen 1:26; 2:18–20). However, the wonderful and good relationship they had with God suddenly and sadly was lost and thrown into oblivion as recorded in the sixth verse in Genesis 3, as the sin of disobedience overpowered them and took control of their whole beings.

The pivotal purpose of Christ Jesus' earthly mission is to undo what Adam and Eve did (sin of disobedience). Christ Jesus came to put the seeds of Adam and Eve back to their original intended state of perfection (without sin) to restore the good Creator-creatures relationship which Adam and Eve had with the Creator God before their fall.

The only and ultimate way for God to make that possible was to send his one and only son, Christ Jesus, to the cosmos to undergo indescribable suffering and eventual death on the cross and burial. But that was not the end of the Son of God. God raised his son from the power of the grave and freed him from the clutches of death, completing the divine and most important task ever undertaken by bringing human beings back to their original and perfect state without sin. This phenomenal event is recorded in the sixth verse in the last chapters in all the three synoptic gospels.

What I observe is that the motif of sixth is not simply a synchronistic event; rather, it shows or confirms God's righteousness in his divine plan for the work of salvation through the resurrection power of Christ Jesus. This power of the resurrection of Christ Jesus is so important to Apostle Paul who desired "to know Christ and the power of his resurrection and the fellowship of sharing his suffering, becoming like him in his death, and so, somehow, to attain the resurrection from death" (Phil. 3:10–11). To know Christ means to experience him as "life giving spirit, the one who here and now is conquering the forces of death and making Christians to be ready for the eschatological resurrection."[16]

The motif of the glorious sixth which connects the two testaments is God's own divine plan of redemptive action to restore fallen human beings from their sins through the birth, death on the cross, and eventual resurrection which wrought salvation that is in our Lord and God who is Christ Jesus.

I conclude this chapter by stating that there is power in the resurrected Christ Jesus. It is this wonderful power that gives salvation to all people in all nations who believe in his name. Salvation in Christ Jesus is the main and only link between the Old and the New Testaments, and between the Creator God and humanity. This confirms the grand and divine understanding of the first and the second Adam analogy, and the work of Christ Jesus through his obedience by his voluntary action of dying on the cross, and by his resurrection which brings salvation to all who believe in him (1 Cor. 15:21–22; Rom. 8:18–25).

---

[16] Brendan Byrne, "The letter to the Philippians", in The New Jerome Bible Commmentary, 796.

# Bibliography

Allison, Dale C., "Matthew", *The Oxford Bible Commentary*, ed. John Barton and John Muddiman (Oxford, 2011).

Barton, John, and John Muddiman, eds, *The Oxford Bible Commentary* (Oxford, 2011).

Bunyan, John, *The Pilgrim's Progress: The Classic Allegory of the Christian Life* (Buckingham, 2010).

Douglas, J. D., *New Bible Dictionary: Second Edition* (Leicester, 1994).

Dunn, James D. G., *The Partings of the Ways between Christianity and Judaism and their Significance for the Character of Christianity* (London, 2006).

———, *The Theology of Paul the Apostle* (London, 2008).

Fitzgerald, Allen D., *Augustine through the Ages: An Encyclopaedia* (Cambridge, 1999).

Gerhart, Mary, and Udoh, Fabian E., *The Christianity Reader* (London, 2007).

Gunton, Colin E, *The Actuality of the atonement* (London, 1988).

Harrington, J. Daniel, "The Gospel According to Mark", in *The New Jerome Bible Commentary*, ed. Raymond E. Brown, Joseph A. Fitzmyer, and Roland E. Murphy (London, 2013).

Hendriksen, William. *New Testament on Matthew, Mark, Luke, and John* (Edinburgh, 1978).

Henry, Matthew, *Matthew Henry's Commentary on the Whole Bible* (Peabody, Massachusetts, 2008).

McGrath, Alister E., *Christian Theology: An Introduction* (4th edn, Oxford, 2007).

Moltmann, Jurgen, *The Crucified God* (London, 2011).

Sankey, Ira D., *Sacred Songs and Solos* (Basingstoke, 1987).

Spurgeon, Charles Haddon, *Spurgeon's Commentary on the Bible*, comp. and ed. Robert Backhouse (London, 1997).

Verney, Stephen, *Into the New Age* (Glasgow, 1976).

Wright, N.T, *Jesus and the Victory of God,* (London, 1996).